Flying the Icon: Spitfire

Published in 2016 by Fighting High Ltd
www.fightinghigh.com

British Library Cataloguing-in-Publication
data. A CIP record for this title is available
from the British Library.

ISBN – 13: 978–0993212987

Designed by Michael Lindley
www.truthstudio.co.uk

Designed and typeset in 10/12pt Adobe
Minion and 9/10pt Berthold Akzidenz
Grotesk by TruthStudio Limited.
www.truthstudio.co.uk

Printed and bound in Wales by
Gomer Press.

Acknowledgements
This book would not have been possible
without the help of many people, but
particular thanks (in alphabetical order)
must go to:

Andrew Bishop
Guy Bourke
Flight Lieutenant Charlie Brown
Stephen J. Burt
Steve Death
Brendon Deere
Andrea Featherby
Dale Featherby
Bill Giles
Kenny Love
David Lowy
Squadron Leader Duncan Mason
Flight Lieutenant Antony Parkinson, MBE
Richard Paver
Keith Perkins
Squadron Leader Sean Perrett
Squadron Leader Al Pinner, MBE
Dave Ratcliffe
John Romain
Squadron Leader Clive Rowley, MBE
Squadron Leader Paul Simmons
Squadron Leader Ian Smith, MBE
Air Commodore Cliff Spink
Geoffrey Wellum

Flying the Icon: Spitfire
Jarrod Cotter

'I have often wondered who the genius was who christened it Spitfire. It was a name that resounded round the free world in those dark days of Hitler's tyranny, and perfectly symbolized the mood of Britain's defence.'

'…in the dark days of the German domination of Europe, the word "Spitfire" became synonymous with eventual freedom to the citizens of the occupied countries across the English Channel and North Sea. It was a symbol that good would triumph over evil.'

Sir Douglas Bader, from his book *Fight for the Sky*

Contents

Introduction

I was born thirty years after the first flight of the Spitfire and have lived through, enjoyed and worked on many of the commemorative anniversary events since firstly as a young aircraft enthusiast, then as a serving member of the Royal Air Force and most recently as an aviation author. I have always looked forward to the Spitfire flying activities to mark these occasions and also to the latest book to be published, packed with information and superb pictures of this most iconic of British aircraft.

So fondly is the Spitfire thought of, that perhaps it can best be described as the perfect example of a paradox; it is of an ultra-efficient design for its time, was and is still beautiful in its looks and fondly loved by a countless many of those whom it defended, yet at the same time its purpose was of course to be a highly efficient weapon of war. Generations of schoolboys grew up dreaming of flying a Spitfire, and in that statement I can include myself!

For this, the eightieth anniversary year of the Spitfire first taking flight, I decided that it was time that I produced a book myself to mark the occasion – but what could I put together that would be different from all that's gone before? There have been so many books on the Spitfire that most aspects have been done several times over – detailed histories of the type, biographies of famous Spitfire people, pilots' memoirs, descriptions of the numerous campaigns in which the Spitfire played a key part, technical write-ups, glossy coffee table picture books and more.

During my years of writing about aircraft, I have been privy to all that goes on behind the scenes to provide the end result of an audience seeing a Spitfire in the sky. In that time I got to know many Spitfire veterans and a large proportion of today's pilots who still fly this fighter, a great number of whom have become good friends. I have listened with great care to after-dinner talks by Battle of Britain veterans at RAF functions, attended Spitfire

pilot training courses and experienced the thrill of flying along-side these wonderful aircraft. I had never flown in a Spitfire, though, and so the mystique of just what that felt like remained in my imagination for many years.

In 2014 that became a reality, when I received a telephone call from Dale Featherby explaining that he was part of a new organisation called Aero Legends that had negotiated an agreement with the British Civil Aviation Authority to allow passengers to be flown in a Spitfire Tr.IX. Aero Legends was holding a launch event at Headcorn in Kent in June 2014 and Dale invited me along to see what this new organisation had to offer – part of which might include a flight in a Spitfire!

On arrival I saw that my name was on the list for a Spitfire flight, and after a lifetime's waiting the moment was perhaps here. And so it was, as I lifted off in the Aircraft Restoration Company's PV202 with good friend Dave 'Rats' Ratcliffe at the controls. Once up at height Rats handed the controls over to me, and talked me through a 'victory roll' – I was left in disbelief that I was actually flying a Spitfire. At that moment all the information I had gleaned from present and former pilots sunk into place, and I realised that I needed to compile a book solely on flying the Spitfire!

This was to be a book about how the Spitfire was, and is, flown – the wartime instructions given to pilots as to how it should be operated and what its pilots thought, and now think, of its flying characteristics. I surmised that this type of information contained within a glossy souvenir book would mark this historic anniversary occasion in a way that hadn't been done before. I have, however, chosen to include a brief historical background leading up to the first flight of the prototype K5054, as I felt this would help to set the scene of how this supreme design came about.

I have chosen a variety of the more well-known marks to be

Above: Spitfire Vbs of No. 417 Squadron RCAF on patrol over the Tunisian desert in April 1943. These aircraft are armed with two 20mm Hispano cannons and four 0.303in machine-guns. Note also the clearly visible Vokes tropical air filter fitted to AN-V closest to the camera. British Official

Left: The Spitfire Vc was fitted with the 'universal' wing which was able to befitted with four 20mm cannons as shown here. Jarrod Cotter

included, which cover an extreme range of the fighter's evolution: the prototype K5054; early Mk I; Mk IIa; Mk Vb; Mk VIII; Mks IXe and XVIe; PR.XIX; and, to highlight the extreme evolution of the Spitfire, the F.22/24. A point worth clarifying is the reason for my inclusion of the Mk VIII. This was a modified version of the high-altitude Mk VII and only served with units based overseas and especially with the RAAF, so might not seem one of the most predominant variants to feature here at first glance. However, Jeffrey Quill, who piloted all the marks of Spitfire, thought that the Mk VIII with standard wings was his personal favourite from a flying point of view, so I think it should be there among the more familiar variants covered for that reason. It has proved a fascinating exercise to compile this information together in one place and appreciate the differences as the type evolved.

Of course, that means that many of the well-known personalities involved with the Spitfire's design and production do not get recognised, but as already mentioned this is not a type history. The most prominent pilot's name here is Jeffrey Quill, as he flew every mark of the Spitfire and Seafire from the prototype to the furthest stage of its evolution, and so gained a truly comprehensive knowledge of the type, and a great deal of the credit for developing R.J. Mitchell's concept into a true fighting machine must go to him. There were, of course, also a number of women who had the same desire to fly this icon of aviation, and some of these are featured to highlight the important work they did flying with the Air Transport Auxiliary in delivering Spitfires to RAF stations during the Second World War. Other aspects that I felt needed to be included were a visual presentation of a Spitfire sortie, and an inclusion of that most famous of aviation poems 'High Flight', conceived by nineteen-year-old Pilot Officer John Gillespie Magee while flying a Spitfire at 30,000ft. This young pilot is buried just a few miles from where

I live in Lincolnshire, and before writing that part of the book I visited his grave to pay my tribute.

To complement the theme of this book it predominantly comprises pictures of Spitfires flying and pilots in Spitfires – I have deliberately included relatively few static pictures of unattended aircraft on the ground as this is a book about flying the Spitfire. I do hope that this idea to mark the eightieth anniversary of the first flight of K5054 on 5 March 1936 pays a fitting tribute to the genius of R.J. Mitchell and to all those who have flown and fought for this country in what is a true icon of not just British aviation, but world aviation.

Previous page 11, clockwise from left: One of the RAF's most coveted Battle Honours is Battle of Britain 1940. Here it seen emblazoned on the Standard of a very famous fighter unit, No. 74 Squadron, which flew Spitfires from Hornchurch and Biggin Hill during the Battle. On August 11, 1940 the squadron went into combat four times, and by the end of that day alone scored 24 enemy aircraft destroyed and 14 damaged. Jarrod Cotter

For many years aircraft enthusiasts have delighted at the sight and sound of Spitfires in the sky. In recent years they have been able to take to air in a helicopter and fly alongside Spitfire Vb BM597 over the White Cliffs of Dover courtesy of Action Stations! This has given people the readily available opportunity to see a Spitfire in its natural environment in an area where much of the air-to-air combat took place during the Battle of Britain. Jarrod Cotter

The Spitfire was controlled using the iconic spade grip, which to roll aircraft was moved on a separate axis to the control column. Jarrod Cotter

Left: Sometimes during the hectic testing of Spitfires coming off the production line at Castle Bromwich there was very little time between flights – here famous test pilot Alex Henshaw grabs a quick cup of tea in the cockpit a Spitfire.
Via François Prins

Below: A late 1930s postcard describing the Spitfire as the 'fastest aeroplane in the Air Force'.
British Official

Bottom: The centrepiece of the National Battle of Britain Memorial at Capel le Ferne on the south coast of Kent is a statue of a lone fighter pilot looking out to sea in a contemplative mood, as if waiting for his missing comrades to return.
Jarrod Cotter

High Flight

Most people interested in or connected with aviation will be familiar with the poem 'High Flight', composed in 1941 by Pilot Officer John Gillespie Magee. However, what might not be quite so well known is that he penned it aged just nineteen, and the poem was conceived during a high-altitude test flight in a Spitfire over Lincolnshire.

In a letter home to his parents he told them: 'I am enclosing a verse I wrote the other day. It started at 30,000ft, and was finished soon after I landed. I thought it might interest you.' On the back of the letter was 'High Flight', written on 3 September 1941.

John Gillespie Magee was born on 9 June 1922 in Shanghai, China, to an American father and a British mother, who both worked as Anglican missionaries. He was the eldest of four brothers. In 1931 he moved with his mother to the UK and spent the following four years at St Clare, a boarding school for boys, near Walmer in Kent.

He attended Rugby School from 1935 to 1939. He developed his poetry while there and in 1938 he won the school's poetry prize. He was deeply moved by the roll of honour of Rugby pupils who had fallen in the First World War, a list of names that included the celebrated war poet Rupert Brooke (1887–1915), whose work Magee greatly admired. Brooke had won the school poetry prize thirty-four years earlier. The prize-winning poem by Magee referred to Brooke's burial at 11 o'clock at night in an olive grove on the Greek island of Skyros.

Magee visited the United States in 1939. Because of the outbreak of the Second World War he was unable to return to Rugby for his final school year, and as an alternative attended Avon Old Farms School in Avon, Connecticut. He earned a scholarship to Yale University in July 1940, but did not enrol, choosing instead to cross the border into Canada and enlist in the Royal Canadian Air Force in October of that year.

The poem High Flight was conceived by Pilot Officer John Gillespie Magee while flying in a Spitfire over Lincolnshire at 30,000ft. Here Spitfire XIX PM631 of the RAF's Battle of Britain Memorial Flight is being flown at altitude by Squadron Leader Ian Smith, and silhouetted again the sun captures much of the emotion of the poem.
Jarrod Cotter

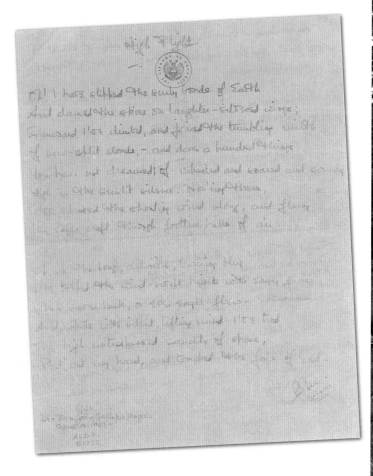

Below: Royal Canadian Air Force Pilot Officer John Gillespie Magee, who died on 11 December 1941 when his Spitfire fell out of the sky. He baled out, but his parachute did not open.

Left: John Gillespie Magee's war grave at Scopwick in Lincolnshire.
Jarrod Cotter

Far left: The young Spitfire pilot wrote the poem in a letter home to his parents in which he stated: 'I am enclosing a verse I wrote the other day. It started at 30,000ft, and was finished soon after I landed. I thought it might interest you.' On the back of the letter was 'High Flight', which was written on 3 September 1941. This is the original letter, which is held by **The Library of Congress.** The Library of Congress

John received flight training in Ontario at No. 9 Elementary Flying Training School, located at RCAF Station St Catharine's, and at No. 2 Service Flying Training School at RCAF Station Uplands in Ottawa. He was awarded his wings in June 1941, was promoted to the rank of pilot officer and was then sent to Britain where he was posted to No. 53 Operational Training Unit at RAF Llandow, in Wales. After graduation he transferred to No. 412 (Fighter) Squadron, RCAF, at RAF Digby, on 30 June 41.

On 11 December 1941 Magee was killed in a flying accident when his Spitfire fell out the sky. A farmer witnessed seeing the young pilot bale out, but his parachute didn't open and he sadly lost his life. John Gillespie Magee is buried among the war graves at Scopwick in Lincolnshire, just a couple of miles away from RAF Digby. His award-winning poem written at Rugby in 1938, 'Sonnet to Rupert Brooke', contained a passage which anyone visiting this young poet/pilot's grave in Lincolnshire could recite and relate to the place where John Magee rests:

We laid him in a cool and shadowed grove
One evening in the dreamy scent of thyme
Where leaves were green, and whispered high above –
A grave as humble as it was sublime. …

High Flight

Oh! I have slipped the surly bonds of Earth
And danced the skies on laughter-silvered wings;
Sunward I've climbed, and joined the tumbling mirth
of sun-split clouds – and done a hundred things
You have not dreamed of – wheeled and soared and swung
High in the sunlit silence. Hov'ring there,
I've chased the shouting wind along, and flung
My eager craft through footless halls of air. …

Up, up the long, delirious, burning blue
I've topped the wind-swept heights with easy grace.
Where never lark, or even eagle flew –
And, while with silent, lifting mind I've trod
The high untrespassed sanctity of space –
Put out my hand, and touched the face of God.

'The aircraft began to slip along as if in skates with the speed mounting up steadily and an immediate impression of effortless performance was accentuated by the low revs of the propeller. ... "Here", I thought to myself, "is a real lady."' Jeffrey Quill

On 5 March 1936, a beautiful-looking sleek new monoplane made its first flight from the Supermarine works airfield at Eastleigh in Hampshire. Attractive as it may have been, this aircraft was designed to be the leading fighter of its time and intended solely for combat. The Spitfire was born.

It had been back in late 1931 that Air Ministry Specification F7/30 was formally put out to industry. This called for a new front-line RAF fighter armed with four 0.303in machine guns that could reach a higher speed than the 225mph Bristol Bulldog biplane.

Supermarine, courtesy of the company's chief designer, R.J. Mitchell, had recently achieved great success with the series of revolutionary high-speed floatplanes that had set world speed records while taking part in the Schneider Trophy races with the RAF's High Speed Flight. The ideas and technological advances used were an ideal basis on which to look into the development of this new fighter – the combination of Mitchell's designs such as the 1931 winning Supermarine S.6B, and the Rolls-Royce 'R' engine that powered it, had formed a world-leading partnership in the production of high-speed aircraft.

While at one point the production of the S.6B was in question due to the refusal of the government to fund that year's Schneider Trophy entry, a lifeline came to Mitchell in the form of a £100,000 donation by Lady Fanny Lucy Houston, a wealthy widow,

Right: The very clean profile of K5054 is seen to good effect in this early side-on view of the revolutionary new aircraft. A&AEE

Below: An early colour advertisement for the Spitfire. Supermarine

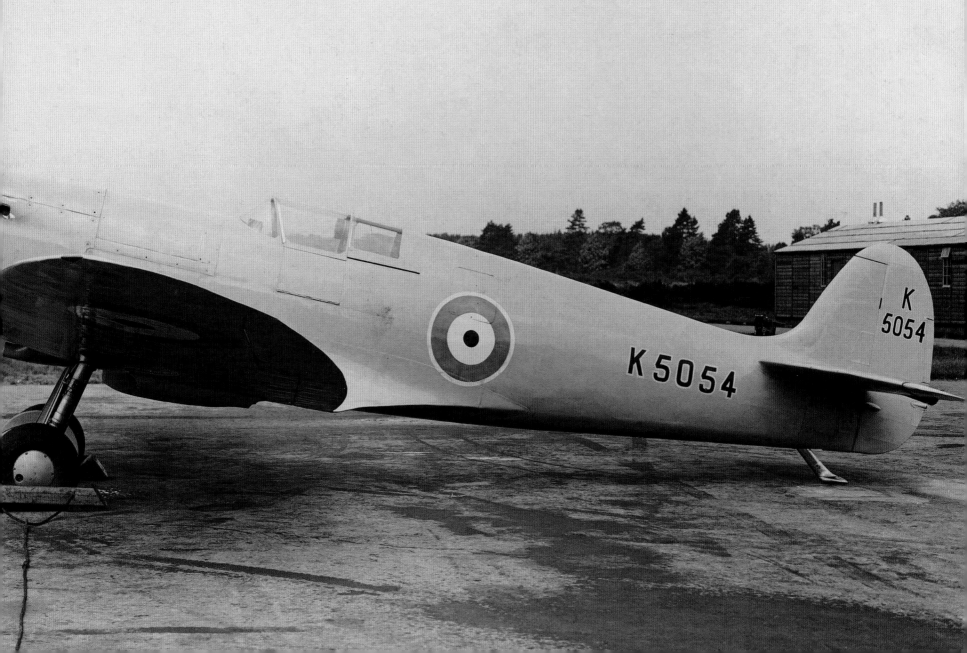

socialite, a one-time suffragette and a high-profile right-wing patriot. He remarked: 'There were dreams, and then there was reality. I had hope, hope to make a difference, hope to make myself part of history. Today, I have been given that chance and all my deepest thanks go to one woman. Her name is Lady Houston. …' This 1931 extract from Mitchell's diary portrays his frustrations. Having dedicated years to designing a racing seaplane superior to any other in the world, in that year he faced government opposition. Funds were not available, and Britain's entry in the 1931 Schneider Trophy contest, which the country had the chance to win outright, was in jeopardy.

When all seemed lost, the donation of £100,000 from Lady Houston came completely out of the blue, and just in time to give Mitchell and his team enough time to work on an advanced design. One of the most significant periods leading up to the production of the Spitfire involved the work behind the record-breaking speed of 407.5mph reached by the S.6B, the aircraft that achieved Britain's outright win of the Schneider Trophy after the third successive victory in 1931. Arthur Sidgreaves, the managing director of Rolls-Royce, commented: 'It is not too much to say that research for the Schneider Trophy contest over the past two years is what our aero-engine department would otherwise have taken six to ten years to learn.' And Rolls-Royce engineer Sir Stanley Hooker later wrote: 'If Mitchell had not set his heart on gaining the speed record; if Lady Houston had not donated £100,000; if Sir Henry Royce had not complete faith in Mitchell as an aircraft designer, then the history of this country might have taken a very different turn.' Marshal of the Royal Air Force, Lord Trenchard, once even suggested that there should be three monuments erected on the White Cliffs of Dover: 'They should glorify Winston Churchill, an Unnamed Airman and Lady Lucy Houston.'

Meanwhile, numerous manufacturers offered prototypes to meet F7/30 and Supermarine's example was the Type 224, an open-cockpit gull-winged monoplane with fixed undercarriage and powered by a Rolls-Royce Goshawk engine. K2890 carried out its maiden flight on 20 February 1934. However, its performance was lacking and the Gloster SS.37 biplane, which became the Gladiator, won the contract.

R.J. Mitchell looked at the requirement again, and used his genius to design an aircraft with far cleaner lines and a retractable undercarriage. By then Rolls-Royce had also developed its PV 12 engine, later named the Merlin. Mitchell was already seriously ill, but persevered with putting everything into the design of a fighter he thought would make a vital contribution to the defence of his country as another war with Germany was already looking ominous.

The new fighter was designated the Type 300 and was initially a private venture funded by parent company Vickers and under development at Woolston, although the Air Ministry soon saw its potential and issued a contract for the construction of a prototype, which was given the designation F37/34. As the design progressed, the type's characteristic elliptical wings were developed as aerodynamicists worked on achieving an overall wing structure that was as thin as possible, but which could still accommodate the fighter's requirement to carry eight guns.

Taking flight

After ground runs had been satisfactorily completed at Woolston, the fighter was dismantled and trucked to the company's airfield at Eastleigh (now Southampton Airport). It was given the RAF serial number K5054. At 16:30 hours on 5 March 1936, Vickers' chief test pilot, Captain Joseph 'Mutt' Summers, took the fighter aloft. In his book *Spitfire: A Test Pilot's Story*, Jeffrey Quill describes this first flight:

There was a light wind blowing across the aerodrome which meant that Mutt had to take the short run and taxied towards one of the four Chance lights which (in those days) were situated round the perimeter, turned into wind and opened the throttle. The aeroplane was airborne after a very short run and climbed away comfortably. Mutt did not retract the undercarriage on that first flight – deliberately, of course – but cruised fairly gently around for some minutes, checked the lowering of the flaps and the slow flying and stalling characteristics, and then brought K5054 in to land. Although he had less room than he would probably have liked, he put the aeroplane down on three points without too much 'float', in which he was certainly aided by the fine-pitch setting of the propeller. He taxied towards the hangar and the point where we in the group of Supermarine spectators were standing. This included R.J. Mitchell,

C99/736/34

Mr Faddys Copy

MR. MITCHELL. MR. .... MR. SMITH (2)

SUPERMARINE AVIATION WORKS (VICKERS)
1 9 MAR 1936
CHIEF DESIGNER

SPITFIRE II - F. 37/34.

5 & 6.3.36.   Fine pitch airscrew for take-off fitted.

10 & 14.3.36. Airscrew Drawing No. 300300.

Handling Trials - light load.

Machine was loaded to load data sheet No. 36.

The following points were noted:-

Taxying: Chassis was quite smooth in operation   B
No tendency for the machine to swing at any period
during the run on the ground. There is slight
tendency when across wind for the machine to roll.

Flying: The handling qualities of this machine
are remarkably good.

Ailerons: These are powerful and quite light to   C
operate balanced at .27 chord, and restore when
disturbed to the central position.

Elevators: These are very effective and light   C
throughout the speed range and are in harmony
with the ailerons.

Rudder: This is also very effective but owing to   C
the design requirements for stressing on the
fuselage, full rudder at 1.2 times stalling speed,
it is considered that the rudder is on the light
side, as it would be possible to apply full rudder
at top speed. It is perfectly satisfactory to
complete tests but it may be necessary to reduce
the balance on this control.

Trimming flaps: At the c. of g. position already   C
flown, the flap is quite ample to compete with
different conditions of flight. This also applies
to the rudder trimming flap.

Wing flaps: These are very effective. No   C
comparison of the gliding angle with or without
flaps has been made. This will be done at a later
date. There is a very slight change of trim
when the flaps are applied, giving a nose down
tendency. This is quite easily trimmed out on the
elevators.

Wheel Brakes: Further braking power could be   B
safely applied on the hand. It was noticed that
after the flaps had been operated twice from the
air supply reservoir, there was no air left for
the brakes on landing. This is considered a
disadvantage and it may be necessary to instal a
separate bottle for wheel brakes.

Stability. The machine is stable laterally and   C
directionally up to a speed of 260 indicated.

Pitching. No pitching tests have been carried out.   C

Cockpit. This is very comfortable: all controls   B
are accessible and very well laid out.

Sliding Hood over the pilot: This requires modifi-   St.
cation. It is possible for the back lock on the
pilot's door to become unfastened in flight,
thus allowing the hood to come out of its runner

C99/736/34

when sliding backwards. It is also considered   St.
that some quick means of releasing the hood
at high speed should be devised, as the load on
the hood at high speed makes it practically
impossible to open.

Retractable chassis operation in the air. This is   St.
very light to operate and handle. The point at
the moment which appears to require investigating
is the emergency method of lowering the wheels
should fracture occur in any of the hydraulic
pipe lines. At the present time, should a pipe
line break, it is not possible to get the chassis
into the down position. It is considered that
an emergency system should be installed, since a
failure to the chassis would mean the loss of
the aircraft.

Engine Installation. No remarks can be made   I
on this at the moment as to running qualities,etc.
until the final propeller and engine are installed.
On the last flight, part of the cowling became
detached and tore backwards. Certain other pieces
of the cowling show signs of cracking and it is
felt that this requires modification. It is
thought that safety straps round the cowling would
be a certain advantage until this machine has
finished its experimental flight.

Performance: The following figures have been taken   P
and supplied to the Technical Office:-

10.3.36.   Height: 3000'   270 A.S.I.   2700 revs. 6lb. Boost.

(Visibility was very bad and it was discovered
that the aneroid fitted was defective. This speed
cannot therefore be relied upon.)

14.3.36.   Height 17,000'.   255 A.S.I.   Air Temp. -15°
Revs. 3100   6½ lbs. boost.

(As part of the engine cowling had torn away and
turned backwards, most likely the indicated speed
given here is low owing to the extra drag of the
cowling.)

(SGD.) J. SUMMERS.

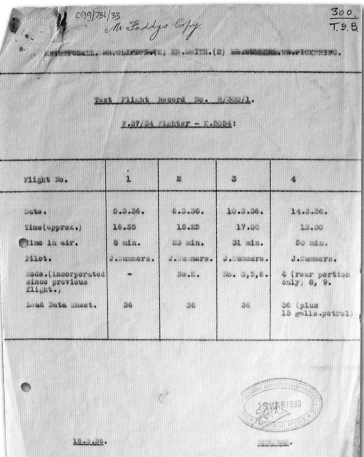

C99/734/33

Mr Faddys Copy.

300.
T.9.B

MR.MITCHELL. MR.CLIFTON.(2), MR.SMITH.(2) MR.SHENSTONE. MR.PICKERING.

Test Flight Record No. R/300/1.

F.37/34 Fighter - K.5054:

Flight No.	1	2	3	4
Date.	5.3.36.	6.3.36.	10.3.36.	14.3.36.
Time(approx.)	16.35	15.25	17.00	13.30
Time in air.	8 min.	23 min.	31 min.	50 min.
Pilot.	J.Summers.	J.Summers.	J.Summers.	J.Summers.
Mods.(incorporated since previous flight.)	-	No.2.	No. 3,5,6.	4 (rear portion only) 8, 9.
Load Data Sheet.	36	36	36	36 (plus 15 galls.petrol)

15.3.36.

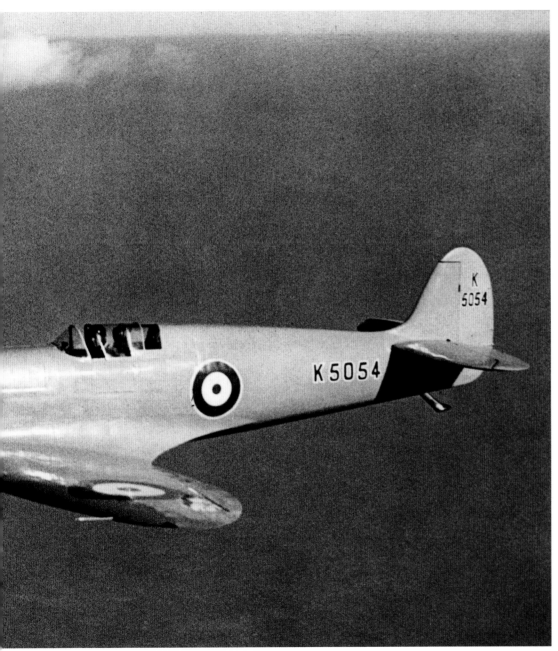

Alan Clifton, Beverley Shenstone, Alf Faddy and Ken Scales, the foreman in charge of the aeroplane. There must also have been quite a few other people there but there was certainly not a crowd. It was very much a Supermarine 'family affair'.

When Mutt shut down the engine and everybody crowded round the cockpit, with R.J. foremost, Mutt pulled off his helmet and said firmly, 'I don't want anything touched.' This was destined to become a widely misinterpreted remark. What he meant was that there were no snags which required correction or adjustment before he flew the aircraft again. The remark has crept into folklore implying that the aeroplane was perfect in every respect from the moment of its first flight, an obviously absurd and impracticable idea. After the 15 minute first flight the aircraft was still largely untested and unproven, having done one take-off and one landing. Mutt was far too experienced a hand to make any such sweeping statement at that stage in the game.

Over the following weeks further tests were carried out and in late May K5054 went to the Aeroplane and Armament Experimental Establishment (A&AEE) at Martlesham Heath in Suffolk for RAF service trials. By this time the aircraft had gained its familiar all-over light blue paintwork. It lived up to all expectations and achieved a maximum speed of 349mph at 16,800ft – an order was placed for 310 examples of this new breed of all-metal fighter.

On 11 June 1937, having given the development of the Spitfire his all despite deteriorating health, R.J. Mitchell died aged just forty-two. At the time K5054 was still the only airworthy Spitfire; sadly, its designer did not live to see the aircraft's full potential put to use in the defence of Britain and its freedom, although he did at least get to see his design fly. Supermarine's Joseph Smith took the lead over the further development of the type, and with his team made sure of its war-winning contribution.

The prototype was later modified to be a more representative example of a production machine. Modifications included fitting eight Browning 0.303in machine guns, progressively more powerful examples of the Merlin and a tailwheel rather than a simple skid; it also lost its pale blue colour scheme in favour of camouflage.

It was not until 14 May 1938 that the first production Spitfire I, K9787, took to the air. K5054 was retained for continued testing until October that year, then sent to Farnborough, Hampshire, where it was destroyed in a fatal landing accident on 4 September 1939, ironically one day after the war for which it was designed had begun.

Jeffrey Quill, *Spitfire: A Test Pilot's Story*

Jeffrey Kindersley Quill was an RAF pilot who was chosen to become a test pilot, and became the second aviator to fly the Spitfire prototype after Mutt Summers. Jeffrey went on to operate every variant of the Spitfire, and so keen was he to understand the service pilots' needs of the Spitfire that during the Battle of Britain he sought an attachment to an operational squadron so that he had a better understanding of the type's capabilities in the environment for which it was designed. What follows is Jeffrey's description of his first flight in K5054, which was published in his brilliant book *Spitfire: A Test Pilot's Story*:

I primed the Merlin engine carefully and it started first time. I began taxying out to the north-east end of the airfield which, of course, was entirely of grass. Never before had I flown a fighter with such a very long nose; with the aircraft in its ground attitude vision directly ahead was completely obscured so I taxied slowly on a zig-zag course in order to ensure a clear path ahead.

The great two-bladed wooden propeller, by this time of maximum coarse pitch, seemed to turn over very slowly and from the stub exhausts, one for each of the 12 cylinders, came a good powerful crackle whenever a small burst of power was applied for taxying followed by a lot of popping in the exhausts as the throttle was closed again. On arrival at the edge of the field I turned the aircraft 45° off the wind and did my cockpit checks which, at that stage, really consisted only of fuel cocks, trimmer and flap settings, radiator shutter, tightening the throttle friction grip and a quick check over the engine instruments. With a last look round for other aircraft I turned into wind and opened the throttle.

With that big fixed-pitch propeller able to provide only very low revs during take-off, the acceleration was sluggish and full right rudder was required to hold the aeroplane straight. The torque reaction tended to roll the aircraft on its narrow undercarriage but soon we were airborne and climbing away. At once it was necessary to re-set the rudder trimmer and then to deal with the undercarriage retraction and the canopy. This presented a minor problem insofar as the undercarriage had to be raised with a hydraulic hand pump, so it was necessary to transfer the left hand from the throttle to the stick and operate the hand pump with the right. This was difficult to do without inducing a longitudinal oscillation of the whole aircraft.

However, once fully airborne and 'tidied up' the aircraft began to slip along as if on skates with the speed mounting up steadily and an immediate impression of effortless performance was accentuated by the low revs of the propeller at that low altitude. The aeroplane just seemed to chunter along at an outstandingly higher cruising speed than I had ever experienced before, with the engine turning over very easily and in this respect it was somewhat reminiscent of my old Bentley cruising in top gear. I climbed up to a few thousand feet and carried out some steep turns and some gentle rolls and found the aeroplane light and lively but with a tendency to shear about a bit directionally. I put it into a gentle dive and it accelerated

Opposite, clockwise from top:
The impressive fixed pitch two-bladed propeller is shown clearly in this study picture of K5054.

Jeffrey Quill, who flew every variant of the Spitfire from the Prototype to the F.24.

Jeffrey Quill at the controls of K5054 during night flying trials.

K5054 puts on a little bank to show off the Spitfire's iconic elliptical wings.

with effortless ease and then I came back to rejoin the circuit for landing. The flaps, which I had already tried out in the air, came down on the prototype to only 60° which was the maximum lift, but not the maximum drag, position so the glide angle on the approach was very flat and the attitude markedly 'nose-up'. This feature was accentuated by the fact that the big wooden propeller ticked over extremely slowly and produced no noticeable drag or deceleration.

The approach, with the use of a little power and very 'nose-up', meant the view straight ahead was almost non-existent as one got close to the ground, so I approached the airfield in a gentle left-hand turn, canopy open, and head tilted to look round the left-hand side of the windscreen. Mutt had warned me about this so I was able to get myself on the right line at the outset. As I chopped the throttle on passing over the boundary hedge the deceleration was hardly discernible and the aeroplane showed no desire to touch down – it evidently enjoyed flying – but finally it settled gently on three points and it wasn't until after the touchdown that the mild aerodynamic buffeting associated with the stalling of the wing became apparent. 'Here', I thought to myself, 'is a real lady'.

Tucking Up their Trousers …

K5054's first public appearance in the New Types Park at Hendon on 27 June 1936 was reported on in the 1 July edition of *The Aeroplane* by editor C.G. Grey: 'The New Types Park was no longer the Amusement Park [nicknamed so due to the regular appearance of "technical curiosities" – Author]. All the inmates were serious and some of them were quite new – albeit of types which we were advocating years back. One could not help remarking that our latest war-machines in the air look remarkably like the Percival Gulls and Miles Hawks of four or five years ago – except that they tuck up their trousers. And at least two years ago our soundest aerodynamic specialists said definitely that a middle-wing monoplane is the most efficient type of all.' He went to comment on the Spitfire in particular: 'Mr Mitchell's little Supermarine fighter, like a baby Schneider Racer which folds up its feet, is a sweet little job all over.' He left the more specific reporting to others, commenting: 'The various turns (forgive me, items on the programme) are criticised hereafter by members of my staff who are better qualified than I am, by their service in the Air Force, to discuss such things.'

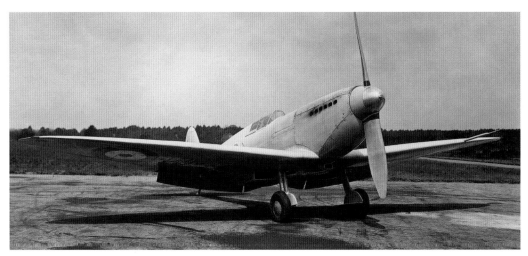

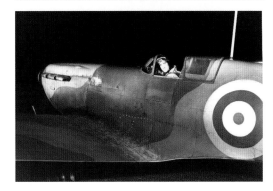

'Monoplanemania'

In his report under the title 'Monoplanemania', in the same issue of *The Aeroplane*, Thurston James began: 'Complete elimination of the biplane and the presence of potential World-record-breakers for speed and distance were significant features of the New Types Park at the 1936 RAF Display, for military design is catching up the lead established by commercial types or at least profiting by the experience so gained. The contrast between the obsolete machines in the air, whose perfectly timed and co-ordinated evolutions made the Display, as they have for years past, and the sleek monoplanes in which next year's pilots will give their show – if there is one – surely was the most striking aspect of the whole performance.' Showing the signs of the times, he continued: 'There was not a single biplane on the sacred ground. Last year there were six, half the total number of exhibits … for the present monoplanemania is absolute.

Bombers, 300mph fighters and trainers now, or about to be, in production for Service, are all monoplanes.' Of K5054 he reported: 'The Supermarine Spitfire (Rolls-Royce Merlin) in the air certainly looked as if it were the fastest fighter in this country, and consequently in the World. Developed from the successful Schneider Trophy designs, the Spitfire which is of remarkably small size has a stress-carrying skin on fuselage and wings alike. Its makers claim that the low weight of its structure has never been achieved before. The perfectly smooth outer surface is the result of much practical experience with counter-sunk riveting.'

In late May 1936, K5054 went to the Aeroplane and Armament Experimental Establishment at Martlesham Heath in Suffolk for RAF service trials. An A&AEE report was published in September 1936. What follows are extracts from that report, with the 'Flying Qualities' section used in its entirety.

Report No. M/692/Int.2.

September 1936.

AEROPLANE AND ARMAMENT EXPERIMENTAL ESTABLISHMENT.

MARTLESHAM HEATH.

Handling trials of the Spitfire K-5054.

A.M. Ref:- 431708/35/R.D.A.1.
A. & A.E.E. Ref:- M/4493/20 - A.S.56.

———

Handling trials were done at a total weight of 5332 lb., the centre of gravity was 9.7 inches aft of the datum point.

Limits 8.25" - 9.9" aft - extended by .01 chord to 10.8 inches aft.

CONTROLS.

Ailerons.

On the ground the aileron control works freely and without play. Full movement of the control column can be obtained when the pilot is in the cockpit.

In the air the ailerons are light to handle when climbing and on the glide they become heavier with increase in speed, but by no more than is required to impart good "feel".

The aeroplane was dived to 380 m.p.h. A.S.I. and up to that speed the ailerons were not unduly heavy, and gave adequate response.

The ailerons are effective down to the stall and give adequate control when landing and taking off. The response is quick under all conditions of flight, and during all manoeuvres required from a fighting aeroplane.

Handling trials of Spitfire K5054

Handling trials were done at a total weight of 5,332lb, the centre of gravity was 9.7in aft of the datum point. Limits 8.25in–9.9in aft – extended by .01 chord to 10.8in aft.

Controls

Ailerons On the ground the aileron control works freely and without play. Full movement of the control column can be obtained when the pilot is in the cockpit.

In the air the ailerons are light to handle when climbing and on the glide they become heavier with increase in speed, but by no more than is required to impart good 'feel'.

The aeroplane was dived to 380mph A.S.I. and up to that speed the ailerons were not unduly heavy, and have adequate response.

The ailerons are effective down to the stall and give adequate control when landing and taking off. The response is quick under all conditions of flight, and during all manoeuvres required from a fighting aeroplane.

Flying Qualities

Stability Laterally the aeroplane is stable. If one wing is depressed and the control column released the aeroplane will return to a level keel in a reasonable time. Directionally the aeroplane is stable under all conditions of flight, engine on or off. Longitudinally the aeroplane is neutrally stable with engine on and stable in the glide. The aeroplane is unstable in the glide with flaps and undercarriage down.

In general the stability characteristics are satisfactory for a fighting aeroplane and give a reasonable compromise between controllability and steadiness as a gun platform.

Characteristics at the stall As the elevator control is very powerful the aeroplane will stall long before the control column is moved

right back. The stall is normal. There is no vice nor snatch on the controls. In tight turns, giving approximately 3g as registered on the accelerometer, at speeds from 140mph A.S.I. downwards there was a distinct juddering on the whole aeroplane. Under these conditions the aeroplane is probably in a semi-stalled condition and this juddering effect may be due to slight buffeting on the tail. This can be stopped at once if the control column is eased forward.

Tests according to A.D.M. 293 were done with the following results: On No. 1 test with the undercarriage and flaps up it is difficult to keep the aeroplane steady when the control column is right back. It wallows from side to side and there is a snatch on the control column from the elevators. With the undercarriage and flaps down the aeroplane is steadier in the stalled glide and there is no snatch. In test No. 2 with the undercarriage and flaps down it was possible to pull the wing up when ailerons were applied to unbank, but in turns both to the left and to the right, the aeroplane tends to take charge at the stall and cannot be said to comply with these tests when the control column is pulled right back.

In the third test with the undercarriage and flaps up, the wing can be pulled up, but in this test again the aeroplane takes charge to such an extent that the pilot found it almost impossible to make sure of centralising the rudder. With the undercarriage and flaps down the aeroplane's behaviour was much the same.

In tests Nos 2 and 3 the movements of the aeroplane are more violent to the right than to the left after applying the controls. No spin resulted in either of these two tests.

This aeroplane, in common with other fighters tested at this Establishment, cannot be said to fully comply with tests Nos 2 and 3, as its behaviour depends so much on the way the pilot uses his controls. Its behaviour in test No. 1 indicates that there is sufficient lateral control at the stall for a heavily loaded high speed aeroplane of this type.

Aerobatics Loops, half rolls off loops, slow rolls and stall turns have been done. The aeroplane is very easy and pleasant to handle in all aerobatics.

Landing and take-off The aeroplane is easy and normal to take off. There is a slight tendency to swing, but this is not so pronounced as on a Fury and is automatically and easily corrected by the pilot. The aeroplane is simple and easy to land, but requires very little movement of the control column as the elevator control is so powerful, and it is not necessary to have the control column fully back.

Left: The first page of the handling trials report for K5054 made at Martlesham Heath in September 1936.

If the engine is opened up with the flaps and undercarriage down, the aeroplane can be easily held by the control column. The aeroplane does not swing when landing.

Sideslipping The aeroplane does not sideslip readily.

Ground handling The ground handling is extremely good. The aeroplane is easy to turn and taxi in fairly strong winds. It is a more satisfactory aeroplane for operating in high winds than the normal biplane fighter.

Undercarriage

The undercarriage has excellent shock absorbing qualities, and good rebound damping.

The controls for the hydraulically retracting mechanism are simple and well arranged. The undercarriage can be raised in about 10 seconds and lowered in about 15 seconds, without undue effort. The indicators were satisfactory. The wheels cannot be seen, but when the undercarriage is lowered two small rods project through the wings to show its position.

When the undercarriage is fully up or down, the hand lever of the oil pump can no longer be moved, and this is a useful additional indication that the undercarriage is in the required position.

A Klaxon to warn the pilot that the undercarriage is up works when the throttle is pulled back beyond two thirds, but is not loud enough to be heard by him with the cockpit open and the engine on.

Flying View

View forwards is fair and upwards is good. View to the rear is fair for a covered cockpit.

The present windscreen gives great distortion. If a curved windscreen of this shape cannot be made in either moulded glass or in suitable material to give no distortion, it is considered that it should be replaced by a flat sided type, even though this might involve a slight reduction in performance.

With the cover open, the cockpit is remarkably free from draught, and it is possible to land and take off with the cockpit cover open without losing goggles.

Cockpit Comfort

The cockpit is comfortable and there is plenty of room, even for a big pilot. The head room is somewhat cramped for a tall pilot. It is not unduly noisy and the instruments and controls are well arranged. The cockpit is easy to enter and leave when the aeroplane is on the ground and footsteps on the wing are not considered necessary.

At speeds over 300mph A.S.I. the cockpit cover is very difficult to open, although it has been opened at 320mph A.S.I. and will stay open. Attention should be given to this question, as it is most important that the pilot should be able to get out of the aeroplane at the very highest speeds without difficulty. A small air flap operated by the handles on the sliding cover might make it easier to open at high speeds.

Although no heating is provided the cockpit was kept warm by heat from the engine and exhaust at 25,000ft. Gloves were not necessary.

Instruments

All instruments are well arranged and are clearly visible to the pilot. The compass is steady at all speeds.

Summary of Flying Qualities

The aeroplane is simple and easy to fly and has no vices. All controls are entirely satisfactory for this type and no modification to them is required, except that the elevator control might be improved by reducing the gear ratio between the control column and elevator. The controls are well harmonised and appear to give an excellent compromise between manoeuvrability and steadiness for shooting. Take-off and landing are straightforward and easy.

The aeroplane has rather a flat glide, even when the undercarriage and flaps are down and has a considerable float if the approach is made a little too flat. This defect could be remedied by fitting higher drag flaps.

In general the handling of this aeroplane is such that it can be flown without risk by the average fully trained service fighter pilot, but there can be no doubt that it would be improved by having flaps giving a higher drag.

Later in its life K5054 gained camouflage and was also fitted with a tailwheel instead of its early tailskid.

'I was pleased with that little episode, partly because I was damn sure that the first 109 was not going to get home and, secondly, because I was now absolutely sure the Spitfire Mk I could readily out-turn the 109, certainly in the 20,000ft area, and probably at all heights.' Jeffrey Quill

Spitfire Mark I
Performance Trials

Spitfire N3171. Merlin III fitted with a Rotol Constant Speed Airscrew. Aeroplane & Armament Experimental Establishment Boscombe Down, 19 March 1940
A&AEE Ref: 4493/44 – AS.56/8
AM Ref: B.8242/39/AD/RDL

In accordance with Air Ministry letter, reference B.9242/39/AD/R/DL, dated 4 November 1939, performance trials have been carried out to compare this aeroplane with the standard Spitfire I fitted with a two-pitch airscrew.

1.0 Comments on Trials
As delivered, this aeroplane was fitted with a bulletproof windscreen, armour plating over the fuel tank, and a domed top on the sliding hood to allow more headroom for the pilot. None of these modifications had been made to K9793 fitted with a two-pitch metal airscrew the performance of which was given in Report M692/B dated 12 July, 1939. Consequently changes in performance, particularly in level speed cannot be attributed solely to the change in airscrew.

2.0 Take-off
The take-off run in zero wind and under standard atmospheric conditions is better than that of the two-pitch airscrew Spitfire. The accompanying table gives the take-off for the three types of airscrews.

Airscrew	Take-off run (yards)	Distance to clear 50ft screen (yards)
Rotol	225	370
Two-pitch Metal	320	490
Wooden Fixed Pitch	420	790

3.0 Climb
It was found that the best climbing speed as determined from partial climbs was not suitable owing to the instability, uncomfortably steep attitude, and poor view at this speed. This

climbing speed was increased by 22mph to a more suitable speed which improved the handling qualities of the aeroplane in the climb.

The following table gives comparative times in minutes to reach various heights for the best climbing speed and the recommended climbing speed. Also included are the times to height for Spitfires with two-pitch and fixed pitch airscrews.

Airscrew	Time to Height (Feet)				
	10,000	15,000	20,000	25,000	30,000
Rotol Best Climb		3	4	7	13
Rotol Recommended				4	8
Two-pitch Metal				4	8
Wooden Fixed Pitch				4	8

Best climbing speed: 140mph ASI to 12,000ft thereafter decreasing by 1mph per 1,000ft.

Recommended climbing speeds: 162mph ASI to 12,000ft thereafter decreasing by 2½mph per 1,000ft.

4.0 Level Speeds
In addition to the routine speed tests on this aeroplane as it was delivered, subsidiary tests were made to determine the effect of the bulletproof windscreen, and engine rpm on the top level speed.

4.1 Windscreen Test
The bulletproof windscreen was replaced by the prototype Spitfire pattern of windscreen.

As delivered the aeroplane was fitted with a bulletproof windscreen which has a flat front panel protruding about 1½ inches beyond the framework. After level speed tests had been completed this was replaced by the prototype pattern of windscreen. This consists of a windscreen with a curved front panel and is perhaps slightly better aerodynamically than the production pattern which has a flat, though flush-fitting, front panel. The loss of speed resulting from the projecting bulletproof windscreen is 6mph.

4.2 Controlling RPM
Speed tests were made at three heights below full throttle height with the boost pressure maintained constant at 6¼lb/in^2 whilst the rpm was varied over a range from 2,600 to 3,000.

The results show that the maximum level speed is reached with the airscrew controlling at 2,800 engine rpm. On increasing the rpm to 3,000 the speed was reduced, on the average by 4mph.

Previous Page: Restored Spitfire I P9374 lifts off from Duxford. Pilot John Romain has begun the process of hand cranking the undercarriage up and the starboard main wheel can be seen to be partially retracted with the port wheel only just beginning to retract. Jarrod Cotter

Right: Spitfire Is of No. 610 (County of Chester) Squadron on patrol from RAF Hornchurch during the Battle of Britain in the summer of 1940. British Official

Below right: The cockpit of a very early Spitfire I which is equipped with a hand-cranked undercarriage lever and a ring and bead sight. British Official

Left: Flight Sergeant George 'Grumpy' Unwin of No. 19 Squadron climbs out of his Spitfire Mark I at Fowlmere, Cambridgeshire, after a sortie. Unwin shot down 14½ enemy aircraft between May and September 1940. British Official

Below left: Pilots of No. 19 Squadron perform a mock scramble to their Spitfire Is at Duxford. British Official

For the particular engine fitted there is a reduction of 17bhp at constant boost (+6¼lb) when the rpm are increased from 2,800 to 3,000. The loss of speed is therefore probably due to the loss of power accompanied by a slight decrease in airscrew efficiency. The matter is being further investigated by Messrs Rolls-Royce and Messrs Rotols. It will be noted that reducing the rpm from 3,000 to 2,800 lowers the full throttle height by 2,000ft.

4.3. Engine Power
The engine installed in the aeroplane develops slightly less power under test bed conditions than that in K9793, the aeroplane fitted with the two-pitch airscrew. This could have the effect of reducing the top level speed by about 2mph.

Summary of Trials

Aeroplane	Spitfire I No. N3171
Spec. No	16/36
Contractor	Vickers-Armstrong (Supermarine) Ltd
Type	Landplane DUTY Single Seater Fighter.
Engine	Merlin III
	Normal BHP 950/990 at Rated Altitude 12,250ft
	At 2,600 RPM at rated boost pressure +6¼lb/in² boost

	Lb
Tare weight	4,713.0
Weight light	4,476.5
Fixed military load	236.5
Service Load	657.5
Fuel 84 gallons*	630.0
Oil 5½	49.5
Flying weight on trials	6,050.0

*Based on 7.5lb per gallon.

At Full Throttle

Height Feet	Top Speed MP	Time to Climb Mins	Rate of Climb Ft/Min
Sea Level	–	–	–
2,000	–	0.7	2820
5,000	–	1.8	2850
10,000	320.5	3.5	2895
15,000	339	5.3	2430
20,000	353.5	7.7	1840
25,000	345	10.9	1250
30,000	319	16.4	660

Stalling speed

flaps up	78 MPH	Gliding in ASI	87 MPH
flaps down	68 MPH		
Best landing ASI	66 MPH		

Landing and take-off tests corrected to zero wind and standard atmosphere

Aircraft Spitfire I N3171
Engine Merlin III Airscrews

Position	Centre
Variable Pitch airscrew	Rotol
Type	Merlin
Serial No.	2572
Maker's No.	–
Diameter	10ft 9in
No of Blades	Three
Direction of Blades	Right-hand
A.M. Serial Nos Hub	2572
A.M. Serial Nos Blade 1	A-4184
A.M. Serial Nos Blade 2	A-4185
A.M. Serial Nos Blade 3	A-4136
Basic Pitch Setting	–
Pitch Range	35° 0'
High Pitch Setting	58° 20' (estimated)
Low Pitch Setting	23° 20'

Climbing Trials Spitfire N3171

Height in Standard Atmosphere Feet	Time from Start Min	Rate of Climb Ft/Min	True Air Speed MPH	ASI MPH	PEC	Comp	RPM	Boost Lb/in²
Sea Level	0							
1,000	0.4	2,810	163	161	-0.7	-0.1		6.4
2,000	0.7	2,820	165	161	-0.7	-0.1		6.4
3,000	1.1	2,830	167.5	161	-0.7	-0.1		6.4
5,000	1.8	2,850	172.5	161	-0.7	-0.1	Controlled at 2,600	6.4
6,500	2.3	2,860	176.5	161	-0.7	-0.1		6.4
10,000	3.5	2,895	186.5	161	-0.7	-0.1		6.4
11,000	3.9	2,905	189	161	-0.7	-0.1		6.4
13,000	4.6	2,665	193.5	159.5	-0.4	-0.7		5.2
15,000	5.3	2,460	195.5	155.5	+0.2	-0.7		3.9

Climbing Trials Spitfire N3171 continued

Height in Standard Atmosphere Feet	Time from Start Min	Rate of Climb Ft/Min	True Air Speed MPH	ASI MPH	PEC	Comp	RPM	Boost Lb/in²
16,500	6.0	2,250	197.0	152.5	+0.7	-0.8		3.1
18,000	6.7	2,075	198.5	149.5	+1.2	-0.8		2.2
20,000	7.7	1,840	201.0	146	+1.8	-0.9		1.0
23,000	9.5	1,480	205.0	140	+2.9	-0.0	Controlled at 2,600	-0.8
26,500	11.8	1,130	209.0	134.5	+3.9	-1.0		-2.5
28,000	13.8	895	212.0	130.5	+4.7	-1.1		-3.6
30,000	16.4	660	214.0	126.5	+5.4	-1.1		-4.7

Estimated absolute ceiling	35,600
Greatest height reached	30,000
RPM stationary on ground	2,850
Boost pressure lb/in²	+6½
Service ceiling	34,700ft

Speed Trials At 3,000 RPM and 6¼lb/in² boost (nominal) Spitfire N3171

Height in Standard Atmosphere Feet	True Air Speed MPH	ASI MPH	Compressibility and Position Error Correction MPH PE	CE	RPM	Boost Lb/in²
Sea Level						
1,000						
2,000						
3,000						
5,000						
6,500						
10,000	320.5	286	-8.5	-2.1		+6.1
13,000	332	283.5	-8.5	-2.9		+6.1
15,000	339	280.5	-8.5	-3.4		+6.1
16,500	345	279	-8.5	-3.8		+6.1
18,000	350.5	277.5	-8.5	-4.2	Controlling at 3,000	+6.1
20,000	353.5	271	-8.5	-4.6		+5.25
23,000	350	255.5	-8.4	-4.8		+3.15
26,000	341.5	237.5	-8.0	-4.7		+1.1
28,000	332	222.5	-7.4	-4.5		-0.3
30,000	319	205	-6.3	-4.0		–
18,900*	354	276	-8.5	-4.4		+6.1

Right: Six Spitfire Is of No. 65 Squadron in a close starboard echelon formation. British Official

Landing and take-off tests corrected to zero wind and standard atmosphere.

Take-off run	225yds
Distance from rest to clear	50ft screen 370yds
Gliding in ASI	87MPH
Best landing ASI	66MPH
Landing run with brakes	310yds

T/O and Landing Runs under actual conditions of tests, i.e: wind 4mph, Temp +8°C, Press 30.0" Hg..

T/O Run	195yds in 9.1 secs.
Distance to 50ft screen	335yds.
Landing run	265yds in 16.7 secs.

*Full throttle height

Conclusions

1.This aeroplane has a much better take-off and climbs faster than other Spitfires fitted with wooden fixed pitch or metal two pitch airscrews.

2.There is a drop of 13mph in maximum level speed compared with the two-pitch airscrew aeroplane, but of this, 8mph can be attributed to sources other than the airscrew.

3.Below full throttle height an increase in speed of about 4mph can be attained by controlling the engine RPM at 2,800 instead of 3,000.

4.The limiting diving speed can be reached much more rapidly with this aeroplane than with Spitfires fitted with fixed pitch wooden and two-pitch metal airscrews.

Clockwise from top left: This early Spitfire I shows various features that were soon to be modified on later examples – a 'broomstick' aerial, flat-sided canopy and two-bladed propeller. British Official

The beautifully restored cockpit of Spitfire I P9374 at Duxford. Note the large hand cranking lever on the right which needs to be cranked about 19 times to raise or lower the fighter's undercarriage.
Jarrod Cotter

A pleasant study of Jeffrey Quill climbing into the cockpit of a Spitfire I.

First thoughts on flying the Spitfire

Flight Sergeant George Unwin, 19 Squadron, RAF Duxford: 'It was a bit frightening to start with because we had the two-bladed, fixed pitch prop. You went as far back as you could and opened up on the brakes and then let it go. There was a little hawthorn hedge on the western side of Duxford, and when you saw that you were going through that, unless you did something, you eased it back. But once you were up, she was an absolute delight to fly. …But of course, that didn't last long. When they fitted the three-bladed prop everything changed.'

Seventy years on …

In October 2010, following a summer of commemorations to mark the seventieth anniversary of the Battle of Britain, former Spitfire pilot Squadron Leader Geoffrey Wellum, DFC, made a very moving and typically modest after-dinner speech at the RAF Battle of Britain Memorial Flight's (BBMF's) end of season guest night. With Geoffrey's kind permission, what follows are extracts from one of the most moving speeches that even many of the serving RAF personnel present had ever been privileged to hear, spoken by a veteran who was the youngest RAF fighter pilot during the Battle of Britain:

By the time 92 Sqn arrived at Biggin, I was more or less conversant with the Spitfire, but apart from chasing one or two isolated enemy aircraft, I was still un-blooded and had yet to experience real fighter combat. Consequently, I was very much aware that my personal most testing time was still to come. Did I have the courage, and of course a courage that had to be sustained for weeks and possibly months?

One recalls having to settle into some sort of routine, memories of which had we realised it, were to remain with us most vividly for the remainder of our lives, but for many of us, of course, there was to be no remainder. Never to be forgotten is the transport taking those on dawn readiness around the perimeter track to the dispersal hut, the tranquillity and peace of the pre-dawn, and the beginning of a new day. The muffled talk as the ground crews prepared their charges for the testing hours to come. The chug, chug of the petrol bowsers refuelling or topping up the Spitfires, the clink of a spanner. Even little things, like dew on your flying boots as you carried your parachute across the grass to your waiting Spitfire, looking at the sky and thinking at the time it's going to be a lovely day again. Resignation, total resignation. Oh God … another dawn.

More often than not one offered up a little prayer. 'It's going to be a very busy day, O Lord, and if I forget you, please don't forget me. Just give me this day please, please give me this day.'

An early scramble and at 20,000ft you would see the sunrise. And for those of us who returned to an earth, still shrouded in the pre-dawn twilight, suppressing the thoughts of friends unaccounted for, you would see the sunrise again, the second time in one morning. We had lived to see two dawns, and between those dawns, time was packed with enough incident to last a lifetime, of possibly being killed and most certainly avoiding being killed. A time literally packed with life or death. And the day had just begun, and so it went on for the remainder of that day, and of course, for those of us still around, there was another day tomorrow, and the day after that.

Well-known warbird pilot John Romain describes operating the earliest-configured Spitfire flown since 1940:

Looking through my logbook reminded me that I have test-flown quite a few Supermarine Spitfires. The marks vary, and include both Rolls-Royce Merlin and Griffon engined examples. Some were clipped-wing variants and two are Tr.IX two-seaters.

In all cases, though, the various Spitfire marks had similarities. They all had the engine-driven hydraulic system to retract and lower the undercarriage. All were fitted with constant-speed units to control the propeller rpm, and all had the later metal covered ailerons.

Restored to exacting standards, P9374 is a true Spitfire I. For me as the test pilot this provided a few areas of discovery over the 'standard' Spitfire air test. A Spitfire I fitted with all the early systems, engine and propeller, has not flown since the end of 1940, as any aircraft flying after this had been 'field modified' to enhance their modification state.

The aircraft is powered by a Rolls-Royce Merlin III driving a two-pitch de Havilland propeller. The early engines were not the 'power horses' of the later marks, this example giving 940hp at +6¼lb of boost. They are also delicate engines to handle, the early one-piece heads and banks being particularly prone to cracking and losing coolant.

A two-pitch propeller brings its own problems. There is no constant-speed unit to govern the engine rpm, and therefore the pilot becomes the 'governor', constantly monitoring rpm against boost or throttle settings. Any speed change in addition gives an rpm change.

The airframe is simply early Spitfire design. I expected the controls to be quite light and responsive, thinking that a comparatively light aircraft and early design would probably reflect Mitchell's intent closer than the later types.

Undercarriage retraction is a manual, hand-pumped affair. Testing in the hangar showed this to be a very simple and easy operation. Whether this would change with the aircraft airborne and having air loads applied I did not know.

The ailerons are fabric covered, rather than the later metal-covered assemblies. This in itself I did not expect to give problems, but I had asked Alex Henshaw about them just in case. He simply asked how fast I intended flying! 'Anything up to 400mph is fine John. Over that they get a bit heavy.'

Reading the quite sparse Spitfire I pilot's notes did not show any areas of additional concern, so I prepared for the first flight with a balance of excitement and trepidation.

Just like the 'old days'

Walking up to P9374 really impresses on you the fact that it is a Spitfire I. The straight legs of the undercarriage, balloon tyres and 'baby' engine/propeller combination were highlights of the many wartime pictures I had seen of Spitfire Is on the grass at Duxford. With full fuel, myself and parachute the aircraft weighed 5,991lb and the c.g. position was 6.6in aft of datum. Compared with the Spitfire I's all-up weight of 6,200lb the aircraft was not too far from wartime operational weight.

Strapping-in was carried out easily, and it was not long before I was at last on my own, in the 'office'. Taking a few minutes to settle down, I carried out my normal left-to-right check of everything.

Cockpit side door closed and locked
Rudder trim tab at neutral
Elevator trim tab, 1 division nose-up
Propeller pitch control at coarse
Throttle, full and free and closed
Mixture control – auto rich

Right: Although the Rolls-Royce Merlin has six exhaust ports on each side of the engine, on early aircraft the normal practice was to use 'Siamese' exhaust stubs which each incorporated two exhausts and meant that only six stubs were used. Later aircraft had a smaller stub for each exhaust port. *Jarrod Cotter*

Throttle friction adjusted
Electrical power switch – on
Undercarriage indicator light switch – on
Magnetos – off, starter magneto – on
Radiator door – open
Flap control – up and air pressure – checked
Flight instruments – checked
Engine instruments – checked
Fuel selector – on
Undercarriage selector at 'down' position
Seat height – adjusted
Headset lead – connected
Canopy – free to slide and open
Flight controls – full and free
Brakes – on and checked – air pressure – check.

'Clear to start!'

With that done I am ready for engine start. The engine had been run earlier, so was still quite warm. If it had been cold then a good five loaded primes of fuel would have been required, but when hot or warm much less priming fuel is needed. I therefore give three pumps of the primer and then screw it back in the closed position. Opening the throttle ½in, I check brakes on and with the stick hard back call 'Clear to start!'

With the propeller turning through its third blade the engine surges into life with a cloud of oil smoke and exhaust. What a lovely smell! Somehow you never get tired of starting a Merlin.

The oil pressure is instantly checked and is sitting happily at 60lb/in². Selecting the propeller from coarse to fine position sees the oil pressure drop slightly and then return to normal. The engine is now running very smoothly and all the engine instruments are showing normal readings.

As the engine is already warm I know I do not have a lot of time before take-off. The coolant temperature will rise quite quickly, and with that in mind I wave away the chocks, release the brakes and start taxying out to the runway.

Directional control is good, and only small amounts of brake are necessary to weave from side to side on the way to the runway. Temperatures are rising now towards 95°C on the coolant, so not too much time left!

Stopping near the end of the runway, I quickly go through the pre-take-off checks.

Trims – set
Throttle friction – set
Propeller – fine pitch
Magnetos – on, starter magneto – off
Flaps – up
Radiator door – open
Fuel – on, pressure 2½lb/in^2
Instruments – set and checked
Controls – full and free
Harness – tight
Canopy – open and latched

I leave the engine run-up until last, as this will warm up the coolant even more. So, with the stick fully back, I throttle up to 1,800rpm and check the two-position propeller and then the magnetos. All is fine, so I throttle back to idle at 550rpm.

Lining up on the grass, I gradually push the throttle forward and the aircraft starts to accelerate nicely. The first impressions are very important at this stage; I start to feel the controls come 'alive' and concentrate on whether they feel normal. Any large out-of-trim tendencies are better identified here on the ground rather than in the air!

The first flight of P9374

The aircraft accelerates quickly, and a quick glance shows +5lb of boost and 2,600rpm. I leave the throttle there and, following a few bumps from Duxford's grass, we are airborne.

I had briefed the engineers that I would not retract the undercarriage until I was happy with the engine and initial trim of the flying controls, so, climbing steadily on the downwind leg, I throttle back to +2lb boost and select coarse pitch on the propeller. It is like changing gear in a car from first to fourth! The rpm drops from 2,700 to 2,050 very smoothly, and the aircraft now wants to accelerate beyond the undercarriage-down speed of 160mph. The ailerons are not in trim, so I am holding a 2–3lb roll left tendency. However, I feel this is acceptable for now, and select under-carriage up and start to pump the handle. There is no increase in

Left: The Merlin of Spitfire I P9374 in full song above its home base at Duxford. Jarrod Cotter

Right, from the top: Spitfire I K9814 possibly seen on delivery to No. 66 Squadron at Duxford. British Official

A superb study of No. 19 Squadron's Spitfire I K9795 after the unit had become the first RAF squadron to receive the Spitfire in 1938. British Official

Following an air show display at Duxford, Spitfire I N3200 is seen on approachto land on the airfield's grass runway. Jarrod Cotter

the loads over that experienced in the hangar, and in good order the undercarriage retracts and the 'two-up' lights show red on the indicator.

Closing the hood, I now scan the instruments for any signs of a problem. All is well, so I climb the aircraft up to 3,000ft to carry out a stall check. In the climb I start to 'feel' the controls some more, and realise that this aircraft feels really nice. It is well balanced, and apart from the out-of-trim aileron the controls are nice.

Different from other Spitfires

Other things start to register as 'different' from the other Spitfires. The canopy is the original flat-sided type, and I am aware of a limitation to my head movement; I keep banging my head on the canopy sides! Also, the aircraft is relatively quiet compared with some of the later marks. The coarse-pitch propeller and Siamese exhaust stacks obviously keep the noise levels lower.

Once 3,000ft is reached it is time to slow down for the stalls. The first is a 'clean' stall, with undercarriage retracted and flaps up. I first trim the aircraft to fly at 105mph and put the propeller back into 'fine' pitch. If I need the engine to recover from the stall I will need the instant acceleration that fine pitch will give.

As the aircraft slows through 75mph the elevators give a slight buffet, and the nose and left wing drop at 70mph. Very nice! The book figure is 73mph; so a perfect result. Accelerating away, I select undercarriage down and start pumping. It takes more pumps to get the undercarriage down than it does to raise it, but still it is a painless exercise and I have not yet lost the skin off my knuckles, which was an apparent injury for many early Spitfire pilots.

Slowing below 140mph, I select flaps down. Wow! They go down very quickly and the aircraft instantly has a nose-down pitch. Trimming back, I note the flap extension time as 1–1½sec.

The stall is again very benign, and occurs at a little under 60mph. The book figure is 64, so again this is a good result.

I have been airborne for about 20min, and it is time to return for the first landing. We can then check for leaks that may have shown up and adjust the aileron trim before testing the aircraft further.

Flying through the airfield overhead at 500ft, I slow down to below 160mph and lower the undercarriage. Propeller into fine pitch, radiator door open. Check for green down lights on the

undercarriage, and slow to below 140mph for flaps. I am ready for their rapid deployment this time, and trim the aircraft to 90mph. Opening the hood causes a windy buffet through the cockpit, but what a feeling! A Spitfire I on finals to Duxford, the first airfield at which the Spitfire became operational in 1939, a lovely sunny evening and an aircraft that is flying beautifully. I pinch myself and get on with the landing.

The fighter flares at 75mph and settles on to the grass. Fantastic; no problems keeping it straight, and it slows to a walking pace for the taxi back. Puffs of oil smoke cough from the exhaust stacks as I taxi in. The warmth and smell of the engine enhance my imagination of what it must have felt like for a 20-year-old RAF pilot let loose in a Spitfire I before the Battle of Britain. It must have been unbelievable, frightening and exhilarating, all at the same time. With no slow-running cut-out on the Mark I, it is magnetos 'off', and the engine slows and stops, with a momentary kick just to burn of the last bit of fuel.

Everyone is ecstatic; they should be. This is a fantastic restoration of which everyone should be very proud. A lovely aircraft that flies beautifully.

Follow-up testing

After the first flight came the official air-testing. The content was discussed with the Civil Aviation Authority's (CAA) flight-test department, and a format agreed.

After a thorough inspection and the first attempt at trimming the ailerons, I flew P9374 for another 20min sortie. The aileron trim had not changed very much, so I noted the need for a larger addition of cord to the trailing edge of the port aileron. In addition I tried the first climb. The pilot's notes mentioned that the aircraft should climb at +6¼lb boost and an rpm above 2,080. They did not, however, mention a speed. From other Spitfire flying I knew that 160–180mph was normal, but at these speeds I was suffering from low rpm. What I did not want to do was 'over-boost' the engine by running a high boost setting (+6¼lb) with only 2,050rpm.

With little information in the notes, I tried to obtain some original testing notes from the Boscombe Down archive. They were not forthcoming, so I tried the internet. To my surprise I found a lot of original Spitfire test data on the websites, including a test carried out by the Aeroplane and Armament Experimental Establishment at Martlesham Heath on a Spitfire I with the de Havilland two-pitch propeller. This document gave me the data I needed, and also revealed that the two-pitch propeller 'coarse setting' needed adjustment. It also gave me the climb speed of 185mph, noting that this was necessary to obtain a favourable rpm in the climb! Things were finally starting to make sense.

With the propeller adjusted and another piece of cord on the aileron, I took off for the third air-test. The aileron was much better, and the rpm in the climb sat at the correct level. This allowed further testing, so I climbed to 6,000ft for the various stall checks and the start of the higher-speed handling. Copious notes later I landed back at Duxford, content that the aircraft was now settling down very nicely.

The next four flights entailed more climbing and stick-force tests, plus the start of some aerobatics. The roll rate was very similar to that of other Spitfire marks, and generally the aircraft was a delight to roll and loop.

I had attained 350mph in one of the dives, but P9374 had to be tested to the full 405mph stated in the notes. A wartime figure of 450mph was allowed, but this meant an engine overspeed of 3,700rpm. This speed and rpm were not necessary for our flight regime, and also I wondered how many engines survived that. An interesting letter found with the web notes, written by Air Chief Marshal Sir Hugh Dowding in early 1940, warned pilots against blowing up their engines at high rpm and boost figures.

The dive to 405mph was started from 9,000ft. As the airspeed went through 380mph, I had 2,900rpm and the angle of dive was fairly steep. Aileron loads were increasing, and I remembered Alex Henshaw saying that above 400mph they were very heavy. Just as this figure was approached there was a loud bang and a rush of air. Reducing power instantly, I pulled out of the dive and regained level flight, wondering, with a lot of anxiety, what had broken.

It very quickly became obvious what the problem was, and I relaxed. The direct-vision panel on the side of the canopy had blown out. It is simply held on with Perspex pins and clips, and the airflow had obviously been too much for it. I returned to Duxford for a few circuits both with and without flaps, and then landed for repairs.

The next day I achieved the 405mph dive and all went fine. However, it is a very noisy and startling thing to do. I can only think that combat conditions would be the sole reason for flying a Spitfire Mark I at 405mph. The controls would be very heavy, the engine screaming and the air noise incredible.

With eight flights completed, the aircraft was flying very well. All the test data was written in a report for the CAA and accepted the next day. Another wonderful achievement.

The Spitfire I is different to fly when compared with its modified, later-mark companions. However, it is a delight in engineering and pure aerodynamic terms. The aircraft is a real piece of 1938 history, and does everything the test flights of 1939 said it would.

'The Mk.II could be described as a refined version of the Mk.I with some alterations introduced for production as well as technical reasons.'
Jeffrey Quill

Above: The cover of AP 1565B, the pilot's notes for the Spitfire Mk.II.

Opposite: Spitfire IIa P7350 of the Battle of Britain Memorial Flight being flown by former Officer Commanding Squadron Leader Ian Smith MBE. The Flight is based at RAF Coningsby and this aircraft actually fought in combat during the Battle of Britain. Richard Paver

Pilot's Notes
Spitfire Mark II
July 1940
Air Publication 1565b

Pilot's Controls and Equipment

Introduction
The Spitfire IIa is a single seat, low wing monoplane fighter fitted with a Merlin XII engine and a de Havilland 20° (PCP) or Rotol 35° constant speed airscrew.

Main Services

Fuel system Fuel is carried in two tanks mounted one above the other (the lower one is self-sealing) forward of the cockpit and is delivered by an engine driven pump. The tank capacities are as follows: Top tank – 48 gallons. Bottom tank – 37 gallons. The top tank feeds into the lower tank, and the fuel cock controls, one for each tank, are fitted below the instrument panel.

Oil system Oil is supplied by a tank of 5.8 gallons capacity fitted below the engine mounting, and two oil coolers in tandem are fitted in the underside of the port plane.

Hydraulic system An engine-driven hydraulic pump supplies the power for operating the undercarriage.

Pneumatic system An engine-driven air compressor feeds two storage cylinders for operation of the flaps, brakes, guns and landing lamps. The cylinders are connected in series, each holding air at 200lb/in^2 pressure.

Electrical system A 12 volt generator, controlled by a switch above the instrument panel, supplies an accumulator which in turn supplies the whole of the electrical installation. There is a voltmeter on the left of the switch.

Aeroplane Controls

Primary flying controls and locking devices (a) The control column is of the spade-grip pattern and incorporates the brake lever and gun firing control. The rudder pedals have two positions for the

feet and are adjustable for leg reach by rotation of star wheels on the sliding tubes.

(b) Control locking struts are stowed on the right-hand side of the cockpit, behind the seat. To lock the control column, the longer strut should be clamped to the control column handle at one end and the other end inserted in a keyhole slot in the right-hand side of the seat. The fixed pin on the free end of the arm attached to this strut at the control column end should then be inserted in a lug on the starboard datum longeron, thus forming a rigid triangle between the column, the seat and the longeron.

(c) To lock the rudder pedals, a short bar with a pin at each end is attached to the other struts by a cable. The longer of the two pins should be inserted in a hole in the starboard star wheel bearing and the shorter in an eyebolt on the fuselage frame directly below the front edge of the seat. The controls should be locked with the seat in its highest position.

Flying instruments A standard blind flying instrument panel is incorporated in the main panel. The instruments comprise air-speed indicator, altimeter, directional gyro, artificial horizon, rate of climb and descent indicator and turn and bank indicator.

Trimming tabs The elevator trimming tabs are controlled by a hand wheel on the left-hand side of the cockpit, the indicator being on the instrument panel. The rudder trimming tab is controlled by a small hand wheel and is not provided with an indicator. The aeroplane tends to turn to starboard when the handwheel is rotated clockwise.

Undercarriage control and indicators (visual and audible)
(a) The undercarriage selector lever moves in a gated quadrant, on the right-hand side of the cockpit. An automatic cut-out in the control moves the selector lever into the gate when it has been pushed or pulled to the full extent of the quadrant.

(b) To raise the undercarriage the lever is pushed forward, but it must first be pulled back and then across to disengage it from the gate. When the undercarriage is raised and locked, the lever will spring into the forward gate.

(c) To lower the undercarriage the lever is pulled back, but it must be pushed forward and then across to disengage it from the gate. When the undercarriage is lowered and locked, the lever will spring into the rear gate.

Electrical visual indicator The electrically operated visual indicator

has two semi-transparent windows on which the words UP on a red background and DOWN on a green background are lettered; the words are illuminated according to the position of the under-carriage. The switch for the DOWN circuit of the indicator is mounted on the inboard side of the throttle quadrant and is moved to the ON position by means of a striker on the throttle lever; this switch should be returned to the OFF position by hand when the aeroplane is left standing for any length of time. The UP circuit is not controlled by this switch.

Mechanical position indicator A rod that extends through the top surface of the main plane is fitted to each undercarriage unit. When the wheels are down the rods, which are painted red, protrude through the top of the main planes, and when they are up the rods are flush with the main plane surfaces.

Warning horn The push switch controlling the horn is mounted on the throttle quadrant and is operated by a striker on the throttle lever. The horn may be silenced, even though the wheels are retracted and the engine throttled back, by depressing the push-button on the side of the throttle quadrant. As soon as the throttle is again advanced beyond about one quarter of its travel the push-button is automatically released and the horn will sound again on its return.

Flap control The split flaps have two positions only, up and fully down. They cannot, therefore, be used to assist take-off. They are operated pneumatically and controlled by a finder lever. A flap indicator was fitted only on early Spitfire I aeroplanes.

Undercarriage emergency operation (a) A sealed high-pressure cylinder containing carbon-dioxide and connected to the under-carriage operating jacks is provided for use in the event of failure of the hydraulic system. The cylinder is mounted on the right-hand side of the cockpit and the seal can be punctured by means of a red painted lever beside it. The handle is marked EMERGENCY ONLY and provision is made for fitting a thin copper wire seal as a check against inadvertent use.

(b) If the hydraulic system fails, the pilot should ensure that the undercarriage selector lever is in the DOWN position (this is essential) and push the emergency lowering lever forward and downward. The angular travel of the emergency lever is about 100° for puncturing the seal of the cylinder and then releasing the piercing plunger; it must be pushed through this movement and allowed to swing downwards. NO attempt should be made to return it to its original position until the cylinder is being replaced.

Wheel brakes The control lever for the pneumatic brakes is fitted on the control column spade grip; differential control of the brakes is provided by a relay valve connected to the rudder bar. A catch for retaining the brake lever in the on position for parking is fitted below the lever pivot. A triple pressure gauge, showing the air pressures in the pneumatic system cylinders and at each brake, is mounted on the left-hand side of the instrument panel.

Engine Controls

Throttle and mixture controls The throttle and mixture levers are fitted in a quadrant on the port side of the cockpit. A gate is provided for the throttle lever in the take-off position and an interlocking device between the levers prevents the engine from being run on an unsuitable mixture. Friction adjusters for the controls are provided on the side of the quadrant.

Automatic boost cut-out The automatic boost control may be cut out by pushing forward the small red painted lever at the forward end of the throttle quadrant.

Airscrew controls The control lever for the de Havilland 20° or Rotol 35° constant speed airscrew is on the throttle quadrant. The de Havilland 20° airscrew has a Positive Coarse Pitch position which is obtained in the extreme aft position of the control lever, when the airscrew blades are held at their maximum coarse pitch angles and the airscrew functions as a fixed airscrew.

Radiator flap control The flap at the outlet end of the radiator duct is operated by a lever and ratchet on the left-hand side of the cockpit. To open the flap, the lever should be pushed forward after releasing the ratchet by depressing the knob at the top of the lever. The normal minimum drag position of the flap lever for level flight is shown by a red triangle on the top of the map case fitted beside the lever. A notch beyond the normal position in the aft direction provides a position of the lever when the warm air is diverted through ducts into the main planes for heating the guns at high altitude.

Slow-running cut-out The control on the carburettor is operated by pulling the ring on the right-hand side of the instrument panel.

Fuel cock controls and contents gauges The fuel cock controls, one for each tank, are fitted at the bottom of the instrument panel. With the levers in the UP position the cocks are open. Either tank can be isolated, if necessary. The fuel contents gauge on the instrument panel indicates the contents of the lower tank, but only when the adjacent push-button is pressed.

Above left: Spitfires scramble from RAF Hornchurch during the Battle of Britain in September 1940. British Official

Left: Geoffrey Wellum, who was the youngest RAF fighter pilot during the Battle of Britain, discusses flying with Flight Lieutenant Antony Parkinson MBE, the BBMF's Operations Officer. Behind them is Spitfire IIa P7350, which at the time was wearing the QJ-K code that was carried on Geoffrey's wartime Spitfire. Jarrod Cotter

Fuel priming pump A hand-operated pump for priming the engine is mounted below the right-hand side of the instrument panel.

Ignition switches The ignition switches are on the left-hand bottom corner of the instrument panel.

Cartridge starter The starter push-button at the bottom of the instrument panel operates the L.4 Coffman starter and the booster coil. The control for reloading the breech is below the right-hand side of the instrument panel and is operated by slowly pulling on the finger ring and then releasing it.

Hand starting A starting handle is stowed behind the seat. A hole in the engine-cowling panel on the starboard side gives access for connecting the handle to the hand starting gear.

Engine instruments The engine instruments are grouped on the right-hand side of the instrument panel and comprise the following: engine-speed indicator, fuel pressure gauge, boost gauge, oil pressure gauge, oil inlet temperature gauge, radiator outlet temperature gauge and fuel contents gauge. On later aircraft the fuel pressure gauge is replaced by a fuel pressure warning lamp which lights when the pressure drops to 6lb/in^2.

Cockpit Accommodation and Equipment

Pilot's seat control The seat is adjustable for height by means of a lever on the right-hand side of the seat.

Safety harness release In order that the pilot may lean forward without unfastening his harness, a release catch is fitted to the right of the seat.

Cockpit door To facilitate entry to the cockpit a portion of the coaming on the port side is hinged. The door catches are released by means of a handle at the forward end. Two position catches are incorporated to allow the door to be partly opened before taking off or landing in order to prevent the hood from sliding shut in the event of a mishap.

Hood locking control The sliding hood is provided with spring catches for holding it either open or shut: the catches are released by two finger levers at the forward end of the hood. From outside, with the hood closed, the catches can be released by depressing a small knob at the top of the windscreen. Provision is made on the door to prevent the hood from sliding shut if the aeroplane overturns on landing.

Left: A dramatic overhead view of Squadron Leader Ian Smith at the controls of P7350 on a local sortie out of RAF Coningsby. Richard Paver

Direct vision panel A small knock-out panel is provided on the right-hand side of the hood for use in the event of the windscreen becoming obscured.

Cockpit lighting A floodlight is fitted on each side of the cockpit. Each is controlled by a switch immediately below the instrument panel.

Cockpit heating and ventilation A small adjustable flap on the starboard coaming above the instrument panel is provided for ventilation of the cockpit. The flap is opened by turning a knurled nut underneath the flap.

Oxygen A standard regulator unit is fitted on the left-hand side of the instrument panel and a bayonet socket is on the right-hand side of the cockpit. A separate cock is provided in addition to the regulator.

Mirror A mirror providing a rearward view is fitted at the top of the windscreen.

Map cases A metal case for a writing pad and another for maps, books, etc are fitted on the left-hand side of the cockpit. Stowage for a height-and-airspeed computer is provided below the wireless remote contactor.

Operational Equipment and Controls

Guns and cannon (a) The machine-guns and cannon are fired pneumatically by means of push-buttons on the control column spade grip. The compressed air supply is taken from the same source as the brake supply, the available pressure being shown by the gauge.

(b) The triple push-button for firing the machine-guns and the cannon on the Spitfire Vb is fitted with a milled finger which extends out of the bottom and is a means of locking the button in the SAFE position, SAFE and FIRE being engraved on the adjacent casing. When the catch is in the FIRE position, a pip also extends out of the top of the casing so that the pilot can ascertain by feel the setting of the push-button.

(c) The cannon cocking valve is mounted on the starboard side of the cockpit.

Reflector gun sight (a) For sighting the guns and cannon a reflector gun sight is mounted on a bracket above the instrument panel. A main switch and the dimmer switch are fitted below the mounting bracket. The dimmer switch has three positions marked OFF, NIGHT and DAY. Three spare lamps for the sight are stowed in the holders on the right-hand side of the cockpit.

(b) When the sight is used during the day the dimmer switch should be in the DAY position in order to give full illumination, and if the background of the target is very bright, a sun-screen can be slid behind the windscreen by pulling on the ring at the top of the instrument panel. For night use the dimmer switch should be in the NIGHT position; in this position a low-wattage lamp is brought into circuit and the light can be varied by rotating the switch knob.

Camera (a) A G.42B cine-camera is fitted in the leading edge of the port plane, near the root end, and is operated by the gun firing button on the control column spade grip, a succession of exposures being made during the whole time the button is depressed. When cannon are fitted the cine-camera is operated off the cannon-firing pipeline.

(b) A footage indicator and an aperture switch are mounted on the wedge plate above the throttle lever. The switch enables either of the two camera apertures to be selected, the smaller aperture being used for sunny weather. A main-switch for the cine-camera is mounted on the left-hand side of the cockpit. The camera can also be controlled independently by means of an electrical push switch on the control column spade grip, below the gun firing control button.

Navigational, Signalling and Lighting Equipment

Wireless (a) The aeroplane is equipped with a combined transmitter-receiver, either type T.R.9D or T.R.1133, and an R.3002 set.

(b) With the T.R.9D installation a type C mechanical controller is fitted on the port side of the cockpit above the throttle lever and a remote contactor and contactor master switch are fitted on the right-hand side of the cockpit. The master contactor is mounted behind the pilot's headrest and a switch controlling the heating element is fitted on the forward bracket of the mounting. The heating element should always be switched OFF when the pilot leaves the aeroplane. The microphone/telephone socket is fitted on the right-hand side of the pilot's seat. The R.3002 push-buttons are on the right-hand side of the cockpit, and the master switch immediately aft of these.

(c) With the T.R.1133 installation the contactor gear and the microphone/telephone socket are as for the T.R.9D installation, but the type C mechanical controller is replaced by a push-button electrical control unit.

Navigation and identification lamps (a) The switch controlling the navigation lamps is on the instrument panel.

(b) The upward and downward identification lamps are controlled from the signalling switch box on the right-hand side of the cockpit. This switch box has a switch for each lamp and a Morsing key, and provides for steady illumination or Morse signalling from each lamp or both. The switch lever has three positions: MORSE, OFF and STEADY.

(c) The spring pressure on the Morsing key can be adjusted by turning the small ring at the top left-hand corner of the switch box, adjustment being maintained by a latch engaging one of a number of notches in the ring. The range of movement of the key can be adjusted by opening the cover and adjusting the screw and locknut at the centre of the cover.

Landing lamps The landing lamps, one on each side of the aeroplanes, are housed in the under surface of the main plane. They are lowered and raised by a finger lever below the instrument panel. Each lamp has an independent electrical circuit and is controlled by a switch above the pneumatic control lever. With the switch in the central position both lamps are off; when the switch is moved to the left or to the right, the port or starboard lamp, respectively, is illuminated. A lever is provided to control the

Above: Flight Lieutenant Antony Parkinson prepares to taxi P7350 out to the active runway at RAF Coningsby. Jarrod Cotter

Right: P7350 performs a banked turn to show the crowd its elliptical wing planform to great effect. Jarrod Cotter

dipping of both landing lamps. On pulling up the lever the beam is dipped. On later aircraft no landing lamps are fitted.

Signal discharger – A straight pull of the toggle control fires the cartridge out of the top of the fuselage, aft of the cockpit.

De-icing Equipment

Windscreen de-icing (a) A tank containing the de-icing equipment solution is mounted on the right-hand side of the cockpit directly above the bottom longeron. A cock is mounted above the tank, and a pump and a needle valve to control the flow of the liquid are mounted below the undercarriage emergency lowering control. Liquid is pumped from the tank to a spray at the base of the windscreen, from which it is sprayed upwards over the front panel of the screen.

(b) The flow of the liquid is governed by the needle valve, after turning ON the cock and pushing down the plunger to its full extent. The plunger will return to the extended position on its own, and if required, it can be pushed down again. When de-icing is no longer required the cock should be turned to the OFF position.

Pressure head heater switch The heating element in the pressure head is controlled by a switch below the trimming tab handwheels. It should be switched off on landing in order to conserve the battery.

Emergency Equipment

Hood jettisoning The hood may be jettisoned in an emergency by pulling the lever mounted inside the top of the hood in a forward and downward movement, and pushing the lower edge of the hood outboard with the elbows.

Forced-landing flare A forced-landing flare is carried in the tube inside the fuselage. The flare is released by means of a ring grip on the left of the pilot's seat.

First aid The first aid outfit is stowed aft of the wireless equipment and is accessible through a hinged panel on the port side of the fuselage.

Section 2
Handling and Flying Notes for Pilot

Engine Data: Merlin Xiii
(i) **Fuel:** 100 Octane (the reduced limitations for use with 87 Octane fuel are shown in brackets)
(ii) **Oil:** See A.P.1464/C.37

(iii) **Engine limitations:**

	Rpm	Boost Lb/In²	Temp. °C Coolant	Oil
Max Take-Off to 1,000ft	3,000	+12.5 (+7)	–	–
Max Climbing 1hr Limit	2,850	+9 (+7)	125	90
Max Rich Continuous	2,650	+7 (+5)	105	90
Max Weak Continuous	2,650	+4 (+2.5)	105	90
Combat 5 Mins Limit	3,000	+12 (+7)	135	105

115°C permitted for short periods if necessary.
Note: +12lb/in² combat boost is obtained by operating the boost control cut-out and is effective up to about 10,500ft.

Oil Pressure: Minimum in flight: 30lb/In².
Minimum Temp for Take-Off: Oil: 15°C. **Coolant:** 60°C.
Fuel Pressure: Normal: 2½-3lb/in².

(iv) **Other Limitations:**

Diving:	Maximum RPM: 3,600
	3,000rpm may be exceeded only for 20 seconds, with the throttle not less than one-third open.

(v) **Combat concession:**

	3,000 RPM may be used above 20,000 feet for periods not exceeding 30 minutes.

2. Flying Limitations
(i) Maximum speeds (MPH–IAS)

Diving:	450
Undercarriage down:	160
Flaps down:	140
Landing lamps lowered:	140

P7350 being flown over Battle of Britain territory around the south coast of England as part of a series of commemorations for the 70th anniversary of the Battle in 2010.
Jim Dooley

Below: After an autumn shower has passed, Squadron Leader Ian Smith climbs aboard P7350 at Goodwood ready to make the transit home to Coningsby. Jarrod Cotter

Right: The cockpit of P7350, which as an RAF operated aircraft has a military VHF radio set fitted as part of its standard operating procedures. Jarrod Cotter

Preliminaries
On entering the cockpit check:

Undercarriage selector lever –	Down
(Check that indicator shows DOWN; switch on light indicator and check that green lights appear).	
Flaps –	Up
Landing lamps –	Up
Contents of lower fuel tank.	

Starting the Engine and Warming Up
(i) Set:

Both fuel cock levers –	On
Throttle –	½ inch open
Mixture control –	Rich
Airscrew speed control –	Fully back DH 20°
Rotol 35° propeller –	Lever fully forward
Radiator shutter –	Open

(ii) Operate the priming pump to prime the suction and delivery pipes. This may be judged by a sudden increase in resistance of the plunger.

(iii) Prime the engine, the number of strokes required being as follows:

Air temperature °C:	+30	+20	+10	0	-10	-20
Normal fuel:		3	4	7	13	
High volatility fuel				4	8	15

(iv) Switch ON ignition and pull out the priming pump handle.
(v) Press the starter push-button and at the same time give one stroke of the priming pump. The push-button also switches on the booster coil and should be kept depressed until the engine is firing evenly.
Note: If the engine fails to start on the first cartridge, no more priming should be carried out before firing the second, but another stroke should be given as the second cartridge is fired.
(vi) As soon as the engine is running evenly, screw down the priming pump.

Testing Engine and Installations
(i) While warming up, exercise the airscrew speed control a few times. Also make the usual checks of temperatures, pressures and controls. Brake pressure should be at least 120lb/in^2.
(ii) See that the cockpit hood is locked open and that the emergency exit door is set at the 'half-cock' position.
(iii) After a few minutes move the airscrew speed control fully forward.
(iv) After warming up, open the throttle to give maximum boost for cruising with WEAK mixture and test the operation of the constant

speed airscrew.

(v) Open the throttle to give maximum boost for cruising with RICH mixture and check each magneto in turn. The drop in rpm should not exceed 150.

(vi) Open the throttle fully momentarily and check static rpm, boost and oil pressure.

(vii) Warming up must not be unduly prolonged because the radiator temperature before taxying out must not exceed 100°C.

When engines are being kept warm in readiness for immediate take-off, de Havilland 20° CS propeller should be left in fine pitch – control lever fully forward.

Taxying Out

It may be found that one wing tends to remain down while taxying. This is due to stiffness in the undercarriage leg, especially in a new aeroplane.

Final Preparation for Take-Off – Drill of Vital Actions

Drill is 'TMP, Fuel, Flaps and Radiator'

T – Trimming tabs –	Elevator about one division nose down from neutral. Rudder fully to starboard.
M – Mixture control –	Rich
P – Pitch –	Airscrew speed control fully forward
Fuel	Both cock levers ON and check contents of lower tank.
Flaps	Up
Radiator shutter	Fully open

Take-Off

(i) Open the throttle slowly to the gate (RATED BOOST position). Any tendency to swing can be counteracted by coarse use of the rudder. If taking off from a small aerodrome with a full load, maximum boost may be obtained by opening the throttle through the gate to the TAKE-OFF BOOST position.

(ii) After raising the undercarriage, see that the red indicator light – UP – comes on (it may be necessary to hold the lever hard forward against the quadrant until the indicator light comes on).

(iii) Do not start to climb before a speed of 140mph ASIR is attained.

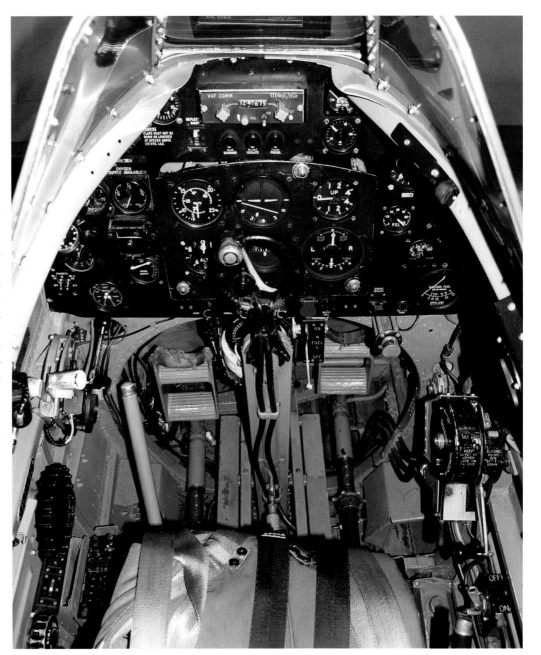

Climbing

Up to 15,000ft the maximum rate of climb is obtained at 160mph ASIR, but for normal climbing the following speeds are recommended:

Ground level to 13,000ft	185mph ASIR
13,000ft to 15,000ft	180
15,000ft to 20,000ft	160
20,000ft to 25,000ft	140
25,000ft to 30,000ft	125
30,000ft to 35,000ft	110

General Flying

Stability and Control

(i) This aeroplane is stable. With metal covered ailerons the lateral control is much lighter than with the earlier fabric covered ailerons and pilots accustomed to the latter must be careful not to overstress the wings. Similar care is necessary in the use of the elevators which are light and sensitive.

(ii) For normal cruising flight the radiator shutter should be in the minimum drag position.

(iii) Change of trim

Undercarriage down –	nose down
Flaps down –	nose down

(iv) Maximum range is obtained with WEAK mixture, 1,700rpm and at 160mph ASIR.

(v) Maximum endurance is obtained with WEAK mixture, 1,700rpm and at the lowest speed at which the machine can be comfortably flown.

(vi) For combat manoeuvres, climbing rpm should be used.

(vii) For stretching a glide in the event of a forced landing, the airscrew speed control should be pulled right back and the radiator flap put at the minimum drag position.

Stalling

(i) At the stall one wing will usually drop with flaps either up or down and the machine may spin if the control column is held back.

(ii) This aeroplane has sensitive elevators and, if the control column is brought back too rapidly in a manoeuvre such as a loop or steep turn, stalling incidence may be reached and a high-speed stall induced. When this occurs there is a violent shudder and clattering noise throughout the aeroplane which tends to flick over laterally and unless the control column is put forward instantly, a rapid roll and spin will result.

(iii) Approximate stalling speeds when loaded to about 6,250lb are:

Flaps and undercarriage	Up	73mph ASIR.
Flaps down –	Down	64mph ASIR.

Left: Former OC BBMF Squadron Leader Dunc Mason signals start-up ready for his first flight in Spitfire IIa P7350, which is always a great honour for the RAF pilots who get to fly this national treasure. Jarrod Cotter

Below: The sun glints off P7350's bodywork above the clouds in the summer skies over England, just as it would have done during the Battle of Britain in 1940. Jim Dooley

Right: A splendid view of P7350 being flown by Squadron Leader Ian Smith. Richard Paver

Spinning

(i) Spinning is permitted by pilots who have written permission from the CO of their squadron (or CFI of an OTU). The loss of height involved in recovery may be very great, and the following height limits are to be observed:

(a) Spins are not to be started below 10,000ft

(b) Recovery must be started not lower than 5,000ft

(ii) A speed of over 150mph IAS should be attained before starting to ease out of the resultant dive.

Aerobatics

(i) This aeroplane is exceptionally good for aerobatics. Owing to its high performance and sensitive elevator control, care must be taken not to impose excessive loads either on the aeroplane or on the pilot and not to induce a high-speed stall. Many aerobatics may be done at much less than full throttle. Cruising rpm should be used, because if reduced below this, detonation might occur if the throttle is opened up to climbing boost for any reason.

(ii) The following speeds are recommended for aerobatics:

Looping – speed should be about 300mph IAS but may be reduced to 220–250mph when the pilot is fully proficient.

Rolling – speed should be anywhere between 180 and 300mph IAS. The nose should be brought up about 30° above the horizon at the start, the roll being barrelled just enough to keep the engine running throughout.

Half roll off loop – Speed should be 320–350mph IAS.

Upward roll – Speed should be about 350–400mph IAS.

Flick manoeuvres – Flick manoeuvres are not permitted.

Diving

(i) The aeroplane becomes very tail heavy at high speed and must be trimmed into the dive in order to avoid the dangers of excessive acceleration in recovery. The forward trim should be wound back as speed is lost after pulling out.

(ii) A tendency to yaw to the right should be corrected by use of the rudder trimming tab.

Landing Across Wind

The aeroplane can be landed across wind but it is undesirable that such landings should be made if the wind exceeds about 20mph.

After Landing

(i) After taxying in, set the propeller control fully back and open up the engine sufficiently to change pitch to coarse. DH 20°.

(ii) Allow the engine to idle for a few seconds, then pull the slow-running cut-out and hold it out until the engine stops.

(iii) Turn OFF the fuel cocks and switch OFF the ignition.

Fuel and Oil Capacity and Consumption

(i) Fuel and oil capacities:

Fuel capacity: Two main tanks – top tank		48 gallons
	bottom tank	37 gallons
Total effective capacity		85 gallons

(ii) Fuel consumption

Max rpm and boost for	Height feet	Approx. consumption gallons/hour
Climbing	13,000	94
Cruising RICH	13,000	78
Cruising WEAK	18,000	56
All-out Level	14,500	98

Right: P7350 being flown around the south of England in the company of Hawker Hurricane II LF363. While the BBMF personnel regularly change the paint schemes of their aircraft, P7350 and LF363 always wear the markings of a Battle of Britain aircraft. Jim Dooley

Below right: Following another successful sortie to commemorate the fallen RAF airmen of World War Two, P7350 taxies back to the BBMF hangar at RAF Coningsby. Jarrod Cotter

Flying the nation's aviation heritage

Squadron Leader Duncan Mason, officer commanding the RAF Battle of Britain Memorial Flight at RAF Coningsby in Lincolnshire, describes his thoughts on flying P7350, which is the world's only airworthy Spitfire that fought in the Battle of Britain:

For those of us lucky enough to be allowed to fly the Spitfires of the BBMF, it is always a very special thing to fly P7350, the Flight's very special 'baby' Mk II Spitfire.

Walking out to the aircraft, I am always struck by the beauty of it. Approaching from behind the elliptical wing, the cockpit nestled behind the long nose which is pointing skyward, there is no doubt that this aircraft is a masterpiece. There is a poignancy and reverence about taking this aircraft into the skies. Maybe this is because she is the sole airworthy Spitfire of the world's greatest ever air battle; perhaps it is because she has an airborne elegance that belies her ferocious nature. Whatever the reason, the expectation is always palpable. The feeling is very difficult to describe; excitement like that of a young boy who has been given the most amazing aircraft to wheel around the sky, mixed with a great responsibility to keep her safe at all costs. After all, if anything happened to this irreplaceable artefact of the nation's heritage, even if it was not the pilot's fault, he would probably never be forgiven!

In the air she is different from other Spitfires. She is lighter and more 'twitchy' if you are not steady handed with her and she purrs more than the harsh growl of the later-engine Spitfires. She accelerates faster and, especially on the ground, with her small rudder, she is more skittish and requires more attention than her weightier younger sisters with their bigger rudders.

Safely back on the ground, as I walk away I have to turn and have one last look at this beautiful aircraft – the Spitfire of all Spitfires – with which I'm completely enchanted.

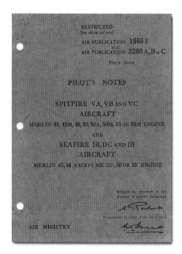

'The Mk.V, in its various forms, was produced in very large numbers and became the workhorse of RAF Fighter Command for 1941 and 1942.'
Jeffrey Quill

Spitfire Vb BL628 was restored in New Zealand before moving to Texas in the USA. It is seen here being flown by Keith Skilling.
Gavin Conroy

Pilot's Notes
Spitfire Mark V
May 1941
Air Publication 1565E

Section 1 Pilot's Controls and Equipment

Introduction
The Spitfire Va, Vb and Vc are single seat, low-wing monoplane fighters, each fitted with a Merlin 45 or 46 engine and a de Havilland 20° (PCP), Rotol 35° or de Havilland hydromatic constant speed propeller. Mark Vb aeroplanes are fully tropicalised and particulars of additional equipment are given in the Addendum at the end of this section.

Fuel system Fuel is carried in two tanks mounted one above the other (the lower one is self-sealing) forward of the cockpit. The top tank feeds into the lower tank and fuel is delivered to the carburettor by an engine-driven pump. The tank capacities are as follows:

Top tank:	48 gallons.
Bottom tank:	37 gallons.

On early aeroplanes the top tank is fitted with a separate cock and an immersed pump is fitted in the lower tank. On tropicalised aeroplanes the main fuel tanks are pressurised and these and later aeroplanes are fitted to carry a long-range jettisonable tank of 30 or 90 gallons capacity under the fuselage.

Oil system Oil is supplied by a tank of 5.98 gallons capacity under the engine mounting and two oil coolers in tandem are fitted in the underside of the port plane. The above tank is replaced by one of 8.5 gallons capacity when the aeroplane is fitted with a 90 gallons jettisonable fuel tank.

Hydraulic system An engine-driven hydraulic pump supplies the power for operating the undercarriage.

Pneumatic system An engine-driven air compressor feeds two storage cylinders for operation of the flaps, brakes, guns and landing lamps. The cylinders are connected in series, each holding air at 300lb/in² pressure.

A war-torn looking Spitfire
Vb R6923/QJ-S of No. 92 Squadron
based at RAF Biggin Hill banking
away from the camera. R6923 was
originally a Mk.I which served with
No19 Squadron, and was later
converted to Mk.V configuration.
It was shot down over the sea by
a Messerschmitt Bf 109 on
22 June 1941. British Official

Electrical system A 12 volt generator, controlled by a switch above the instrument panel, supplies an accumulator which in turn supplies the whole of the electrical installations. There is a voltmeter in the left of the switch.

Aeroplane Controls

Primary flying controls and locking devices (a) The control column is of the spade-grip pattern and incorporates the brake lever and gun cannon firing control. The rudder pedals have two positions for the feet and are adjustable for leg reach by rotation of star wheels on the sliding tubes. Control locking struts are stowed on the right-hand side of the cockpit, behind the seat.

(b) To lock the control column, the longer strut should be clamped to the control column handle at one end and the other end inserted in a keyhole slot in the right-hand side of the seat. The fixed pin on the free end of the arm attached to this strut at the control column end should then be inserted in a lug on the starboard datum longeron, thus forming a rigid triangle between the column, the seat and the longeron.

(c) To lock the rudder pedals, a short bar with a pin at each end is attached to the other struts by a cable. The longer of the two pins should be inserted in a hole in the starboard star wheel bearing and the shorter in an eyebolt on the fuselage frame directly below the front of the seat. The controls should be locked with the seat in its highest position.

Flying instruments A standard blind flying instrument panel is incorporated in the main panel. The instruments comprise: air-speed indicator, altimeter, directional gyro, artificial horizon, rate of climb and descent indicator, and turn and bank indicator.

Trimming tabs The elevator trimming tabs are controlled by a hand wheel on the left-hand side of the cockpit, the indicator being on the instrument panel. The rudder trimming tab is controlled by a small hand wheel and is not provided with an indicator. The aeroplane tends to turn to starboard when the hand wheel is rotated clockwise.

Undercarriage control and indicators (a) The undercarriage selector lever moves in a gated quadrant, on the right-hand side of the cockpit. An automatic cut-out in the control moves the selector lever into the gate when it has been pushed or pulled to the full extent of the quadrant. A hydraulic valve indicator in the quadrant shows DOWN, or IDLE, or UP depending upon the position of the hydraulic valve. UP or DOWN should normally show only when the selector lever is operated to raise or lower the undercarriage, and IDLE when the lever has automatically sprung back into the gate after raising or lowering the undercarriage. If, with the engine not running, the indicator shows DOWN, it should return to IDLE when the engine is started.

(b) To raise the undercarriage the lever is pushed forward, but it must first be pulled back and then across to disengage it from the gate. When the undercarriage is raised and locked, the lever will spring into the forward gate.

(c) To lower the undercarriage the lever is pulled back, but it must first be pushed forward and then across to disengage it from the gate. When the undercarriage is lowered and locked, the lever will spring into the rear gate.

(d) Electrical visual indicator – The electrically operated visual indicator has two semi-transparent windows on which the words UP on a red background and DOWN on a green background are lettered; the words are illuminated according to the position of the undercarriage. The switch for the DOWN circuit of the indicator is mounted on the inboard side of the throttle quadrant and is moved to the ON position by means of a striker on the throttle lever; this switch should be returned to the OFF position by hand when the aeroplane is left standing for any length of time. The UP circuit is not controlled by this switch.

(e) Mechanical position indicator – A rod that extends through the top surface of the main plane is fitted to each undercarriage unit. When the wheels are down the rods – which are painted red – protrude through the top of the main planes and when they are up, the top of the rods are flush with the main plane surfaces.

(f) Warning horn – The push switch controlling the horn is mounted on the throttle quadrant and is operated by a striker on the throttle lever. The horn may be silenced, even though the wheels are retracted and the engine throttled back, by depressing the button on the side of the throttle quadrant. As soon as the throttle is again advanced beyond about one quarter of its travel the push-button is automatically released and the horn will sound again on its return.

Flap control The split flaps have two positions only, up and fully down. They cannot, therefore, be used to assist take-off. They are operated pneumatically and are controlled by a finger lever.

Undercarriage emergency operation (a) A sealed high-pressure cylinder containing carbon-dioxide and connected to the undercarriage operating the jacks is provided for use in the event of failure of the hydraulic system. The cylinder is mounted on the right-hand side of the cockpit and the seal can be punctured by means of a red painted lever beside it. The handle is marked EMERGENCY ONLY and provision is made for fitting a thin copper wire seal as a check against inadvertent use.

(b) If the hydraulic system fails, the pilot should ensure that the undercarriage selector lever is in the DOWN position (this is essential) and push the emergency lowering lever forward and downward. The angular travel of the emergency lever is about 100° for puncturing the seal of the cylinder and then releasing the piercing plunger; it must be pushed through this movement and allowed to swing downwards. NO attempt should be made to return it to its original position until the cylinder is being replaced.

Wheel brakes The control lever for the pneumatic brakes is fitted on the control column spade grip: differential control of the brakes is provided by a relay valve connected to the rudder bar. A catch

for retaining the brake lever in the on position for parking is fitted below the lever point. A triple pressure gauge, showing the air pressure in the pneumatic system cylinders and at each brake, is mounted on the left-hand side of the instrument panel.

Engine Controls

Throttle and mixture controls The throttle and the mixture levers are fitted in a quadrant on the port side of the cockpit. A gate is provided for the throttle lever in the take-off position and an interlocking device between the levers prevents the engine from being run on an unsuitable mixture. Friction adjusters for the controls are fitted on the side of the quadrant. On later aircraft there is no mixture control or, if fitted, it is rendered inoperative.

Automatic boost cut-out The automatic boost control may be cut out by pushing forward the small red painted lever at the forward end of the throttle quadrant.

Right: This series of 3 pictures shows BL628 caught breaking away from the camera aircraft in fine style. Gavin Conroy

Left: Spitfire Vb AB910 of the RAF Battle of Britain Memorial Flight. Built at Castle Bromwich in 1941, AB910 has a remarkable operational history. Initially allocated to No. 222 (Natal) Squadron at North Weald in August 1941, the fighter soon moved to No. 130 Squadron with which its tasks included escort patrols for the daylight bombing raids against the battle cruisers *Scharnhorst* and *Gneisenau* in December 1941. In June 1942, AB910 was delivered to No. 133 (Eagle) Squadron at Biggin Hill from where it flew 29 operations including four sorties on 19 August 1942 during the fierce aerial battles in support of the Dieppe raid. On that day its pilots scored one Dornier Do 217 destroyed and one damaged. Other units it served with include No. 402 (RCAF) Squadron, with which it flew numerous cover patrols over the Normandy invasion beach heads on D-Day, 6 June 1944. This Spitfire is seen in one of its former paint schemes while wearing the markings Mk.Vb EN951/RF-D, the aircraft of Squadron Leader Jan Zumbach, OC No. 303 (Kosciuszko) Squadron in 1942. Jim Dooley

Airscrew controls The control levers for the de Havilland 20° or Rotol 35° constant speed airscrew is on the throttle quadrant. The de Havilland 20° airscrew has a Positive Coarse Pitch position which is obtained in the extreme aft position of the control lever, when the airscrew blades are held at their maximum coarse pitch angles and the airscrew functions as a fixed airscrew. Some aircraft are fitted with a de Havilland hydraulic propeller.

Radiator flap control The flap at the outlet end of the radiator duct is operated by a lever and the ratchet on the left-hand side of the cockpit. To open the flap, the lever should be pushed forward after releasing the ratchet by depressing the knob at the top of the lever. The normal minimum drag position of the flap lever for the level flight is shown by a red triangle on the top of the map case fitted beside the lever. A notch beyond the normal position in the aft direction provides a position of the lever when warm air is diverted through ducts into the main planes for heating the guns at high altitude.

Slow-running cut-out The control on the carburettor is operated by pulling the ring on the right-hand side of the instrument panel.

Fuel cock controls and contents gauges The fuel cock controls, one for each tank, are fitted at the bottom of the instrument panel. With the levers in the up position the cocks are open. Either tank can be isolated, if necessary. The fuel contents gauge on the instrument panel indicates the contents of the lower tank, but only when the adjacent push-button is pressed. On later aircraft there is only one fuel cock control.

Immersed fuel pumps An immersed fuel pump is fitted in the lower fuel tank for use at the heights over 25,000ft, when the fuel pressure falls. The pump is electrically operated and the switch controlling it is mounted on the left-hand side of the cockpit, adjacent to the seat.

Fuel priming pump A hand-operated pump for priming the engine is mounted below the right-hand side of the instrument panel.

Ignition switches The ignition switches are on the left-hand side bottom corner of the instrument panel.

Electric starting On early aeroplanes the starting magneto switch is at the right-hand bottom corner of the instrument panel and the engine starting push-button is under a shield above the fuel cock controls. On later aeroplanes the starting magneto switch is not provided but a booster coil push switch is fitted adjacent to the starter push-button. Current for the starter motor is normally supplied by an external battery which is connected to the socket

on the engine mounting U-frame, accessible through a door in the engine cooling panel on the starboard side. The general service accumulator carried in the aeroplanes is also connected to the starter, but as its capacity is small for such heavy duty it should be used only as a stand-by.

Hand starting A starting handle is stowed behind the seat. A hole in the engine cowling panel in the starboard side gives access for connecting the handle to the hand starting gear.

Oil dilution A push-button for operating the solenoid valve is on the left-hand side in the cockpit.

Engine instruments The engine instruments are grouped on the right-hand side of the instrument panel and consist of an engine speed indicator, fuel pressure gauge, boost gauge, oil pressure gauge, oil inlet temperature gauge, radiator outlet temperature gauge, and fuel contents gauge. On later aircraft the fuel pressure gauge is replaced by a fuel pressure warning lamp which lights when the pressure drops to 6lb/in^2.

Cockpit Accommodation and Equipment

Pilot's seat control The seat is adjustable for height by means of a lever on the right-hand side of the seat.

Safety harness release In order that the pilot may lean forward without unfastening his harness, a release catch is fitted to the right of the seat.

Cockpit door To facilitate entry to the cockpit a portion of the coaming on the port side is hinged. The door catches are released by means of a handle at the forward end. Two position catches are incorporated to allow the door to be partly opened before taking off or landing in order to prevent the hood from sliding shut in the event of a mishap.

Hood locking control The sliding hood is provided with spring catches for holding it either open or shut: the catches are released by two finger levers at the forward end of the hood. From outside, with the hood closed, the catches can be released by depressing a small knob at the top of the windscreen. Provision is made on the door to prevent the hood from sliding shut if the aeroplane overturns on landing.

Direct vision panel A small knock-out panel is provided on the right-hand side of the hood for use in the event of the windscreen becoming obscured.

Right: The cockpit of Mk.Vb BM597. Jarrod Cotter

Far right: Spitfire Vb BM597 of the Historic Aircraft Collection is a UK air show favourite and has become very familiar wearing Polish markings. Jarrod Cotter

Cockpit lighting A floodlight is fitted on each side of the cockpit. Each is controlled by a switch immediately below the instrument panel.

Cockpit heating and ventilation A small adjustable flap on the starboard coaming above the instrument panel is provided for ventilation of the cockpit. The flap is opened by turning a knurled nut underneath the flap.

Oxygen A standard regulator unit is fitted on the left-hand side of the instrument panel and a bayonet socket is on the right-hand side of the cockpit. A separate cock is provided in addition to the regulator.

Mirror A mirror providing a rearward view is fitted at the top of the windscreen.

Map cases A metal case for a writing pad and another for maps, books, etc are fitted on the left-hand side of the cockpit. Stowage for a height-and-airspeed computer is provided below the wireless remote contactor.

Operational Equipment and Controls

Guns and cannon (a) The machine-guns and cannon are fired pneumatically by means of push-buttons on the control column spade grip. The compressed air supply is taken from the same source as the brake supply, the available pressure being shown by the gauge.

(b) The triple push-button for firing the machine-guns and the cannon on the Spitfire Vb is fitted with a milled finger which extends out of the bottom and is a means of locking the button in the SAFE position, SAFE and FIRE being engraved on the adjacent casing. When the catch is in the FIRE position, a pip also extends out of the top of the casing so that the pilot can ascertain by feel the setting of the push-button.

(c) The cannon cocking valve is mounted on the starboard side of the cockpit.

Reflector gun sight (a) For sighting the guns and cannon a reflector gun sight is mounted on a bracket above the instrument panel. A main switch and the dimmer switch are fitted below the mounting bracket. The dimmer switch has three positions marked OFF, NIGHT and DAY. Three spare lamps for the sight are stowed in the holders on the right-hand side of the cockpit.

(b) When the sight is used during the day the dimmer switch

should be in the DAY position in order to give full illumination, and if the background of the target is very bright, a sun-screen can be slid behind the windscreen by pulling on the ring at the top of the instrument panel. For night use the dimmer switch should be in the NIGHT position; in this position a low-wattage lamp is brought into circuit and the light can be varied by rotating the switch knob.

Camera (a) A G.42B cine-camera is fitted in the leading edge of the port plane, near the root end, and is operated by the gun firing button on the control column spade grip, a succession of exposures being made during the whole time the button is depressed. When cannon are fitted the cine-camera is operated off the cannon-firing pipeline.

(b) A footage indicator and an aperture switch are mounted on the wedge plate above the throttle lever. The switch enables either of the two camera apertures to be selected, the smaller aperture being used for sunny weather. A main-switch for the cine-camera is mounted on the left-hand side of the cockpit. The camera can also be controlled independently by means of an electrical push switch on the control column spade grip, below the gun firing control button.

Navigational, Signalling and Lighting Equipment

Wireless (a) The aeroplane is equipped with a combined transmitter-receiver, either type T.R.9D or T.R.1133, and an R.3002 set.

(b) With the T.R.9D installation a type C mechanical controller is fitted on the port side of the cockpit above the throttle lever and a remote contactor and contactor master switch are fitted on the right-hand side of the cockpit. The master contactor is mounted behind the pilot's headrest and a switch controlling the heating element is fitted on the forward bracket of the mounting. The heating element should always be switched OFF when the pilot leaves the aeroplane. The microphone/telephone socket is fitted on the right-hand side of the pilot's seat. The R.3002 push-buttons are on the right-hand side of the cockpit, and the master switch immediately aft of these.

(c) With the T.R.1133 installation the contactor gear and the microphone/telephone socket are as for the T.R.9D installation, but the type C mechanical controller is replaced by a push-button electrical control unit.

Navigation and identification lamps (a) The switch controlling the navigation lamps is on the instrument panel.

Left: Flight Lieutenant Laurie of No. 222 Squadron fires up Spitfire Vb BM202/ZD-H *Flying Scotsman* at RAF North Weald in May 1942. The aircraft was the second bearing this name to be paid for from donations made by LNER personnel.
British Official

(b) The upward and downward identification lamps are controlled from the signalling switch box on the right-hand side of the cockpit. This switch box has a switch for each lamp and a Morsing key, and provides for steady illumination or Morse signalling from each lamp or both. The switch lever has three positions: MORSE, OFF and STEADY.

(c) The spring pressure on the Morsing key can be adjusted by turning the small ring at the top left-hand corner of the switch box, adjustment being maintained by a latch engaging one of a number of notches in the ring. The range of movement of the key can be adjusted by opening the cover and adjusting the screw and locknut at the centre of the cover.

Landing lamps The landing lamps, one on each side of the aeroplanes, are housed in the under surface of the main plane. They are lowered and raised by a finger lever below the instrument panel. Each lamp has an independent electrical circuit and is controlled by a switch above the pneumatic control lever. With the switch in the central position both lamps are off; when the switch is moved to the left or to the right, the port or starboard lamp, respectively, is illuminated. A lever is provided to control the dipping of both landing lamps. On pulling up the lever the beam is dipped. On later aircraft no landing lamps are fitted.

Signal discharger A straight pull of the toggle control fires the cartridge out of the top of the fuselage, aft of the cockpit.

De-icing Equipment

Windscreen de-icing A tank containing the de-icing equipment solution is mounted on the right-hand side of the cockpit directly above the bottom longeron. A cock is mounted above the tank, and a pump and a needle valve to control the flow of the liquid are mounted below the undercarriage emergency lowering control. Liquid is pumped from the tank to a spray at the base of the windscreen, from which it is sprayed upwards over the front panel of the screen.

(b) The flow of the liquid is governed by the needle valve, after turning ON the cock and pushing down the plunger to its full extent. The plunger will return to the extended position on its own, and if required, it can be pushed down again. When de-icing is no longer required the cock should be turned to the OFF position.

Pressure head heater switch The heating element in the pressure head is controlled by a switch below the trimming tab handwheels. It should be switched off on landing in order to conserve the battery.

Emergency Equipment

Hood jettisoning The hood may be jettisoned in an emergency by pulling the lever mounted inside the top of the hood in a forward and downward movement, and pushing the lower edge of the hood outboard with the elbows.

Forced-landing flare A forced-landing flare is carried in the tube inside the fuselage. The flare is released by means of a ring grip on the left of the pilot's seat.

Section 2
Handling and Flying Notes for Pilot

Engine Data: Merlins 45, 45M and 46
Fuel: 100 octane only

Engine limitations:

	Rpm	Boost Lb/In^2	Temp. °C Coolant	Oil
Max Take-Off to 1,000ft	3,000	+12	–	–
Max Climbing 1hr Limit	2,850	+9	125	90
Max Rich Continuous	2,650	+7	105 (115)	90
Max Weak Continuous	2,650	+4	105 (115)	90
Combat 5 Mins Limit	3,000	+16	135	105
		+18	135	105

Note: (a) +18lb/in^2 boost is obtained only on 'M' type engines, by moving the throttle lever through the gate. On other engines +16lb/in^2 boost is obtained by operating the boost control cut-out.
(b) Combat boost is permitted only at 2,850 to 3,000rpm.
(c) The figure in brackets is permitted for short periods if necessary.

Top right: BM597 flies over Duxford and is seen about to break into circuit to land. Jarrod Cotter

Right: RAF ground crew help the pilot of Spitfire Vb BM202/ZD-H strap into the fighter's cockpit ready for a sortie in June 1942. British Official

Following page: Spitfire Vb AB910 and Hurricane I R4118 fly by the National Battle of Britain Memorial at Capel le Ferne, Kent, while commemorating the 70th anniversary the Battle of Britain in 2010. Jim Dooley

Oil Pressure

Normal:	60/80lb/in^2
Min:	45lb/in^2

Min temp for Take-Off

Oil:	15°C
Clnt:	60°C

Min temp for Take-Off	8–10lb/in^2

Flying Limitations
i. Maximum speeds:

Diving:	450mph IAS
Undercarriage down:	160mph IAS
Flaps down:	160mph IAS
Landing lamps lowered:	140mph IA

ii. Restrictions:
a) When fitted with a 90-gallon drop tank the aircraft is restricted to 'straight flying' until the tank is jettisoned. This restriction does not apply when fitted with a 30-gallon drop tank.
b) Drop tanks should be jettisoned only in straight and level flight, and then only if absolutely necessary.
c) When carrying a bomb, spinning is not permitted and violent manoeuvres must be avoided. The angle of dive must at no time exceed 40°.

Management of Fuel System
When fitted with a drop tank:
i. Start and warm up in the normal way on the main tanks.
ii. Take off on the main tanks and change over to the drop tank at a safe height (2,000ft). Turn OFF the main tanks.
iii. Normally the aeroplane should be flown on the jettisonable tank until the fuel is exhausted. When the engine cuts turn ON the main tanks and turn OFF the jettisonable tank at once.
iv. If the tank is to be jettisoned before the fuel in it is exhausted, first turn ON the main tanks and then move the jettisonable tank cock control to OFF before operating the jettison lever.
Note: The jettisonable tank cock must be kept OFF when the tank is jettisoned or when the fuel in it is exhausted, otherwise air may be sucked into the main fuel system.
v. For maximum range and endurance the tank should be jettisoned as soon as the fuel in it has been exhausted.

Preliminaries
On entering the cockpit check:

Undercarriage selector lever –	Down
(Check that indicator shows DOWN; switch on	
light indicator and check that green lights appear).	
Flaps –	Up
Landing lamps –	Up
Contents of lower fuel tank.	

Starting the Engine and Warming Up
(i) Set:

Both fuel cock lever(s) –	On
Throttle –	½ inch open
Mixture control (if fitted) –	Rich
Propeller speed control –	Fully back (DH 20°) or fully forward Rotol 35° or DH hydromatic
Radiator shutter –	Open

ii. High volatility fuel should be used if possible for priming at air temperatures below freezing. Work the priming pump until the suction and delivery pipes are full; this may be judged by a sudden increase in resistance.

iii. Switch on the ignition and starting magneto (if fitted) and press the starter and booster coil buttons (if fitted). Turning periods must not exceed 20 seconds, with a 30 seconds wait between each. Work the priming pump as rapidly and as vigorously as possible while the engine is being turned, and it should start after the following number of strokes:

Air temperature °C:	+30	+20	+10	0	-10	-20
Normal fuel:		3	3½	7	12½	
High volatility fuel:				4	7½	15

iv. At temperatures below freezing it will probably be necessary to continue priming after the engine has fired and until it picks up on the carburettor.
v. When the engine is running satisfactorily, release the booster coil button, or switch off the starting magneto (if fitted), and screw down the priming pump.
vi. Run the engine as slowly as possible for half a minute, then warm up at a fast tick-over.
vii. If fitted with a DH 20° CS propeller, move the speed control slowly fully forward when the engine has been running for a minute or more.

Testing Engine and Installations

While warming up

i. Make the usual checks of temperatures, pressures and controls. Brake pressure should be at least 120lb/in².

ii. See that the cockpit hood is locked open and the emergency exit door is set at the 'half-cock' position.

After warming up:

iii. See that there are TWO men on the tail, and with the propeller speed control fully forward, test as follows:

a) Open up to maximum boost for WEAK mixture cruising; exercise and check operation of constant speed propeller.

b) Open the throttle fully and check take-off boost and rpm.

c) Act maximum boost for RICH mixture cruising test each magneto in turn. The drop should not exceed 150rpm.

iv. Running of the engine must not be unduly prolonged because, if the coolant temperature before taxying out exceeds 100°C, it may become excessive before take-off is completed.

v. When engines are being kept warm in readiness for immediate take-off, de Havilland 20° CS propeller should be left in fine pitch – control lever fully forward.

Final Preparation for Take-Off

The Drill of Vital Actions is 'T, M, P, Fuel, Flaps and Radiator'.

T – Trimming tabs –	Elevator; about one division nose down from neutral. Rudder: fully to st'bd.
M – Mixture control (if fitted) –	Rich
P – Pitch –	Propeller speed control fully forward
Fuel	Cock levers ON and check contents of lower tank.
Flaps	Up
Radiator shutter	Fully open

Take-Off

i. Open the throttle slowly to the gate (RATED BOOST position). Any tendency to swing can be counteracted by coarse use of the rudder. If taking off from a small airfield with a full load, maximum boost may be obtained by opening the throttle through the gate to the TAKE-OFF BOOST position.

ii. After raising the undercarriage, see that the red indicator light – UP – comes on (it may be necessary to hold the lever hard forward against the quadrant until the indicator light comes on).

iii. Do not start to climb before a speed of 140mph IAS is attained.

Climbing

The speeds for maximum rate of climb are as follows:

From SL to 10,000ft	170mph IAS
10,000ft to 16,000ft	160mph IAS
16,000ft to 21,000ft	150mph IAS
21,000ft to 26,000ft	140mph IAS
26,000ft to 31,000ft	130mph IAS
31,000ft to 37,000ft	120mph IAS
Above 37,000ft	115mph IAS

General Flying

i.   Stability: The aircraft is stable about all axes.
ii. For normal cruising flight the radiator shutter should be in the minimum drag position.

iii. Change of trim

Undercarriage down –	nose down
Flaps down –	nose down

iv. For combat manoeuvres climbing rpm should be used.
v.   For stretching a glide in the event of a forced landing, the propeller speed control should be pulled right back and the radiator flap set at the minimum drag position.

Maximum Range

i.   Climbing:
Climb at +9lb/in² boost and 2,850rpm at the speed recommended for maximum rate of climb. Mixture control (if fitted) at RICH.
ii. Cruising:
Maximum range will be obtained at intermediate heights. The recommended speeds are as follows:

a) Without auxiliary tanks, or if fitted with 30 gallon drop tank:

Below 8,000ft:	180mph IAS
Between 8,000 and 18,000ft:	160mph IAS
Above 15,000ft:	150mph IAS

At very low altitudes the speed may be increased to 200mph IAS without seriously affecting range.

b) If fitted with 90 gallon drop tank:

Below 8,000ft:	180mph IAS
Above 8,000ft:	170mph IAS

Fly in WEAK mixture (if control fitted) at maximum obtainable boost not exceeding +4lb/in² (the mixture richens automatically at higher boosts)

and reduce speed by reducing rpm which may be as low as 1,800 if this will give the recommended speed, but check that generator is charging. If at 1,800rpm the speed is higher than that recommended, reduce boost.

Stalling

i.   At the stall one wing will usually drop with flaps either up or down and the aircraft may spin if the control column is held back.

ii. This aircraft has sensitive elevators, and if the control column is brought back too rapidly in a manoeuvre such as a loop or a steep turn, stalling incidence may be reached and a high speed stall induced. When this occurs there is a violent shudder and clattering noise throughout the aircraft which tends to flick over laterally, and unless the control column is put forward instantly, a rapid roll and spin will result.

iii. Stalling speeds when loaded to about 6,400lb are:

Flaps and undercarriage	Up	73mph ASIR.
	Down	64mph ASIR.

Spinning

i.   Spinning is permitted by pilots who have written permission from the CO of their squadron (CFI of an OTU). The loss of height involved in recovery may be very great, and the following height limits are to be observed:
a) Spins are not to be started below 10,000ft.
b) Recovery must be started not lower than 5,000ft.

ii. A speed of over 150mph IAS should be attained before starting to ease out of the resultant dive.

Aerobatics

The following speeds are recommended:
Looping: Speed should be about 300mph IAS, but may be reduced to 220–250mph IAS when the pilot is fully proficient.
Rolling: Speed should be anywhere between 180 and 300mph IAS. The nose should be brought up about 30° above the horizon at the start, the roll being barrelled just enough to keep the engine running throughout.
Half-roll off loop: Speed should be 320–350mph IAS.
Upward roll: Speed should be about 350–400mph IAS.
Flick manoeuvres: Flick manoeuvres are not permitted.

Diving

i.   The aircraft becomes very tail heavy at high speed and must be trimmed into the dive in order to avoid the dangers of excessive acceleration in recovery. The forward trim should be wound back as speed is lost after pulling out.

ii. A tendency to yaw to the right should be corrected by use of the rudder trimming tab.

Approach and Landing

i. During the preliminary approach see that the cockpit hood is locked open, and the emergency exit door is set at the half-cock position. Take care not to get the arm out into the airflow.

ii. Reduce speed to 140mph IAS and carry out the Drill of Vital Actions 'U, M, P and Flaps'.

U – Undercarriage –	DOWN (Watch indicators and check green lights).
M – Mixture control (if fitted) –	Rich
P – Propeller Control –	Fully forward
Flaps	Down

iii. Approach Speeds (mph IAS)

		(flaps up)
Engine assisted:	85	(95)
Glide:	95	(100)

iv. When lowering the undercarriage hold the lever fully forward for about two seconds. This will take the weight off the locking pins and allow them to turn freely when the lever is pulled back. The lever should then be pulled back smartly to the down position and left there. It should NOT be pushed into the gate by hand. As soon as the undercarriage is locked down the lever should automatically spring into the gate and the hydraulic valve indicator return to IDLE. If it cannot be pulled fully back, hold it forward again for at least two seconds. If it becomes jammed it may generally be released by a smart blow of the hand. If this fails it is necessary to take the weight of the wheels off the locking pins, either by pushing the nose down sharply or by inverting the aircraft. The lever can then be pulled straight back.

v. If the green indicator light does not come on hold the lever fully back for a few seconds. If this fails, raise the undercarriage and repeat the lowering. If this fails also, use the emergency system.
Note: Before the emergency system can be used, the control lever must be in the down position. It may be necessary to push the nose down or invert the aircraft in order to get the lever down.

vi. If the undercarriage is lowered too late on the approach, with insufficient engine speed to develop full hydraulic pressure, the selector lever may not automatically spring from the fully back position into the gate, so indicating that the operation is not complete. This may cause the undercarriage to collapse on landing.

(As previously mentioned, the lever must NOT be pushed into the gate by hand). It is advisable, therefore, to lower the undercarriage early on

the circuit prior to landing and not in the later stages of the approach.

vii. Mislanding: Climb at about 120mph IAS.

After Landing

i. Raise the flaps before taxying.

ii. If fitted with a DH 20° CS propeller, after taxying in set the speed control fully back and open up the engine sufficiently to change pitch to coarse.

iii. Run the engine at 800–900rpm for two minutes, then pull the slow-running cut-out and hold it out until the engine stops.

iv. Turn OFF the fuel cocks and switch OFF the ignition.

Oil Dilution

The dilution period should be:
Atmospheric temperatures above -10°C: 1 minute
Atmospheric temperatures below -10°C: 2 minutes

Flying at Reduced Airspeeds

In conditions of bad visibility near the ground, reduce speed to about 120mph IAS and lower the flaps. The radiator shutter must be opened to keep the temperature at about 100°C and the propeller speed control should be set to give cruising rpm.

Position Error

From	100	140	160	180	200	240	270	mph IAS
To	140	160	180	200	240	270	& over	mph IAS
Add	4	2	0	–	–	–	–	mph
S'tract	–	–	–	2	4	6	8	mph

Right: AB910 flies over the BBMF hangar at RAF Coningsby in some rare clear blue skies over England.
Jarrod Cotter

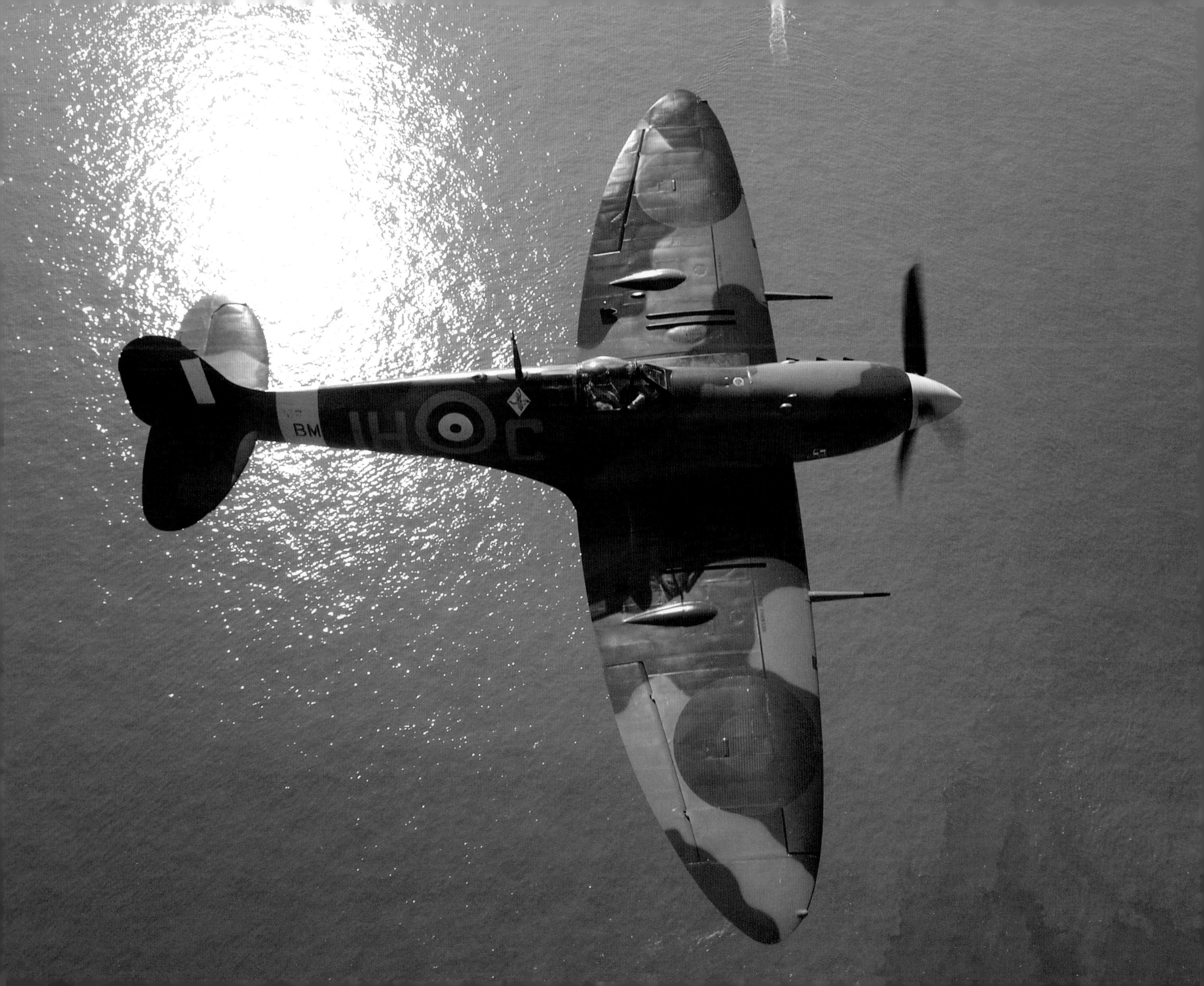
BM
IH
C

Fuel and Oil Capacity and Consumption

i. Fuel: Normal Capacity:

Top tank	48 gallons
Bottom tank	37 gallons
Total	85 gallons

Long-range capacities:

With 30 gallons drop tank:	115 gallons
With 90 gallons drop tank:	175 gallons
With 170 gallons drop tank and 29 gallons rear fuselage tank:	284 gallons

ii. Oil: Normal Capacity:

	5.8 gallons

Long-range capacity:

With 90 gallon tank:	0.5 gallons
With 170 + 29 gallon tank:	14.5 gallons.

Fuel consumptions (approximate gals/hr):

a) WEAK mixture (or as obtained at +4lb/in^2 boost and below if control not fitted) at 6,000–20,000ft:

Boost lb/in^2 rpm	2,650	2,400	2,200	2,000	1,800
+4	56	53	51	47	43
+2	51	48	46	43	39
0	47	44	42	39	35
-2	43	40	38	35	31
-4	39	36	34	31	26

b) RICH mixture (or as obtained above +4lb/in^2 boost if control not fitted):

rpm	Boost lb/in^2	gals/hr
3,000	+9	88
2,850	+9	84
2,650	+7	67

With the sun reflecting off the water of the English Channel, BM597 skirts the south coast of England close to Folkestone. Jarrod Cotter

Jeffrey Quill's Last Spitfire Flight

It was in 1966 when I made my last flight in a Spitfire. It was in an old Mk V aeroplane AB910, which we had restored at Supermarine in the early 1950s. ... As I taxied in afterwards and shut down the engine I remained for a few moments in the cockpit, listening to the gentle ticking noises as the engine cooled off, and savoured the indefinable yet so familiar smells of the Spitfire cockpit. It had been 30 years since my first flight in a Spitfire. ...

My mind went back to the day in 1936 when I stood with R.J. Mitchell and Mutt Summers around the unfinished prototype in the old works at Woolston and to the day, some two months later, when, as a very young test pilot, I had made my own first flight in it. ... Looking back on it I began to realise the extent to which the Spitfire had dominated my life and energies during those ten years from 1936. I had come to know the aeroplane intimately and thoroughly, not only as a test pilot but by flying it in the RAF. ...

As I climbed out of the cockpit of AB910, I had that feeling of sadness of bidding farewell to an old friend.

'When the Merlin 66 engine was brought in on the Mk VIII we reverted to the standard wing tip configuration. We then had an excellent aeroplane, very pleasant to handle and of performance as good as the Mk IX with many other advantages added on'
Jeffrey Quill

Above: RAAF Publication 443, which contains the pilot's notes for the Spitfire Mk.VIII.

Right: The strikingly painted Spitfire Mk.VIII A58-758 of the Temora Aviation Museum in New South Wales, Australia, which wears the markings of No. 457 Squadron RAAF, complete with a shark's mouth. This beautiful aircraft is seen here being flown by Guy Bourke on a local sortie out of Temora.
Courtesy Temora Aviation Museum

Pilot's Notes
for Spitfire Mark F VIII
December 1943
Air Publication 1565G & H

Section 1 Descriptive

Introduction
The Spitfire Mk VIII is fitted with the following Marks of Merlin engine:

F.VIII	Merlin 63
LF.VIII	Merlin 66
HF.VIII	Merlin 70

Merlin 63 engines have SU carburettors and Merlin 66 and 70 engines have Bendix-Stromberg carburettors. All are fitted with Rotol 35° four-bladed propellers. The Spitfire VIII is fully tropicalised. The aircraft controls, including the undercarriage, flaps and brakes, are identical with those on earlier Marks.

Fuel Oil and Coolant Systems

Fuel tanks Fuel is carried in four self-sealing tanks, two (one above the other) forward of the cockpit and one in each wing. The top tank feeds into the lower tank and fuel in the wing tanks is transferred to the top tank by means of air pressure through a transfer valve controlled by the pilot. It is delivered to the carburettor, through a filter, by an engine-driven pump. On Merlin 63 engine installations there is a fuel cooler, and on Merlin 66 and 70 installations a de-aerator in the carburettor which is vented to the top tank.

The tank capacities are as follows:

Top tank	47 gallons
Bottom tank	49 gallons
2 wing tanks (13 gallons each)	26 gallons
Total	122 gallons

An auxiliary drop tank of 30, 90 or 170 gallons capacity can be fitted under the fuselage. To meet the possibility of engine cutting due to fuel boiling in warm weather at high altitudes, the fuselage top and bottom tanks can be pressurised (operative above 20,000ft). Pressurising, however, impairs the self-sealing of tanks and should, therefore, be turned off in the event of a tank being holed.

Fuel cocks The cock control for the main tanks is a lever fitted below the engine- starting push-buttons: the pressurising cock is below the right-hand side of the instrument panel. The transfer valve selector lever for admitting pressure to either wing tank, is next to the main cock control. The cock control lever and jettison lever for the auxiliary drop tank are mounted together on the right-hand side of the cockpit, below the undercarriage control unit. The jettison lever is pulled up to jettison the drop tank, but cannot be operated until the cock control lever is moved forward to the OFF position.

Fuel pumps On Stromberg carburettor installations an electric booster-pump, operated by a switch on the left-hand side of the cockpit, is fitted in the lower main tank for facilitating engine starting and engine recovery during combat, and should, therefore, be left on in flight. On early aircraft, where this pump is not fitted, a hand-wobble pump, just forward of the remote contactor, is provided.

NOTE: The idle cut-off lever must be in the fully aft position before the pump is operated with the engine stationary.

Fuel contents gauge and warning light (a) The contents gauge on the right-hand side of the instrument panel has two dials, one for the top tank and another for the bottom tank. A red mark on the former indicates the level of fuel at which fuel should be transferred from the wing tanks. On early aircraft there is only one dial showing the combined contents of both tanks.
(b) The fuel pressure warning light comes on when the pressure drops to $6lb/in^2$ ($10lb/in^2$ on Stromberg carburettor installations) and is switched off by the undercarriage indicator switch.
(c) Provision is made on later aircraft for a fuel tank low-level warning light.

Oil system On early aircraft the oil tank is housed in the rear fuselage, immediately aft of the cockpit, and has an oil capacity of 7.5 gallons. On later aircraft it is fitted below the engine mounting, and the oil capacity is increased to 8.5 gallons. Either tank has an air space of approximately 3 gallons. The oil tank is pressurised to $2\frac{1}{2}lb/in^2$ and the supply passes through a filter before entering the engine. A cooler is fitted inside the fairing of the port wing radiator and oil pressure and temperature gauges are fitted on the instrument panel. When carrying an auxiliary fuel tank of 170 gallons capacity a larger oil tank of either 8.5 or 14.5 gallons capacity must be fitted.

Engine coolant system The system is thermostatically controlled, the under-wing radiators being by-passed until the coolant reaches a certain temperature. The header tank is mounted above the reduction gear casing and is fitted with a relief valve. The radiator flaps are fully automatic and are designed to open at a coolant temperature of 115°C. A push-button on the electrical panel is fitted for ground testing, and there is a coolant temperature gauge on the instrument panel.

Main Services

Hydraulic system Oil is carried on the fireproof bulkhead and passes through a filter to an engine-driven pump for operation of the undercarriage and tailwheel.

Electrical system A 12-volt generator supplies an accumulator which in turn supplies the whole of the electrical installation. A voltmeter across the accumulator is fitted at the top of the instrument panel and a red light on the electrical panel, marked POWER FAILURE, is illuminated when the generator is not charging the accumulator.

NOTE: If the electrical system fails or is damaged the supercharger will be fixed in M ratio and the radiator flaps will remain closed.

Pneumatic system An engine-driven air compressor feeds two storage cylinders for the operation of the flaps, radiator flaps, supercharger operating ram, brakes and guns. The cylinders each hold air at $300lb/in^2$ pressure.

NOTE: If the pneumatic system fails, the supercharger will be fixed in M ratio, but the position of the radiator flaps will depend on the nature of the failure.

Aircraft Controls

Flying controls The control column is of the spade-grip pattern and incorporates the brake lever, gun and cannon firing control and camera gun push-button. The rudder pedals have two positions and are adjustable for leg reach by rotation of star wheels on the sliding tubes.

Trimming tabs The elevator trimming tabs are controlled by a handwheel on the left-hand side of the cockpit, the indicator being on the instrument panel. The rudder trimming tab is controlled by a small handwheel and is not provided with an indicator. The aircraft tends to turn to starboard when the handwheel is rotated clockwise.

Undercarriage control The undercarriage selector lever moves in a gated quadrant on the right-hand side of the cockpit. To raise the undercarriage, the lever must be moved downwards and across, to disengage it from the gate, and then moved forward to the full extent of the quadrant. When the undercarriage operation is completed the lever will automatically spring into the forward gate.

To lower the undercarriage the operation is reversed and the lever will spring into the rear gate when the undercarriage is down.

The lever must never be moved into either gate by hand, as this will cut off the hydraulic pressure. An indicator in the quadrant shows DOWN, IDLE or UP, depending on the position of the hydraulic valve. UP or DOWN should show only during the corresponding operation of the undercarriage, and IDLE when the lever is in either gate. If, when the engine is not running, the indicator shows DOWN, it should return to IDLE when the engine is started; if it does not, probable failure of the hydraulic pump is indicated.

Undercarriage indicators (a) Electrical visual indicator – The electrically operated visual indicator has two semi-transparent windows on which the words UP on a red background and DOWN on a green background are lettered; the words are illuminated according to the position of the undercarriage. The master switch incorporates a sliding bar which prevents the ignition switches from being switched on until the indicator is illuminated. The switch also operates the tailwheel indicator light and the fuel pressure warning light.
(b) Mechanical position indicators – A rod that extends through the top surface of the main plane is fitted to each undercarriage unit. When the wheels are down the rods – which are painted red – protrude through the top of the main planes and when they are up, the tops of the rods are flush with the main plane surface.
(c) Tailwheel indicator – A green light below the undercarriage indicator is illuminated when the tailwheel is in the fully down position.

Undercarriage warning horn The horn sounds when the throttle lever is nearly closed and the undercarriage is not lowered. It may be silenced, however, by depressing the push-button on the side of the throttle quadrant. As soon as the throttle is opened again the push-button is automatically released and the horn will sound when the throttle is again closed.

Flap control The split flaps have two positions only, up and fully down. They are controlled by a finger lever on the instrument panel.

Wheel brakes The brake lever is fitted on the control column spade grip and a catch for retaining it in the on position for parking is fitted below the lever pivot. A triple pressure gauge, showing the air pressures in the pneumatic system and at each brake, is mounted on the instrument panel.

Flying control locking struts Two struts are stowed on the right-hand side of the cockpit, aft of the seat. The longer strut and the arm attached to it lock the control column to the seat and to the starboard datum longeron, and the shorter strut, attached to the other strut by a cable, locks the rudder pedals. The controls should be locked with the seat in its highest position.

Engine Controls

Throttle The throttle lever is gated at the take-off position. There is a friction adjuster on the side of the quadrant. The mixture control is automatic and there is no pilot's control lever.

Propeller control The speed control lever on the throttle quadrant varies the governed rpm from 3,000 down to below 1,800. Speeds below this figure should, however, not be used except in the event of a forced landing, when it is necessary to lengthen the glide. The friction adjuster is on the side of the quadrant.

Later Mk VIII aircraft have interconnected throttle and propeller controls. The interconnection is controlled by a lever similar to the normal speed control lever, known as the override lever. When this lever is set fully back to the AUTOMATIC position the rpm are controlled by the positioning of the throttle lever. When pushed fully forward to the MAX RPM position it overrides the inter-connection device and rpm are then governed at 3,000.

The override lever can also be used in the same way as the conventional propeller speed control lever to enable the pilot to select higher rpm than those given by the interconnection. The automatic controlling of rpm is effected only when the override lever is set fully back and indiscriminate use of the lever in any other position will increase fuel consumption considerably.

At low altitudes the corresponding rpm for a given boost with the override lever set at AUTOMATIC are as follows:

Boost (lb/in^2)	rpm
Below +3	1,800 to 1,850
At +7 (cruising)	2,270 to 2,370
At +11½ to +12½ (at the gate)	2,800 to 2,900
At +17½ to +18½ (fully open)	3,000 to 3,050

Left: Temora's Spitfire VIII wears the markings of A58-602/RG-V, the aircraft flown by Wg Cdr R.H. 'Bobby' Gibbes OAM DSO DFC*. He is seen in the fighter here after his arrival back in Australia from the war in the Pacific in April 1945. Via Keith Webb

Below, left: A wartime photograph of the underside of a Spitfire VIII. British Official

Right: The Temora Spitfire VIII is seen here being flown by Temora Aviation Museum's Founder and President David Lowy AM. Note that in this view the aircraft can be seen to be wearing the serial number A58-602. Courtesy Temora Aviation Museum

Supercharger controls The two-speed two-stage supercharger automatically changes to S ratio at about 21,000ft (14,000ft on Merlin 66 installation) on the climb, and back to M ratio at about 19,000ft (12,500ft on Merlin 66 installation) on the descent. An override switch is fitted on the instrument panel by means of which M ratio may be selected at any height. There is a push-button on the electrical panel for testing the gear change on the ground, and a red light on the instrument panel comes on when S ratio is engaged, on the ground or in flight.

Radiator flap control The push-button for testing the radiator flaps is on the electrical panel.

Slow-running cut-out (Merlin 63 installations) The control on the carburettor is operated by pulling the ring below the left-hand side of the instrument panel.

Idle cut-off control (Merlin 66 and 70 installations.) The idle cut-off is operated by moving the lever on the throttle quadrant to the fully aft position.

Cylinder priming pump A hand operated pump for priming the engine is fitted below the right-hand side of the instrument panel.

Ignition switches and starter buttons The ignition switches are on the left-hand side of the instrument panel and the booster coil and engine starter push-buttons immediately below the panel. Each push-button is covered by a safety shield.

Ground battery starting The socket for starting from an external supply is mounted on the starboard engine bearer.

Hand starting A starting handle is stowed behind the seat and a hole in the starboard side of the engine cowling gives access for connecting the handle to the hand-starting gear.

Carburettor air-intake control On early aircraft the filter in the air intake can be bypassed, in the event of it becoming choked, by moving the control lever in the cockpit from COLD to HOT. Unfiltered air is then admitted from the engine bay. On later aircraft the normal air intake (OPEN position of the control lever) is not filtered and is used at all times except for take-off and landing on sandy or dusty aerodromes, or when flying through sand storms, when the CLOSED position should be used. Filtered air is then taken from the engine bay.

Oil dilution A push-button for operating the solenoid valve is fitted on the electrical panel.

Left: A close-up of A58-758's fearsome shark's mouth and eyes. Courtesy Temora Aviation Museum

Below, left: An Australian pilot from No. 457 Squadron climbs into his Spitfire VIII at Darwin. British Official

Other Controls

Cockpit door The cockpit door is provided with a two-position catch which allows it to be partly opened and so prevents the hood from sliding shut when taking off and landing, and in the event of a forced landing. It will be found that the catch operates more easily when the aircraft is airborne than when on the ground.

Identification lamp The downward identification lamp is fitted flush with the under surface of the starboard wing and is controlled by the forward switch and Morsing key on the signalling switchbox. A colour (red, green and amber) selector lever is fitted just aft of the switchbox for operation of the colour disc.

Signal discharger The recognition device fires one of six cartridges out of the top of the rear fuselage when the handle to the left of the pilot's seat is pulled upwards. On some aircraft a pre-selector control is mounted above the operating handle.

Bomb release controls On Mk VIII aircraft equipped for the carriage of bombs, the master switch and the fusing switch are mounted together on the left-hand side of the cockpit, just forward of the door. The bomb release push-button is incorporated in the top of the throttle lever.

Section 2
Handling

Management of the fuel system
i. Flying restrictions:
a) When fitted with a 90-gallon drop tank the aircraft is restricted to 'straight flying' until the tank is jettisoned. This restriction does not apply when fitted with a 30-gallon or 45-gallon drop tank.
b) Drop tanks should be jettisoned only in straight flight and at a speed of not more than 300mph IAS.

ii. Management of tanks:
Main fuel system only
a) Start and warm up on the main tanks.
b) Take-off on the main tanks and when the contents of these drop to 80 gallons or less (to the red mark on the contents gauge on later aircraft), fuel should be transferred to the top tank from one of the wing tanks. The transfer valve selector cock should be turned OFF after three minutes.
c) Repeat the above procedure with the second wing tank when the contents of the main tanks again drop to 80 gallons or less (to the red mark on the gauge on later aircraft). It is important to leave the transfer selector cock OFF, or pressurising of the main tanks will not be effective.

Right: David Lowy AM standing in front of Spitfire VIII A58-758.
Courtesy Temora Aviation Museum

Below, right: Guy Bourke bears down on the camera aircraft in A58-758.
Courtesy Temora Aviation Museum

When fitted with a drop tank:

d) Start, warm up and take-off on the main tanks and change over to the drop tank at a safe height (2,000ft). Turn OFF the main tanks.

e) Owing to a possible delay in picking up after the engine-driven pump has run dry, it is recommended that the main tanks are turned ON and the drop tank is turned OFF before the drop tank is completely empty, working on a time basis. If it is essential to use all fuel from the drop tank, proceed as follows:

i. It must be run dry only at a safe height.

ii. The drop tank cock should be turned OFF immediately and the main cock then turned ON.

iii. On Bendix-Stromberg carburettor installations (Merlin 66 and 70 engines) the booster pump should be ON, or the wobble pump operated until the engine is running satisfactorily. Windmilling at high rpm will assist the engine to pick up.

f) If a drop tank has to be jettisoned before it is empty, first turn ON the main tanks and then turn OFF the drop tank.

NOTE: It is necessary to ensure that the drop tank cock is in the fully OFF position when the tank is empty or has been jettisoned; otherwise air may be sucked into the main fuel system.

Preliminaries

i. Check contents of fuel tanks. If fitted with a drop tank check that the cock is OFF.

ii. Check that the undercarriage selector lever is down; switch on the indicator and see that the DOWN and tailwheel light show green. Check voltmeter: 12 volts min.

iii. Test operation of flying controls.

iv. In order to avoid damage to the propeller, the ground immediately below it should be cleared of any small stones or rubble before starting the engine.

Starting the engine and warming up – F.VIII (Merlin 63 engine)

i. Set main fuel cock ON and wing tank selector cock OFF.

ii. **Set the controls as follows:**

Throttle	½ inch open
Propeller control	Fully forward
Supercharger over-ride switch	AUTO

iii. If an external priming connection is fitted, high volatility fuel should be used for priming at temperatures below freezing. Work the Ki-gass priming pump until the fuel reaches the priming nozzles; this may be judged by a sudden increase in resistance.

iii. Switch ON the ignition and press the starter and booster-coil buttons. Turning periods must not exceed 20 seconds, with a 30 second wait between each. Work the priming pump as rapidly and vigorously as possible while the engine is being turned; it should start after the following number of strokes if the engine is cold:

Air temperature °C:	+30	+20	+10	0	-10	-20
Normal fuel:			3	4	7	12
High volatility fuel:				4	8	15	18

i. At temperatures below freezing it will probably be necessary to continue priming after the engine has fired and until it picks up on the carburettor.

ii. Release the starter button as soon as the engine starts and as soon as the engine is running satisfactorily release the booster-coil button and screw down the priming pump.

iii. Open up slowly to 1,000rpm then warm up at this speed.

Starting the engine and warming up – LF.VIII and HF.VIII (Merlin 66 and 70 engines)

i. Set main fuel cock ON and wing tank selector cock OFF.

ii. **Set the controls as follows:**

Throttle	½ inch open
Propeller control	Fully forward
Idle cut-off control	Fully aft
Supercharger over-ride switch	AUTO

iii. If an external priming connection is fitted, high volatility fuel should be used for priming at temperatures below freezing. Work the Ki-gass priming pump until the fuel reaches the priming nozzles, this may be judged by a sudden increase in resistance, and then give the following number of strokes:

Air temperature °C:	+30	+20	+10	0	-10	-20
Normal fuel:			3	4	7	12
High volatility fuel:				4	8	15	18

iv. Switch ON the booster pump (or operate the wobble pump until the pressure warning light goes out).

NOTE: Neither the booster pump nor the wobble pump must be operated unless the cut-off valve is closed or the engine is running. The wobble pump may be operated again, if necessary, after the engine has started and the idle cut-off control has been moved forward.

v. Switch ON the ignition and press the starter and booster-coil push-buttons.

vi. As soon as the engine fires release the starter button and move the idle cut-off control forward. Release the booster-coil button and screw down the priming pump as soon as the engine is running satisfactorily.

NOTE: If the engine is over-primed and fails to start, operate the idle cut-off control and switch off the booster pump while the engine is cleared by turning it through two or three revolutions.

vii. Open up slowly to 1,000rpm then warm up at this speed.

RAAF Spitfire Mk.VIIIs, with A58-315 nearest the camera, in formation over Australia during 1945. Australian Official

Testing the engine and installation

While warming up:

i.   Check temperatures and pressures.

ii. Press the radiator test push-button and have ground crew check that shutters open.

iii. Check operation of the flaps.

iv. Test each magneto in turn as a precautionary check before running up.

NOTE: The following comprehensive checks (for which the tail must be tied down) should be carried out after repair, inspection other than daily, or otherwise at the pilot's discretion. Normally they may be reduced in accordance with local instructions, when the tail need not be tied down.

After warming up to at least 15°C oil temperature and 60°C coolant temperature (with the propeller override control fully forward):

v.   Open up to 0lb/in^2 boost and exercise and check operation of the supercharger by pressing the test push-button. Rpm should fall slightly and the red light should come on when S ratio is engaged.

vi. At 0lb/in^2 boost exercise and check operation of the constant speed propeller, but take care not to reduce rpm below 1,800. Check that the generator is charging; the power failure light should be out and the voltage 14 or over. On aircraft on which an interconnection is fitted open the throttle to +3lb/in^2 boost and set the override lever to AUTOMATIC, when rpm should fall to 1,800. Return the lever to MAX RPM.

vii. With the propeller control fully forward open the throttle to the gate and check take-off boost and static rpm which should be 3,000 at take-off boost.

viii.Throttle back to +9lb/in^2 boost, or further if necessary to ensure that rpm fall below 3,000, then test each magneto in turn. The single ignition drop should not exceed 150rpm.

ix. Before taxying, check brake pressure (80lb/in^2) and pneumatic supply pressure (220lb/in^2).

Final Preparation for Take-Off

T – Trimming tabs –	Elevator. Half a division nose down Rudder: fully right.
P – Propeller control interconnection (if fitted) –	Fully forward
F – Fuel	Override lever-Max RPM Check contents of main tanks Main tank cock – ON Transfer cock – OFF Drop tank cock – OFF Electric booster pump (if fitted) – ON
F – Flaps	Up
Supercharger	Over-ride switch – AUTO. Red light out
Air intake	As required

Take-off

i. Open the throttle slowly, to the gate if +12lb/in² boost is needed, +7lb/in² is sufficient for a normal take-off.
ii. Any tendency to swing can be counteracted by the rudder.
iii. After raising the undercarriage, see that the red indicator light – UP – comes on and the tailwheel light goes out. It may be necessary to hold the lever hard forward against the quadrant until the red indicator light does come on. Failure of the wheels to lock up may spoil the airflow through the radiators and oil cooler and result in excessive temperatures.
iv. Do not start to climb before a speed of 140mph IAS is attained.

Climbing

i. The speed for maximum rate of climb is 160mph IAS from sea level to 25,000ft, reducing by 3mph per 1,000ft above this height.
ii. The fuel tank pressure cock should normally be kept OFF, but should be turned ON if the fuel pressure warning light comes on.
iii. Regulate the oxygen supply by the cabin altimeter.

General flying

i. Stability: On later aircraft fitted with horn balance elevators and large rudders there is a marked increase in longitudinal and directional stability, particularly at altitude.

ii. Change of trim

Undercarriage down –	nose down
Flaps down –	nose down
Flaps down (if fitted with horn balance elevator)	nose up

iii. In bad visibility near the ground, flaps should be lowered and the propeller set to give 2,650rpm. Speed may then be reduced to 130mph IAS.

Stalling

The stalling speeds (engine off) in mph IAS at normal load (7,850lb) are as follows:

Undercarriage and flaps up:	82
Undercarriage and flaps down:	74

Spinning

i. Spinning is permitted and recovery is normal, but the loss of height involved in recovery may be very great and the following limits are to be observed:
ii. Spins are not to be started below 10,000ft.
a) Recovery is to be initiated before two turns are completed.
b) A speed of 150mph IAS should be attained before starting to ease out of the resultant dive.
iii. Spinning is not permitted when fitted with a drop tank or when carrying a bomb.

Diving

i. The aircraft should be trimmed into and out of the dive.
ii. A tendency to yaw to starboard should be corrected by use of the rudder trimming tab.
iii. When carrying a bomb, the angle of dive must not exceed 60°.

Aerobatics

The following speeds (mph IAS) are recommended:

Loop	280–300
Roll	220–250
Half roll off loop	320–350
Upward roll	330–380

Flick manoeuvres are not permitted.

Check list before landing

i. Reduce speed to 160mph IAS and open the cockpit hood.

U – Undercarriage	DOWN (Check indicator)
Tailwheel	Green light on
P – Propeller control	Fully forward
Supercharger	Red light out
F – Flaps	DOWN

NOTE: The undercarriage operation takes considerably longer with engine off than with engine on. The undercarriage must, therefore, be lowered early on a glide approach.
ii. Check brake pressure (80lb/in²) and pneumatic supply pressure (220lb/in²)

Approach and landing
i. Approach speeds in mph IAS at normal load 7,850lb:

		(flaps up)
Engine assisted	95	(105)
Glide	105	(110)

NOTE: In all cases speed may be reduced by 5mph when cannon ammunition or considerable fuel has been expended.

ii. The aircraft is nose-heavy on the ground; the brakes, therefore, must be used carefully on landing.

Mislanding
i. Raise the undercarriage.
ii. Climb at about 130mph IAS with flaps fully down.
iii. Raise flaps at a safe height of about 200–300ft.
iv. Retrim

After landing
i. Raise the flaps before taxying.
ii. To stop the engine, idle for ½ minute at 800–900rpm then pull the slow-running cut-out and hold it out until the engine stops. On Merlin 66 and 70 installations the booster-pump must be switched off and the idle cut-off control moved fully aft.
iii. Turn OFF the fuel cock and switch OFF the ignition.
iv. Oil dilution
The correct dilution period for this aircraft is:
Atmospheric temperature above -10°C: 1 minute
Atmospheric temperature below -10°C: 2 minutes

Beam approach
i. The recommended speeds (mph IAS), rpm and flap settings are:

	Maintaining height		Final approach
	Prelimenary manoeuvring	Manoeuvring with u/c down	
Speed	180	160	120
Flaps	UP	UP	DOWN Fully forward
RPM	2,650	2,650	

ii. Approach at 900ft over the outer marker beacon, reducing to 200ft over the inner marker beacon.

Section 2
Operating Data

Engine Data: Merlins 63, 66 and 70
i. **Fuel:** 100 octane only

ii. Engine limitation:

		Rpm	Boost Lb/In²	Temp. °C Coolant	Oil
Max Take-Off to 1,000ft	M	3,000	+18*	135	–
Max Climbing 1 Hour Limit	M } S	2,850	+12	125	90
Maximum Continuous	M } S	2,650	+7	105 (115)	90
Combat 5 Mins Limit	M } S	3,000	+18	135	105

* +12lb/in² on Merlin 63, 64 and 66 engined.
Note: The figure in brackets is permitted for short periods.

Minimal Oil Pressure in Flight	30lb/in²

Minimum Temperature for Take-Off
Oil	15°C
Coolant	60°C

Fuel Pressure
Merlin 63	8–10lb/in²
Merlins 66 and 70	14–16lb/in²

Flying limitations
i. Maximum speeds:
Diving	470mph IAS
Undercarriage down	160mph IAS
Flaps down	160mph IAS

ii. Restriction
a) Take-off with three bombs or a drop tank and bombs fitted should be made from a smooth runway.
b) Spinning and aerobatics are not permitted and violent manoeuvres must be avoided when any bomb load is carried, or when a 170-gallon or 90-gallon drop tank is carried. Spinning is not permitted with any drop tank.
c) Before commencing dive-bombing, the 90-gallon drop tank (if carried) must be jettisoned.
d) The angle of dive when releasing a bomb or bombs must not exceed 60°.
e) Except in an emergency the fuselage bomb or drop tank should be jettisoned before landing with wing bombs fitted.

Right: Spitfire VIIIc MV239 arrived in Australia on board the SS *Rangitana* on 8 May 1945 and was allocated the very last RAAF Spitfire serial number, A58-758. It saw no operational service though, and went into storage the very next month. Australian Official

Maximum performance

The speeds for maximum rate of climb are as follows:

SL to 25,000ft:	160mph IAS
25,000 to 30,000ft:	145mph IAS
30,000 to 35,000ft:	130mph IAS
35,000 to 40,000ft:	115mph IAS
Above 40,000ft:	Reduce speed by 3mph per 1,000ft.

Economical flying

i. Climbing – For maximum fuel economy, climb at +7lb/in² boost and 2,650rpm at the speeds for maximum rate of climb. When climbing to altitudes below 30,000ft, however, the climb may be made at +12lb/in² and 2,850rpm without seriously increasing the total fuel consumption over that obtained on a climb at +7lb/in² boost and 2,650rpm.

ii. Cruising – Greatest range will be obtained at medium heights. The recommended speeds are as follows:

a) Without auxiliary tanks, or if carrying a 30 gallon drop tank: 170mph IAS. At low altitudes speed should be increased by 10 to 20mph.

b) If carrying a 90-gallon drop tank: 175mph IAS. At low altitudes 180mph IAS.

c) If carrying a 170-gallon drop tank: 185mph IAS at start of level flight, reducing as fuel is consumed to 170mph IAS when the drop tank is empty. By reducing rpm by 50 at the end of each hour the IAS will be reduced by approximately the correct amount.

NOTE. At low altitudes the recommended speed is 180mph IAS after jettisoning the tank.

Fly at 1,800rpm (but check that the generator is charging) and adjust the throttle to give the recommended speed, but do not exceed +7lb/in² boost. If at 1,800rpm and full throttle the recommended speed cannot be obtained, increase rpm as necessary.

Fuel capacities and consumption

i. Normal fuel capacity:

Top tank	47 gallons
Bottom tank	49 gallons
2 Wing tanks (13 gallons each)	26 gallons
Total	122 gallons

ii. Long range fuel capacities:

With 30-gallon drop tank	152 gallons
With 90-gallon drop tank	212 gallons
With 170-gallon drop tank	292 gallons

iii. Fuel consumptions:
The approximate fuel consumptions (gals/hr) for the Merlin 63 engine are as follows:

Weak mixture (as obtained at +7lb/in² boost and below)

Boost lb/in² rpm	2,650	2,400	2,200	2,000	1,800
+7	80	–	–	–	–
+4	71	66	61	54	49
+2	66	61	57	50	43
0	60	55	51	45	39
-2	53	42	38	34	20
-4	45	42	38	34	20

Rich mixture (as obtained above +7lb/in² boost):

Boost lb/in²	rpm	gals/hr
+18	3,000	150
+15	3,000	130
+12	2,850	105

'By the end of the war Jeffrey Quill had personally test flown all 50-plus variants of Spitfire and Seafire. The rapid increase in performance, armament and all-up weight produced a never-ending stream of design changes, most of which tended to be detrimental to handling qualities and affected the Spitfire's aesthetics. But, as Quill remarked, "We were trying to produce the most effective flying machine, not the most elegant flying machine." His personal favourite mark, from a pure flying point of view, was the Spitfire VIII, with standard wings.'

Richard Riding, from Jeffrey Quill's obituary in The Independent, *published on 5 March 1996– the sixtieth anniversary of the first flight of K5054.*

Shark's mouth 'Spit'

Australia has two airworthy Spitfires, both of which are located at the Temora Aviation Museum in New South Wales. Founder and president of the museum is David Lowy, AM, a well-known Australian businessman whose aviation accolades began in aerobatics, but who has since become a pivotal figure in the country's warbird movement.

Spitfire Mk VIII A58-758 was the first to be acquired back in 2000, when it was bought by David Lowy in May of that year. David then donated it to the Temora Aviation Museum in 2002.

The aircraft is painted in the green and grey camouflage as worn by 453 Squadron, RAAF, aircraft defending Darwin against Japanese attacks during the Second World War and later in operations in the South-west Pacific. The aircraft carries the markings of A58-602 RG-V, the personal mount of Wing Commander R.H. 'Bobby' Gibbes, AM, DSO, DFC*. This sees it adorned with a shark's mouth on the underside of its forward fuselage, making it one of the most strikingly painted Spitfires in the world.

Driven by passion

David Lowy's establishment of the museum at Temora was driven by his passion for aviation heritage, and in its time has set new standards in warbird operation and presentation in Australia.

David spoke to this author about the roots of the museum and in particular what the Spitfire's addition meant:

The museum started off when I finished aerobatic flying. I won the Australian championship in 1998 and was looking for another aim for my aviation passion.

By chance we used do our training at Temora. We were having difficulty finding somewhere to practise, and Temora as a town invited us there because of its aviation heritage.

I had been training there a lot and when I finished with the aerobatics I decided to establish a museum. From the start the goal would be to collect and maintain aircraft in airworthy condition that were either operated by, or used in conjunction with, Australian armed forces.

We acquired a Tiger Moth that was actually used at 10 EFTS

[Elementary Flying Training School] Temora and then a Wirraway. I also had a Cessna A-37, which was often used in Vietnam to support Australian ground forces. We built a hangar and as that was going on I learnt a lot more about the history of Temora and what a significant location it was.

Early on we realised that the museum was much more than just being about the aircraft. I realised that it was more attributed to the men and women who had made sacrifices for Australia. I therefore integrated the veterans into the museum and invite them to every flying day.

The stories of the people are more important than the aircraft. I have met many of them and it's important for later generations to understand their contribution.

About the acquisition of the museum's first Spitfire, Mk VIII A58-758, and its most appropriate colour scheme, David commented:

I had been talking to Colonel Pay for some time and really wanted to have a Spitfire. I first met 'Bobby' Gibbes not long after I acquired it and Peter Anderson, our chief historian and flying day commentator, felt that as a tribute to 'Bobby' we should paint the Spitfire in his colours.

Bobby didn't realise we'd done it and when we rolled the Spitfire out there was a tear in his eye – it was an emotional moment. That's what it's all about. It's a wonderful tribute to the fighting men of Australia.

Temora's flight operations have often been likened to those in the military. There are good reasons for this as David points out:

I've been passionate about flying since I was five years old. My life took a different path from the military, but I always want to operate to the highest standards … to reduce the risks.

Flight operations are run separately from the museum. We have a number of ex-military personnel and use this experience as a base …We try to operate as closely as we can to military standards. Safety is front and centre to us.

In conclusion, David shared his feelings about what it means to fly the Spitfire:

It's a real thrill and privilege to be able to fly the Spitfire. It's every young aviator's dream. It's more than a machine that you're taking into the air; you're taking the history of people's sacrifices up there. It's very emotional.

You have to handle it in a way that means it can be enjoyed for many years to come. It's a blending of a boyhood dream and being conscious that while flying it you're responsible in representing the sacrifices of generations past. It's a huge responsibility, but an absolute joy and privilege.

Left: The cockpit of Spitfire VIII **A58-758.** Courtesy Temora Aviation Museum

Below, right: In this view of **A58-758** being flown by David Lowy it can be clearly seen that a feature of the **Mk.VIII was a retractable tail wheel.** Courtesy Temora Aviation Museum

**Pilot's Notes for
Spitfire IX and XVI
3rd Edition, September 1946**
Air Publication 1565J, P & L

'The appearance of increasing numbers of the Fw 190, which was showing itself more highly manoeuvrable and heavily armed than any other Luftwaffe aircraft, in the early spring of 1942 intensified the need for a greatly improved Spitfire, and the result was a 'crash' programme to convert the Spitfire Vc to Merlin 61 engines and put them into squadron service as quickly as possible. ... The aircraft was designated the Spitfire Mk IX.'
Jeffrey Quill

Descriptive

Introduction
The variants of the Spitfire IX and XVI are distinguished by prefix letters denoting the general operating altitude or role and the suffix letter 'e' is used where 0.5in guns replace 0.303in guns. The aircraft are all essentially similar, but the following table shows the main features that give the various versions their distinguishing letters:

F.IX   Merlin 61, 63 or 63A; two 20mm and four 0.303in guns.
LF.IX   Merlin 66; two 20mm and four 0.303in guns.
LF.IXe   Merlin 66; two 20mm and two 0.5in guns.
HF.IX   Merlin 70; two 20mm and four 0.303in guns.
HF.IXe   Merlin 70; two 20mm and two 0.5in guns.
F.XVI   Merlin 266; two 20mm and two 0.5in guns.

(i) Merlin 61 and 63 engines have SU float-type carburettors, but on Merlin 66, 70 and 266 engines these are replaced by Bendix-Stromberg injection carburettors.
(ii) All these marks of aircraft are fitted with Rotol four-bladed hydraulic propellers and on the majority of the aircraft the wingtips are clipped.
(iii) Later Mk IX and Mk XVIs have 'rear view' fuselages which incorporate 'teardrop' sliding hoods.

Part 1 – Descriptive
Fuel, Oil and Coolant Systems

Fuel tanks Fuel is carried in two tanks mounted one above the other (the lower one is self-sealing) forward of the cockpit. The top tank feeds into the bottom tank and fuel is delivered to the carburettor, through a filter, by an engine-driven pump. On Merlin 61 and 63 engine installations there is a fuel cooler, while on Bendix-Stromberg carburettor installations a de-aerator in the carburettor, for separating accumulated air from the fuel, is vented to the top tank. Later Mk IX and all F.XVI aircraft mount two additional fuel tanks with a combined capacity of 75 gallons

(66 gallons in aircraft with 'rear view' fuselages); they are fitted in the fuselage behind the cockpit. These tanks should only be filled for special operations at the discretion of the appropriate Area Commander and normally their cocks should be wired OFF. If fitted in aircraft with 'rear view' fuselages, they must not be used in any circumstances.

The capacities of the main tanks are as follows:

Top tank	48 gallons
Bottom tank	37 gallons or 47* gallons
Total	85 or 95* gallons

*On some aircraft, generally those which have 'rear view' fuselages, an auxiliary 'blister' drop tank of 30, 45 or 90 gallons capacity can be fitted under the fuselage; the fuel from these tanks feeds the engine direct and does not replenish the main tanks. To meet the possibility of engine cutting due to fuel boiling in warm weather at high altitudes, the main tanks are pressurised; pressurising, however, impairs the self-sealing properties of the tanks and should, therefore, be turned OFF if a tank is holed.

Fuel cocks The cock control for the main tanks is a lever fitted below the engine starting push-buttons and the pressurising control is below the right-hand side of the instrument panel. The cock control and jettison lever for the auxiliary drop tank are mounted together on the right-hand side of the cockpit, below the undercarriage control unit. The jettison lever is pulled up to jettison the drop tank, but cannot be operated until the cock control is moved forward to the OFF position.

Fuel pumps On Bendix-Stromberg carburettor installations an electric booster pump, operated by a switch on the left-hand side of the cockpit, is fitted in the lower main tank. On early aircraft this pump is not fitted, but a hand wobble pump is provided instead, just forward of the remote contactor.
NOTE: On aircraft which have rear fuselage tanks a second pump is fitted (in the lower rear tank) and the control switch described above then has three positions.

Fuel contents gauges and pressure warning light The contents gauge on the right-hand side of the instrument panel indicates the quantity of fuel in the lower main tank when the adjacent push-button is depressed. On aircraft with rear fuselage tanks a gauge (for the lower rear tank only) is mounted beside the main tanks' gauge. This also operates when the main tanks' gauge push-button is depressed. On later LF.XVI aircraft the two gauges are mounted together, the left-hand dial indicating the contents of the main tanks.

The fuel pressure warning light is operative when the switch on the throttle quadrant is on and comes on at any time when fuel pressure at the carburettor falls appreciably below normal.

Oil system Oil is supplied by a tank of 7.5 gallons capacity under the engine mounting, which is pressurised to $2\frac{1}{2}$lb/in^2, and passes through a filter before entering the engine. An oil cooler is fitted in the underside of the port wing and oil pressure and temperature gauges are fitted on the instrument panel. When carrying an auxiliary drop tank of 170 gallons capacity a larger oil tank of either 8.5 or 14.5 gallons capacity must be fitted.

Engine coolant system On early aircraft only, circulation of the coolant through the underwing radiators is thermostatically controlled, the radiators being by-passed until the coolant reaches a certain temperature. The header tank is mounted above the reduction gear casing and is fitted with a relief valve. On all aircraft the radiator flaps are fully automatic and are designed to open at a coolant temperature of 115°C. A push-button is fitted on the electrical panel for ground testing; and there is a coolant temperature gauge on the instrument panel.

Intercooler system On all aircraft the high temperatures resulting from two-stage supercharging necessitate the introduction of an intercooler between the supercharger delivery and the induction manifolds, particularly when S (high) gear is used. An auxiliary pump passes the coolant from a separate header tank to a radiator under the starboard wing, and thence through the supercharger casing to the intercooler, where the charge is cooled by loss of heat passing to the coolant. On early aircraft a thermo-statically operated switch in the induction pipe is connected to the supercharger operating ram and causes it to change the super-charger to M (low) gear in the event of the charge temperature becoming excessive. This change of gear ratio is indicated to the pilot by a push-button, which springs out on the instrument panel. The supercharger will change back to high gear after the temp-erature of the charge has returned to normal and the push-button has been pushed in. If, however, the excessive temperature is of a permanent nature, due to failure of the intercooler system, the push-button will continue to spring out and the flight should be continued in low gear.

Main Services

Hydraulic system Oil is carried in a reservoir on the fireproof bulkhead and passes through a filter to an engine driven pump for operation of the undercarriage.

Electrical system A 12-volt generator supplies an accumulator which in turn supplies the whole of the electrical installation. A voltmeter across the accumulator is fitted at the top of the instrument panel and a red light, on the electrical panel, marked POWER FAILURE, is illuminated when the generator is not delivering current to the accumulator.

NOTE: If the electrical system fails or is damaged, the supercharger will be fixed in low gear and the radiator flaps will remain closed.

Pneumatic system An engine-driven air compressor charges two storage cylinders to a pressure of 300lb/in^2 for operation of the flaps, radiator flaps, supercharger ram, brakes and guns.
NOTE: If the pneumatic system fails, the supercharger will be fixed in low gear, but the position of the radiator flaps will depend on the nature of the failure.

Aircraft Controls

Trimming tabs The elevator trimming tabs are controlled by a handwheel on the left-hand side of the cockpit, the indicator being on the instrument panel. The rudder trimming tab is controlled by a small handwheel and is not provided with an indicator. The aircraft tends to turn to starboard when the handwheel is rotated clockwise.

Undercarriage control The undercarriage selector lever moves in a gated quadrant on the right-hand side of the cockpit. To raise the undercarriage the lever must be moved downwards and inwards to disengage it from the gate, and then moved forward smartly in one movement to the full extent of the quadrant. When the undercarriage is locked up the lever will automatically spring into the forward gate.

To lower the undercarriage the lever must be held forward for about two seconds, then pulled back in one movement to the full extent of the quadrant. When the undercarriage is locked down the lever will spring into the rear gate.

Warning: The lever must never be moved into either gate by hand as this will cut off the hydraulic pressure. An indicator in the quadrant shows DOWN, IDLE or UP depending on the position of' the hydraulic valve. UP and DOWN should show only during the corresponding operation of the undercarriage and IDLE when the lever is in either gate. If, when the engine is not running, the indicator shows DOWN, it should return to IDLE when the engine is started; if it does not, probable failure of the hydraulic pump is indicated.

Undercarriage indicators
(a) Electrical visual indicator – The electrically operated visual indicator (2) has two semi-transparent windows on which the words UP on a red background and DOWN on a green background are lettered; the words are illuminated according to the position of the undercarriage. The switch for the DOWN circuit is moved to the on position by a striker on the throttle lever as the throttle is opened.

(b) Mechanical position indicators – On early aircraft a rod that extends through the top surface of the main plane is fitted to each undercarriage unit. When the wheels are down the rods – which are painted red – protrude through the top of the main planes and when they are up, the tops of the rods are flush with the main plane surfaces.

Undercarriage warning horn The horn, fitted in early aircraft only, sounds when the throttle lever is nearly closed and the under-carriage is not lowered. It cannot be silenced until the throttle is opened again or the undercarriage is lowered.

Flaps control The split flaps have two positions only, up and fully down. They are controlled by a finger lever on the instrument panel.

Wheel brakes The brake lever is fitted on the control column spade grip and a catch for retaining it in the on position for parking is fitted below the lever pivot. A triple pressure gauge, showing the air pressures in the pneumatic system cylinders and at each brake, is mounted on the instrument panel.

Flying controls locking gear Two struts are stowed on the right-hand side of the cockpit aft of the seat. The longer strut and the arm attached to it lock the control column to the seat and to the starboard datum longeron, and the shorter strut, attached to the other strut by a cable, locks the rudder pedals. The controls should be locked with the seat in its highest position.

Engine Controls

Throttle The throttle lever is gated at the climbing boost position. There is a friction adjuster on the side of the quadrant. The mixture control is automatic and there is no pilot's control lever.

Propeller control (a) On early aircraft the speed control lever on the inboard side of the throttle quadrant varies the governed rpm from 3,000 down to 1,800.
(b) On later aircraft the propeller speed control is interconnected with the throttle control. The interconnection is effected by a lever,

Right: A clipped wing Spitfire IX puts on some bank in this publicity photo taken during World War Two.
British Official

similar to the normal speed control lever, which is known as the override lever. When this is pulled back to the stop in the quadrant (the AUTOMATIC position) the rpm are controlled by the positioning of the throttle lever. When pushed fully forward to the MAX RPM position it overrides the interconnection device and rpm are then governed at approximately 3,000. The override lever can be used in the same way as the conventional propeller speed control lever to enable the pilot to select higher rpm than those given by the interconnection. It must be remembered that the interconnection is effected only when the override lever is pulled back to the stop in the quadrant; indiscriminate use of the lever in any position forward of this stop will increase fuel consumption considerably.

At low altitudes (and at altitudes just above that at which high gear is automatically engaged) the corresponding rpm for a given boost with the override lever set to AUTOMATIC are as follows:

Boost (lb/in²)	rpm
Below +3	1,800 to 1,850
At +7 (cruising)	2,270 to 2,370
At +12 (at the gate)	2,800 to 2,900
At +18 (throttle fully open)	3,000 to 3,050

Supercharger controls The two-speed two-stage supercharger automatically changes to high gear at about 21,000ft (14,000ft on Merlin 66 and 11,000ft on Merlin 266 installations) on the climb and back to low gear at about 19,000ft (12,500ft on Merlin 66 and 10,000ft on Merlin 266 installations) on the descent. An override switch is fitted on the instrument panel by means of which low gear may be selected at any height. There is a push-button on the electrical panel for testing the gear change on the ground, and a red light on the instrument panel comes on when high gear is engaged, on the ground or in flight.

Intercooler protector On early aircraft, should excessive charge temperatures cause the push-button to spring out, it may be reset manually to allow the supercharger to return to high gear; it will, however, only remain in if the charge temperature has returned to normal.

Radiator flap control The radiator flaps are fully automatic and there is no manual control. A push-button (41) for testing the radiator flaps is on the electrical panel.

Slow-running cut-out (Merlin 61 and 63 installations only)
The control on the carburettor is operated by pulling the ring below the left-hand side of the instrument panel.

Idle cut-off control (Merlin 66, 70 and 266 installations only) The idle cut-off valve on Bendix-Stromberg carburettors is operated by moving the short lever on the throttle quadrant through the gate to the fully aft position. On early Stromberg carburettor installations this lever is not fitted, but the cut-off valve is operated by the ring which on other aircraft operates the slow-running cut-out.

NOTE: The idle cut-off control must be in the fully aft position, or cut-off position, at all times when a booster pump is on and the engine is not running; otherwise, fuel will be injected into the supercharger at high pressure and there will be, in consequence, a serious risk of fire.

Carburettor air intake filter control On tropicalised aircraft the carburettor air intake filter control on the left-hand side of the cockpit has two positions, OPEN and CLOSED (NORMAL INTAKE and FILTER IN OPERATION on later aircraft). The CLOSED (or FILTER IN OPERATION) position must be used for all ground running, take-off and landing and when flying in sandy or dust-laden conditions.

NOTE: In the air it may be necessary to reduce speed to 200mph IAS or less, before the filter control lever can be operated. The filter control lever must always be moved slowly.

Cylinder priming pump A hand-operated pump for priming the engine is fitted below the right-hand side of the instrument panel.

Ignition switches and starter buttons The ignition switches are on the left-hand side of the instrument panel and the booster-coil and the engine starter push-buttons immediately below it. Each push-button is covered by a safety shield.

Ground battery starting The socket for starting from an external supply is mounted on the starboard engine bearer.

Other Controls

Cockpit door The cockpit door is fitted with a two-position catch which allows it to be partly opened, thus preventing the sliding hood from coming forward in the event of a crash or forced landing. It will be found that the catch operates more easily when the aircraft is airborne than when on the ground.
NOTE: On aircraft with 'teardrop' hoods, the two-position catch should not be used.

Sliding hood controls On later Mk IX and XVI aircraft the 'teardrop' hood is opened and closed by a crank handle mounted on the right-hand cockpit wall, above the undercarriage selector lever. The handle must be pulled inwards before it can be rotated. The hood may be locked in any intermediate position by releasing the crank handle which then engages with the locking ratchet. From outside the cockpit the hood may be opened and closed by hand provided the push-button below the starboard hood rail is held depressed. The hood may be jettisoned in emergency.

Signal discharger The recognition device fires one of six cartridges out of the top of the rear fuselage when the handle to the left of the pilot's seat is pulled upwards. On some aircraft a pre-selector control is mounted above the operating handle.

Part II – Handling

Management of the fuel system NOTE: Except for special operations as directed by the appropriate Area Commander, the rear fuselage tanks must not be used and their cocks should be wired OFF. On aircraft with 'rear view' fuselages they must not be used.

Without a drop tank – Start the engine, warm up, taxi and take off on the main tanks; then, at 2,000ft, change to the rear fuselage tanks (turning off the main tanks cock after the change has been made) and drain them; then revert to the main tanks.

When fitted with a drop tank – (a) Without rear fuselage tanks: Start the engine, warm up, taxi and take off on the main tanks; then at 2,000ft turn ON the drop tank and turn OFF the main tanks cock. When the fuel pressure warning light comes on, or the engine cuts, turn OFF the drop tank cock and reselect the main tanks. (See Note (i) below.)

(b) With rear fuselage tanks: Start the engine, warm up, taxi and take off on the main tanks; then, at 2,000ft change to the rear fuselage tanks and continue to use fuel from them until they contain only 30 gallons. Turn ON the drop tank (turning OFF the rear fuselage tanks cock when the change has been made) and drain it, then change back to the rear fuselage tanks and drain them. Revert to the main tanks.

NOTE: (i) When it is essential to use all the fuel from the drop tank its cock must be turned OFF and the throttle closed immediately the engine cuts; a fresh tank should then be selected without delay. The booster pump in the newly selected tank should be switched ON, or the hand wobble pump operated, to assist the engine to pick up but in addition to this it may be necessary to windmill the engine at high rpm to ensure an adequate fuel supply.

(ii) Drop tanks should only be jettisoned if this is necessary operationally. If a drop tank is jettisoned before it is empty a fresh tank

should be turned ON before the drop tank cock is turned OFF.

(iii) At no time must the drop tank cock and the rear fuselage tanks cock be on together or fuel from the rear fuselage tanks will drain into the drop tank since the connection from these tanks joins the drop tank connection below the non-return valve.

(iv) The drop tank cock must always be off when the tank has been jettisoned or is empty, otherwise air may be drawn into the main fuel system thus causing engine cutting.

Use of the booster pump(s) (a) The main tanks booster pump should be switched ON for take-off and landing and at all times when these tanks are in use in flight.

(b) The rear fuselage tanks booster pump should be switched ON at all times when changing to, or using fuel from, these tanks.

Preliminaries (i) Check that the undercarriage selector lever is down; switch on indicator and see that DOWN shows green.

(ii) Check the contents of the fuel tanks. If fitted with auxiliary tank(s) check that corresponding cock(s) are OFF.

(iii) Test the operation of the flying controls and adjust the rudder pedals for equal length.

(iv) On aircraft with Bendix-Stromberg carburettors ensure that the idle cut-off control is in the fully aft position, or cut-off position, then check the operation of the booster pump(s) by sound.

Starting the engine and warming up (aircraft with Merlin 61 or 63 engines)

Set the fuel cock	ON
Ignition switches	OFF
Throttle	½in–1in open
Propeller speed control lever	Fully forward
Supercharger switch	AUTO, NORMAL POSITION
Carburettor air intake filter	CLOSED or FILTER
Control	IN OPERATION

(i) If an external priming connection is fitted, high volatility fuel should be used for priming at temperatures below freezing. Work the Ki-gass priming pump until the fuel reaches the priming nozzles; this may be judged by a sudden increase in resistance.

(ii) Switch ON the ignition and press the starter and booster-coil buttons. Turning periods must not exceed 20 seconds, with a 30 seconds wait between each. Work the priming pump as rapidly and vigorously as possible while the engine is being turned; it should start after the following number of strokes if cold:

Air temperature °C:	+30	+20	+10	0	-10	-20
Normal fuel:	3	4	7	12	–	–
High volatility fuel:	–	–	–	4	8	18

(iii) At temperatures below freezing it will probably be necessary to continue priming after the engine has fired and until it picks up on the carburettor.

(iv) Release the starter button as soon as the engine starts, and as soon as the engine is running satisfactorily release the booster-coil button and screw down the priming pump.

(v) Open up slowly to 1,000–1,200rpm, then warm up at this speed.

Starting the engine and warming up (aircraft with Merlin 66, 70 or 266 engines)

(i) Set the fuel cock	ON
(ii) Ignition switches	OFF
Throttle	½in–1in open
Propeller speed control (or override) lever	Fully forward
Idle cut-off control	AUTO, NORMAL POSITION
Carburettor air intake filter	CLOSED or FILTER IN OPERATION

(iii) Switch ON the main tanks booster pump for 30 seconds (or operate the hand wobble pump for that period) then switch it OFF and set the idle cut-off control forward to the RUN position.

(iv) An external priming connection is fitted and high volatility fuel should be used for priming at temperatures below freezing. Operate the priming pump until fuel reaches the priming nozzles (this may be judged by a sudden increase in resistance to the plunger) then prime the engine (if it is cold) with the following number of strokes

Air temperature °C:	+30	+20	+10	0	-10	-20
Normal fuel:	3	4	7	12	–	–
High volatility fuel:	–	–	–	4	8	18

(v) Switch ON the ignition and press the starter and booster-coil push-buttons.

(vi) When the engine fires release the starter button; keep the booster-coil button depressed and operate the priming pump (if required) until the engine is running smoothly.

(vii) Screw down the priming pump then open up gradually to 1,000–1,200rpm and warm up at this speed.

(viii) Check that the fuel pressure warning light does not come on then switch ON the main tanks booster pump (if fitted).

Testing the engine and services while warming up
(i) Check all temperatures and pressures and the operation of the flaps.
(ii) Press the radiator flaps test push-button and have the ground crew check that the flaps open.
(iii) Test each magneto in turn as a precautionary check before increasing power further.
(iv) If a drop tank is carried check the flow of fuel from it by running on it for at least one minute.
After warming up to at least 15°C (oil temperature) and 60°C (coolant temperature),
(v) Open up to 0lb/in² boost and exercise and check the operation of the two-speed two-stage supercharger by pressing in and holding the test push-button. Boost should rise slightly and the red warning light should come on when high gear is engaged. Release the push-button after 30 seconds.
(vi) At the same boost, exercise (at least twice) and check the operation of the constant speed propeller by moving the speed control lever over its full governing range. Return the lever fully forward. Check that the generator is charging the accumulator by noting that the power failure warning light is out.
(vii) Test each magneto in turn; if the single ignition drop exceeds 150rpm, the ignition should be checked at higher power.
NOTE: The following additional checks should be carried out after repair, inspection other than daily, when the single ignition drop at 0lb/in² boost exceeds 150rpm, or at any time at the discretion of the pilot. When these checks are performed the tail of the aircraft must be securely lashed down.
(viii) Open the throttle to the take-off setting and check boost and static rpm.
(ix) Throttle back until rpm fall just below the take-off figure (thus ensuring that the propeller is not constant speeding) then test each magneto in turn. If the single ignition drop exceeds 150rpm the aircraft should not be flown.
(x) Where applicable throttle back to +3lb/in² boost and set the override lever to AUTOMATIC; rpm should fall to 1,800–1,850. Return the lever to MAX RPM.
(xi) Before taxying check the brake pressure (80lb/in²) and the pneumatic supply pressure (220lb/in²).

Final Preparation for Take-Off

T – Trimming tabs –	Elevator. One division nose down Rudder: Fully right.
P – Propeller control	Fully forward
Override lever	Fully forward
F – Fuel	Check contents of main tanks
Main tanks cock	ON
Drop tank cock	OFF
Transfer cock	OFF
Main tanks booster pump	ON
F – Flaps	Up
Supercharger	AUTO, NORMAL POSITION, red light out
Carburettor air intake filter control	CLOSED or FILTER IN OPERATION

Take-off
(i) At normal loads +7lb/in² to +9lb/in² boost is sufficient for take-off. After take-off, however, boost should be increased (where applicable) to +12lb/in² to minimise the possibility of lead fouling of the sparking plugs.
(ii) There is a tendency to swing to the left but this can easily be checked with the rudder.
(iii) When the rear fuselage tanks are full the aircraft pitches on becoming airborne and it is recommended that the undercarriage should not be retracted, nor the sliding hood closed, until a height of at least 100ft has been reached.
(iv) After retracting the undercarriage it is essential to check that the red warning light comes on, since if the undercarriage fails to lock UP, the airflow through the radiators and oil cooler will be much reduced and excessive temperatures will result.
NOTE: It may be necessary to hold the undercarriage selector lever hard forward against the quadrant until the red warning light comes on.
(v) If interconnected throttle and propeller controls are fitted move the override lever smoothly back to AUTOMATIC when comfortably airborne.
(vi) After take-off some directional retrimming will be necessary.
(vii) Unless operating in sandy or dust-laden conditions set the carburettor air intake filter control to OPEN (or NORMAL INTAKE) at 1,000ft.

Cimbing
At all loads the recommended climbing speed is 180mph (155kts) IAS from sea level to operating height.
NOTE: (i) With the supercharger switch at AUTO, high gear is engaged automatically when the aircraft reaches a predetermined height. This is the optimum height for the gear change if full combat power is being used, but if normal climbing power (2,850rpm and 12lb/in² boost) is being used the maximum rate of climb is obtained by delaying the gear change until the boost in low gear has fallen to +8lb/in². This is achieved by leaving the supercharger switch at MS until the boost has fallen to this figure.
(ii) Use of the air intake filter reduces the full throttle height considerably.

General flying
(i) Stability
(a) At light loads (no fuel in the rear fuselage tanks, no drop tank)

stability about all axes is satisfactory and the aircraft is easy and pleasant to fly.

(b) When the rear fuselage tanks are full there is a very marked reduction in longitudinal stability, the aircraft tightens in turns at all altitudes and, in this condition, is restricted to straight flying, and only gentle manoeuvres; accurate trimming is not possible and instrument flying should be avoided whenever possible.

(c) When a 90-gallon drop tank is carried in addition to full fuel in the rear fuselage tanks the aircraft becomes extremely difficult and tiring to fly and in this condition is restricted to straight flying and only gentle manoeuvres at low altitudes.

(d) On aircraft which have 'rear view' fuselages there is a reduction in directional stability so that the application of yaw promotes marked changes of lateral and longitudinal trim. This characteristic is more pronounced at high altitudes.

(e) When 90 (or 170) gallon drop tanks are carried on these aircraft, they are restricted to straight flying and gentle manoeuvres only.

(ii) Controls

The elevator and rudder trimming tabs are powerful and sensitive and must always be used with care, particularly at high speed.

iii. Change of trim

Undercarriage up	nose up
Undercarriage down	nose down
Flaps up	nose up
Flaps down	Strongly nose down

There are marked changes of directional trim with change of power and speed. These should be countered by accurate use of the rudder trimming tab control. The firing of salvos of RPs promotes a nose-up change of trim; this change of trim is most marked when the weapons are fired in level flight at about 300mph (258kts) IAS.

(iv) Flying at reduced airspeed in conditions of poor visibility.

Reduce speed to 160mph (140kts) IAS, lower the flaps and set the propeller speed control (or override) lever to give 2,650rpm; open the sliding hood. Speed may then be reduced to 140mph (120kts) IAS.

Stalling

(i) The stalling speeds, engine 'off', in mph (knots) IAS are:

Aircraft without 'rear-view' fuselage

Undercarriage and flaps up:	90	93	100
	(78)	(80)	(86)
Undercarriage and flaps down:	75–79	80	84
	(65–69)	(96)	(72)

Aircraft without 'rear-view' fuselage

Undercarriage and flaps up:	95	08	115–117
	(83)	(85)	(100-102)
Undercarriage and flaps down:	83–84	85	95
	(71–73)	(98)	(83)

The speeds above apply to aircraft which have 'clipped' wings. On aircraft with full-span wings these speeds are reduced (some 3–6mph IAS).

(ii) Warning of the approach of a stall is given by tail buffeting, the onset of which can be felt some 10mph (9kts) IAS before the stall itself. At the stall either wing and the nose drop gently. Recovery is straightforward and easy. If the control column is held back at the stall tail, buffeting becomes very pronounced and the wing drop is more marked.

NOTE: On LF.XVI aircraft warning of the approach of a stall is not so clear; faint tail buffeting can be felt some 5mph IAS before the stall occurs.

(iii) When the rear fuselage tanks are full there is an increasing tendency for the nose to rise as the stall is approached. This self-stalling tendency must be checked by firm forward movement of the control column.

(iv) Warning of the approach of a stall in a steep turn is given by pronounced tail buffeting (and on F.XVI aircraft by hood rattling). If the acceleration is then increased the aircraft will, in general, flick out of the turn.

Spinning

(i) Spinning is permitted, but the loss of height involved in recovery may be very great and the following limits are to be observed:

 (a) Spins are not to be started below 10,000ft.

(b) Recovery must be initiated before two turns are completed.

(ii) A speed of 180mph (156kts) IAS should be attained before starting to ease out of the resultant dive.

(iii) Spinning is not permitted when fitted with a drop tank, when carrying a bomb load, or with any fuel in the rear fuselage tank.

Diving

(i) At training loads the aircraft becomes increasingly tail heavy as speed is gained and should, therefore, be trimmed into the dive. The tendency to yaw to the right should be corrected by accurate use of the rudder trimming tab control.

(ii) When carrying wing bombs the angle of dive must not exceed 60°; when carrying a fuselage bomb the angle of dive must not exceed 40°.

NOTE: Until the rear fuselage tanks contain less than 30 gallons of fuel the aircraft is restricted to straight flight and only gentle manoeuvres.

Aerobatics

(i) Aerobatics are not permitted when carrying any external stores (except the 30-gallon 'blister' drop tank) nor when the rear fuselage tanks contain more than 30 gallons of fuel, and are not recommended when the rear fuselage tanks contain any fuel.

(ii) The following minimum speeds in mph (knots) IAS are recommended:

Loop	300 (260)
Roll	240 (206)
Half roll off loop	340 (295)
Upward roll	330 (286)

iii) Flick manoeuvres are not permitted.

Left: Squadron Leader Dunc Mason puts on some bank to show the elliptical wings of Spitfire IX MK356 while it was wearing an all-over silver paint scheme as was applied to an aircraft of No. 601 Squadron while the unit was based in Italy during World War Two. Jarrod Cotter

Check list before landing

(i) Reduce speed to 160mph (138kts) IAS, open the sliding hood and check:

U – Undercarriage	DOWN
P – Propeller control	Speed control (or override) lever set to give 2,650rpm – fully forward on the final approach
Supercharger	Red light out
Carburettor air intake filter control	CLOSED (or FILTER IN OPERATION)
F – Fuel	Main tanks cock ON
Main tanks booster pump	ON
F – Flaps	DOWN

(ii) Check brake pressure (80lb/in^2) and pneumatic supply pressure (220lb/in^2).
NOTE: The rate of undercarriage lowering is much reduced at low rpm.

Approach and landing

(i) The recommended final approach speeds* in mph (kts) IAS are:
At training load (full main tanks, no ammunition or external stores) 7,150lb
(a) Aircraft without 'rear-view' fuselages

	Engine assisted	Glide
Flaps down	95 (82)	105 (90)
Flaps up	105 (90)	110 (95)

(b) Aircraft with 'rear-view' fuselages

	Engine assisted	Glide
Flaps down	100–105 (86–90)	115–120 (100–104)
Flaps up	115 (100)	120–125 (104–108)

*These are the speeds at which the airfield boundary is crossed; the initial straight approach should, however, be made at a speed 20–25mph (17–21kts) IAS above these figures.
NOTE: The speeds above apply to aircraft which have 'clipped' wings; on aircraft with full-span wings they may be safely reduced by 5mph IAS.
(ii) Should it be necessary in an emergency to land with the rear fuselage

tanks still containing all their fuel, the final engine assisted approach speeds given in (i) above should be increased by 10–15mph (9–13kts) IAS. The tendency for the nose to rise of its own accord at the 'hold-off' must be watched; the throttle should be closed only when contact with the ground is made.
(iii) The aircraft is nose-heavy on the ground; the brakes, therefore, must be used carefully on landing.

Mislanding

(i) At normal loads the aircraft will climb away easily with the undercarriage and flaps down and the use of full take-off power is unnecessary.
(ii) Open the throttle steadily to give the required boost.
(iii) Retract the undercarriage immediately.
(iv) With the flaps down climb at about 140mph IAS.
(v) Raise the flaps at 300ft and retrim.

After landing

(i) Before taxying
Raise the flaps and switch OFF the main tanks booster pump (if fitted).
(ii) On reaching dispersal
(a) Open up to 0lb/in^2 boost and exercise the two-speed two-stage supercharger once.
(b) Throttle back slowly to 800–900rpm and idle at this speed for a few seconds then stop the engine by operating the slow running cut-out or idle cut-off control.
(c) When the propeller has stopped rotating switch OFF the ignition and all other electrical services.
(d) Turn OFF the fuel.
(iii) Oil dilution
The correct dilution periods are

At air temperatures above 10°C	1 minute
At air temperatures below 10°C	2 minutes

Part III Operating Data

Engine Data: Merlins 63, 66 and 70
i. Fuel: 100 octane only
(ii) The principal engine limitations are as follows:

	Sup.	Rpm	Boost Lb/In^2	Temp. °C Coolant	Oil
Max Take-Off to 1,000ft	M	3,000	+18*	135	–
Max Climbing 1Hr Limit	M/S	2,850	+12	125	90
Maximum Continuous	M/S	2,650	+7	105 (115)	90
Combat 5 Mins Limit	M/S	3,000#	+18	135	105

The figure in brackets is permissible for short periods.
* +12lb/in^2 on Merlin 61 and 63 engines.
# +15lb/in^2 on Merlin 61 and 63 engines.

Oil Pressure: Minimal in Flight	30lb/in²

Minimum Temperature for Take-Off

Coolant	60°C
Oil	15°C

Flying limitations

i. Maximum speeds in mph (kts) IAS.
Diving (without external stores), corresponding to a Mach No. of .85:

Between SL and 20,000ft	450 (385)
20,000–25,000ft	430 (370)
25,000–30,000ft	390 (335)
30,000–35,000ft	340 (292)
Above 35,000ft	310 (265)
Undercarriage down	160 (138)
Flaps down	160 (138)

Diving (with the following external stores):
(a) With 1 x 500lb AN/M 58 bomb, or 1 x 500lb AN/M 64 bomb, or 1 x 500lb AN/M 76 bomb, or 1 x 65 nickel bomb Mk II

Below 20,000ft*	440 (378)

(b) With 1 x 500lb SAP bomb or smoke bomb Mk I

Below 25,000ft*	400 (344)

(c) With 10lb practice bomb

Below 25,000ft*	420 (360)

* Above these heights the limitations for 'clean' aircraft apply.

(ii) Maximum weights:

For take-off and gentle manoeuvres only	8,700lb*
For landing (except in emergency)	7,450lb

*At this weight take-off must be made only from a smooth hard runway.

(iii) Flying restrictions

(a) Rear fuselage tanks may be used only with special authority and never on aircraft with 'rear view' fuselages.
(b) Aerobatics and combat manoeuvres are not permitted when carrying any external stores (except the 30-gallon 'blister' type drop tank) nor when the rear fuselage tanks contain more than 30 gallons of fuel.
(c) When a 90 or 170 gallon drop tank or a bomb load is carried the aircraft is restricted to straight flying and only gentle manoeuvres.
(d) When wing bombs are carried in addition to a drop tank or fuselage bomb, take-off must be made only from a smooth hard runway.
(e) When carried, the 90 or 170 gallon drop tank must be jettisoned before any dive bombing is commenced.

Left: One of the most popular Spitfires in the UK is the Old Flying Machine Company's Mk.IX MH434. It is seen here out on the grass at Duxford on a glorious summer's day. Jarrod Cotter

Below left: The first Spitfire to make a formal ceremonial flypast for the Historic Aircraft Flight (now called the Battle of Britain Memorial Flight) was Mk.XVI TE330, seen here on take-off from Biggin Hill in 1957 in the hands of the Flight's founder, Wg Cdr Peter Thompson DFC. Crown Copyright

Right: Spitfire VXI TE311 literally fires up at RAF Coningsby. This is a common occurrence when a Spitfire is started, especially when the Merlin engine is still hot from a previous sortie. SAC Graham Taylor/ Crown Copyright

(f) The angle of dive when releasing a bomb or bomb load must not exceed 60° for wing bombs or 40° for a fuselage bomb.

(g) Except in emergency the fuselage bomb or drop tank must be jettisoned before landing with wing bombs fitted operationally.

(h) Drop tanks should not be jettisoned unless necessary operationally. While jettisoning, the aircraft should be flown straight and level at a speed not greater than 300mph IAS.

(i) Except in emergency, landings should not be attempted until the rear fuselage tanks contain less than 30 gallons of fuel. Should a landing be necessary when they contain a greater quantity of fuel the drop tank (if fitted) should be jettisoned.

Position error corrections

From	120	150	170	210	240	290	mph
To	150	170	210	240	290	350	IAS

Add		4	2	0				mph
Subtract				0	2	4	6	or kts

From	106	130	147	180	208	250	knots
To	130	147	180	208	250	300	IAS

Maximum performance

i. **Climbing.**

(a) The speeds in mph (knots) for maximum rate of climb are:

Sea level–26,000ft	160 (140)
26,000–30,000ft	150 (130)
30,000–33,000ft	140 (122)
33,000–37,000ft	130 (112)
37,000–40,000ft	120 (104)
Above 40,000ft	100 (95)

(b) With the supercharger switch at AUTO, high gear is engaged automatically when the aircraft reaches a predetermined height. This is the optimum height for the gear change if full combat power is being used, but if normal climbing power (2,850rpm +12lb/in^2 boost) is being used the maximum rate of climb is obtained by delaying the gear change until the boost in low gear has fallen to +8lb/in^2. This is achieved by leaving the supercharger switch at MS until the boost has fallen to this figure.

(ii) **Combat**

Set the supercharger switch to AUTO and open the throttle fully.

NOTE: On those aircraft which do not have interconnected throttle and propeller controls the propeller speed control lever must be advanced to the maximum rpm position before the throttle is opened fully.

Economical flying

(i) **Climbing**

On aircraft not fitted with interconnected throttle and propeller controls.

(a) Set the supercharger switch to MS, the propeller speed control lever to give 2,650rpm and climb at the speeds given above, opening the throttle progressively to maintain a boost pressure of +7lb/in^2.

(b) Set the supercharger switch to AUTO when the maximum obtainable boost in low gear is +3lb/in^2, throttling back to prevent overboosting as the change to high gear is made.

On aircraft fitted with interconnected throttle and propeller controls:

(a) Set the supercharger switch to MS, set the throttle to give +7lb/in^2 boost and climb at the speeds given above.

(b) As height is gained the boost will fail and it will be necessary to advance the throttle progressively to restore it. The throttle must not, however, be advanced beyond a position at which rpm rise to 2,650. Set the supercharger switch to AUTO when, at this throttle setting, the boost in low gear has fallen to +3lb/in^2.

NOTE: Climbing at the speeds given above will ensure greatest range, but for ease of control (especially at heavy loads and with the rear fuselage tanks full of fuel) a climbing speed of 180mph (155kts) IAS from sea level to operating height is recommended. The loss of range will be only slight.

(ii) **Cruising**

The recommended speed for maximum range is 170mph (147kts) IAS if the aircraft is lightly loaded. At heavy loads, especially if the rear fuselage tanks are full, this speed can be increased to 200mph (172kts) IAS without incurring a serious loss of range.

On aircraft not fitted with interconnected throttle and propeller controls:

(a) With the supercharger switch at MS fly at the maximum obtainable boost (not exceeding +7lb/in^2) and obtain the recommended speed by reducing rpm as required.

NOTE: (i) Rpm should not be reduced below a minimum of 1,800. At low altitudes, therefore, it may be necessary to reduce boost or the recommended speed will be exceeded.

ii) As the boost falls at high altitudes it will not be possible to maintain the recommended speed in low gear, even at maximum continuous rpm and full throttle. It will then be necessary to set the supercharger switch to AUTO. Boost will thus be restored and it will be possible to reduce rpm again (as outlined in (a) above).

(iii) In both low and high gears rpm which promote rough running should be avoided.

On aircraft fitted with interconnected throttle and propeller controls:

Set the supercharger switch to MS and adjust the throttle to obtain the recommended speed. Avoid a throttle setting which promotes rough running.

NOTE: At moderate and high altitudes it will be necessary to advance the throttle progressively to restore the falling boost and thus maintain the recommended speed.

Now as the throttle is opened rpm will increase and at a certain height the recommended speed will be unobtainable even at a throttle setting which gives 2,650rpm. At this height the supercharger switch should be set to AUTO and the throttle then adjusted as before to maintain the recommended speed.

Fuel capacities and consumption
(i) Normal fuel capacity:

Top tank	48 gallons
Bottom tank	37 gallons
Total	85 gallons

ii. Long range fuel capacities:

With 30 gallon 'blister' drop tank	115 gallons
With 45 gallon 'blister' drop tank	130 gallons
With 90 gallon 'blister' drop tank	175 gallons
With 170 gallon "blister" drop tank	255 gallons
With rear fuselage tanks	
Early aircraft	160 gallons
Later aircraft	151 gallons

NOTE: On some aircraft these capacities are increased by 10 gallons.

(iii) Fuel consumptions:
The approximate fuel consumptions (gal/hr) are as follows:
Weak mixture (as obtained at +7lb/in^2 boost and below):

Boost lb/in^2 rpm	2,650	2,400	2,200	2,000	1,800
+7	80	–	–	–	–
+4	71	66	61	54	–
+2	66	61	57	50	43
0	60	55	51	45	39
-2	53	49	45	40	35
-4	45	42	38	34	30

Rich mixture (as obtained above +7lb/in^2 boost):

Boost lb/in^2	rpm	gals/hr
+15	3,000	130
+12	2,850	105

NOTE: The above approximate consumptions apply for all Marks of engine. Accurate figures giving the variation in consumption with height and as between low and high gear are not available.

Tactical Paper No.1
Air Ministry DDAT
February 1947

Air Fighting Tactics used by Spitfire Fighter Squadrons of 2nd TAF during the campaign in Western Europe.

Introduction
In June 1944, when the Allied forces invaded Normandy, the Royal Air Force had experienced almost five years of aerial warfare and had accumulated a wealth of knowledge upon which to base its plans and tactics. The types of formation flown over Normandy, the tactics the day-fighters used, and the different methods of 'treetop' and high altitude fighting had been slowly and carefully evolved throughout the preceding five years, and a brief outline of this period illustrates the development of the various fighter tactics until there was attained a style, method, and degree of combat flying which inflicted the maximum number of casualties upon the enemy whilst keeping our own losses at a minimum.

Formations

Dunkirk
When carrying out standing patrols over the Dunkirk beaches in May/June 1940, most of the squadrons flew in tight compact formations consisting of four sections of three aircraft in line astern. This was a poor formation as individual aircraft were so close to each other that only the leaders had any opportunity of keeping a sharp lookout: the aircraft in the rearmost section, therefore, were very easy to 'bounce'. The Luftwaffe had already learned the lesson of the 'open' formation in the Spanish Civil War and in Poland. Later, such experienced German leaders as Moelders, Galland and Weike declared that our fighter formations over Dunkirk were far too compact and often presented easy targets. Furthermore, the basic section of three aircraft proved to be cumbersome and unwieldy, and later squadron formations were built upon the pair, similar to the 'rotte' in the Luftwaffe, which proved effective and lasted throughout the war.

Battle of Britain
During the Battle of Britain, although many fighter squadrons still flew in four sections of three, others adopted the three sections of four aircraft flying in line astern. This, undoubtedly, was a better fighting formation

but it was still far from ideal, as Nos 2, 3 and 4 in each section had to pay most of their attention to their leader in order to keep in position, and, therefore, were not able to keep a good lookout. This formation, however, remained very popular for a long time and some squadrons were still using it at the end of the war in Europe. Usually the first man to be hit out of this formation was, of course, No. 4, or 'Tail-end-Charlie', as he was most vulnerable, and for this reason this position was unpopular, particularly with new pilots, who generally carried out their first few operations in this unenviable position. In order to keep a better lookout and to prevent the No. 4 from being picked off, some squadrons adopted the 'weaving' principle, in which each section of four weaved when over enemy territory. Although this did allow the leader to keep a better lookout, 'weaving' seriously affected the radius of action of a Wing or Squadron.

Sweeps

The early sweeps over France in 1941 developed yet another type of formation known as 'finger-fours'. This formation was a step in the right direction as everyone was 'well up' and had an equal chance of spotting the enemy, and, if properly flown, it was difficult to 'bounce'. Each section of four was, if necessary, quite independent, as Nos 1 and 2 guarded Nos 3 and 4, and vice-versa. Similarly in squadron formation, yellow section guarded red and blue sections whilst blue section, out on the port flank, guarded red and yellow sections. The main disadvantage of this formation was that it was unwieldy and covered a large area, especially when a wing operated with three squadrons, and, after any fighting, the wing was seldom reformed as a whole and because of this a large percentage of its striking power was lost. Nevertheless, it was a popular formation with the pilots, both leaders and No. 2s, and it is one of the few formations which survived throughout the remaining four years of air fighting. It was especially popular with ground attack aircraft during the campaign in Western Europe.

1942–43 period

During operations over Europe and North Africa in 1942–43 there emerged what is probably the most nearly perfect fighter formation of the war, the 'fluid-six'. It is a loose manoeuvrable formation suitable for freelander fighter sweeps, bomber escort, fighter-bombing, armed reconnaissance, patrols and strafing. It was extremely popular with pilots, particularly newcomers, as there was no 'Tail-end-Charlie' feeling, and, if the formation is flown properly, all pilots are well-up and in position should a fight be imminent. It is both an offensive and defensive formation, as twelve pairs of eyes are continually searching the sky. It has the great advantage over other formations that the Flight Commander is always leading his own Flight of six aircraft and thus he can watch carefully the flying discipline, skill and development of his pilots. Since the squadron flies in two sixes ('A' and 'B' Flights) it eliminates the vulnerable section of four aircraft found in most other formations when a four is made up of two aircraft from each flight, which is most unsatisfactory.

Red 5 and 6 look after the tails of 3 and 4, and vice versa, thus Red 1 and 2 are doubly covered. Similarly it is Blue Section's duty [to] guard Red Section from a surprise attack, and vice versa. A wing of up to and including three squadrons is easy to operate and lead when this formation is flown.

Formation technique – fluid sixes

Take-off
Throughout the campaign in Western Europe squadrons using the 'fluid-six' formation invariably took off in pairs, the leader waiting until all his squadron was in position behind him on the runway in order to ensure a quick form-up after take-off. The pairs of aircraft behind the leader positioned themselves at a slight angle to the runway to facilitate judgement of the exact moment to turn into wind and open up. The leader executed a long wide climb to port so that Blue Section, particularly Nos 5 and 6, could 'cut-the-corner' and achieve a quick squadron form-up. With this method it was possible to form up a squadron within one-half to three-quarters of the circuit. This form of mass take-off would not, of course, have been possible without complete local air superiority as the squadron forming up on the ground makes an ideal target for a ground strafing attack.

Climbing
When climbing, a squadron flying in 'fluid sixes' in conditions where it was unlikely that 10/10 cloud would be met with, 'B' Flight formed up immediately astern of 'A' Flight. A fairly compact formation was then flown during the climb and when the leader deemed it necessary the formation opened out to its battle positions. When it was necessary to climb the squadron through 10/10 cloud the formation was adopted. It is a very small departure from the previous formation but it ensures that an experienced pilot is leading each 'vic' of three aircraft. The four sections of three aircraft then climbed steadily through cloud at one minute intervals and re-formed above the overcast. When the leader decided to open up into battle formation, Red 2 and 3 and Blue 2 and 3 simply changed positions, Blue Section taking up its position and the battle formation being quickly arrived at.

Landing
After a sortie a squadron would return to its base in two sixes, 'B' Flight line astern of 'A' Flight, and as the circuit was approached 'B' Flight dropped back. The formation leader then, for a left-hand circuit, ordered the sections into echelon starboard, and the squadron landed in the order, Red 1, 2, 3, 4, 5 and 6 followed by Blue 1, 2, 3, 4, 5 and 6.

Battle tactics

General
Fighter tactics vary from month to month and from year to year, but at the end of the campaign in Western Europe there were certain general rules that did apply to all Spitfire squadrons. These were:
(a) The pair had been proved to be the basis of the present day fighter formations, and all later formations were designed and built up on this principle.
(b) Strict flying discipline, good drill and immediate obedience to the formation leader's orders were essential to the success of a fighter squadron.
(c) Strict R/T discipline was most important and with a well trained squadron no air-to-air R/T chatter was necessary until enemy aircraft were sighted. Vectors from Controllers and other ground to air messages were acknowledged with a minimum of speech.

'Ultimate pursuit'
During the air fighting over the occupied countries previous to D-Day, the German fighters generally took evasive action by half rolling and diving to ground level. They could dive at a steeper angle and at a higher speed than the Spitfire, and as a result, during the 1941–43 period, they were seldom pursued to ground level as it was considered highly dangerous to do so. Over Normandy, however, this decision was reversed as it was the aim to destroy the enemy's fighter arm completely and furthermore, as a result of their experience in strafing sorties and low-level 'Rangers', the Royal Air Force fighter pilots were well trained in low-level work. The enemy was surprised to find that he was now followed and engaged at tree-top height, and he showed little skill at this hedge-hopping type of air fighting. As a result he suffered a considerable number of casualties.

Rangers
A very popular type of operation was known as the 'Ranger', and it paid handsome dividends. No more than six aircraft, fitted with long-range tanks, would take off. They would first climb in order to cross the bomb-line and flak belts at a safe height, then having flown well inside enemy territory and flown several widely differing courses to confuse enemy radar, they would go down to ground level. Here they settled down, with No. 2s slightly echeloned from their leaders, to follow the prescribed route. With Spitfire IXs using a 90-gallon jettison tank, the radius of action was about 270–280 miles which made it possible to visit a great many enemy airfields on this type of operation. Enemy aircraft were easy to spot, especially if there was any low cloud, and when one was sighted a pair would be detailed to deal with it and they climbed steadily and attacked from below into the belly of the enemy aircraft. The success of this operation depended entirely on the leader, who was always a first-class low-level navigator, and who naturally spent most of his time map-reading

and checking his navigation. The other members of the formation were thus able to devote all their energies to keeping a sharp look-out for enemy aircraft or other targets of opportunity. The height at which this operation was carried out made detection by radar extremely difficult.

Bomber escort

The size of fighter escorts for bombers varied greatly during the different stages of the war, and whereas in 1941 as many as nine fighter squadrons escorted three Stirlings on daylight bombing operations, in 1944–45 the escort for the medium bombers was cut to a bare minimum. This was due to the fact that the American Air Forces were operating deep into enemy territory whilst our medium bombers, in their role of close support air arm, were bombing targets on, and a few miles inside, the bomb line. It was a generally accepted principle that one-third of the escorting fighters could break away and engage any enemy fighters they could see in the vicinity of the bombers, even though they were some miles away. This was an important factor, as during the Battle of Britain, we are now told, Goering strictly ordered his fighters to stay with the bombers at all costs even when they could see RAF fighters manoeuvring for position some distance away.
If this is true the German fighters were at a great disadvantage as they could not break away and fight until our attack had actually commenced. Close co-operation with the bomber squadrons was essential and visits were paid to their bases to discuss formations and tactics.

Fighter v fighter

The better known German fighters, the Bf 109 and Fw 190, presented little difficulty to the versatile Spitfire IXb, and the Spitfire XIV was vastly superior to either of them as it was faster and could out-turn and out-climb them with ease. Whenever there was a warning of German fighters in the vicinity, as much advantage as possible was taken of the prevailing weather conditions, sun and cloud, and if enemy forces were engaged, one-third of the Spitfires were detailed as high cover in order to keep a look-out for further enemy formations. Occasionally the high cover was brought down into the fight if the leader thought it advisable.

The Me 262 presented quite a different problem as it was very fast and quite impossible to catch even when the Spitfires possessed a good height advantage. Fortunately all of this type of enemy aircraft en-countered appeared to be of the bomber, not fighter, variety, and they did not appear to be interested in attacking the Spitfire formations. The only method of cornering the Me 262 with Spitfires was to discover the airfield from which they were operating, pay frequent visits to it during the day and endeavour to destroy them as they took off or landed. This scheme worked on several occasions, and the operation was extremely interesting, largely because of the efforts of the flak defences of the German airfields.

Fighter v bomber

The Battle of Britain offered the only opportunity for the RAF fighters to develop their tactics in attacking large formations of enemy bombers. Since that time, the day fighters operating from the United Kingdom, and later from the Continent, rarely encountered enemy bombers, and even when they did, the enemy was never present in strength. The Luftwaffe, however, had ample opportunity of developing fighter attacks against the large formations of American day bombers, and a study of the lessons they learned are well worthwhile.

Re-forming

It is very necessary that a fighter wing be able to fight, re-form and proceed with its planned flight after an engagement with the enemy. On many occasions Fighter Wings crossed the bomb line, engaged the enemy and returned in ones and twos to their base within a few minutes of taking-off, very often with nearly full petrol tanks and ammunition drums which is a great waste of effort. To avoid this the leaders of certain Wings always gave, after an engagement, clear and concise instructions as to the rendezvous and height at which he wished the Wing to re-form. For example he might say, 'Wing will re-form over Caen, No. 1 Squadron at Angels 20, No. 2 Squadron at Angels 22, and No. 3 at Angels 24, Course 180.' All aircraft were then able to make their way to the rendezvous which the leader would orbit for two or three minutes before setting course.

Camera guns

When the cine films were developed and returned to the Wing, it was customary for the Wing Commander Flying to show the films to all pilots, compare them with the actual combat report, and criticise range, length of bursts and accuracy of shooting. Unfortunately the films produced by the type of camera in use were generally of such poor quality that it made this task practically impossible, and on most films all that could be seen was a dark blur on a greyish scratched background. Even at the end of the war the Spitfires were carrying a camera which took only 14 frames per second as compared to the camera fitted to the American fighters which took 72 frames per second. Furthermore, on the British camera, there was no 'override' fitted, consequently the best cannon strikes at the end of the combat were never seen.

Gun sights

During 1944–45 all Spitfires were fitted with the gyro-sight and it was discovered that it had several disadvantages when pilots were engaging in 'close fighting'. It consisted of a large piece of mechanism which obstructed the forward view of the pilot, and it required quite a lot of ranging and tracking and rudder and stick juggling in order to get an enemy aircraft correctly lined up in the sight; as a result the pilot was apt to spend too much time over his sight in a combat where every second counted. When used for long steady shots at enemy bombers, however, it was found to be ideal.

Briefing

During the Western European campaign the briefing of a Spitfire Wing fell into two categories.

(a) When the Wing operated together and purely in a fighter role, such as freelance fighter sweeps in Wing strength and escorts to bombers, it was customary for the Wing Commander Flying to brief pilots in detail. On these occasions the procedure followed was:

(i) To give a general description of the operation with special emphasis on other friendly forces likely to be encountered. This was most important as there were numerous cases of American and British aircraft attacking one another through faulty recognition and bad training.

(ii) To discuss the role of the Wing, i.e. close escort, escort cover or sweeping ahead of the bombers.

(iii) To make clear the route, rendezvous, heights and targets, which were always displayed on a map of suitable scale, and the Wing Commander Flying traced the whole operation from start to finish. The squadrons were then given the order to go and exactly what time individual squadrons would press starter buttons and take-off. The time for the whole Wing to set course from base was then given and watches synchronised. (It was found that from most bases with a reasonable runway and taxi tracks a Wing of three squadrons could take-off, form up and set course in ten to twelve minutes.)

(iv) To give the positions of the heavy and light flak – an important point, especially if the bombers were attacking heavily defended targets. Special flak maps were always on view in the briefing tents.

(v) To ensure that all pilots were aware of the correct R/T callsigns, emergency homing and air/sea rescue procedure.

(vi) To give the weather forecast with special reference to high altitude wind speed and direction.

(vii) To give general hints such as any new types of enemy aircraft that may be encountered, decoys and any other items of importance.

(viii) For the senior ALO, who generally wound up the briefing, to point out on his maps the positions of the forward troops, the bomb line, and enemy dispositions. This served to keep all pilots up to date with the land battle and was invaluable when squadrons were switched from a purely fighter role to ground attack or close support duties.

(b) When the day's operations consisted of aircraft operating in section or flight strength only, such as standing patrols, armed reconnaissance, dive bombing and ground attacks, the same flight sometimes flew on three and even four operations of an exactly similar nature in one day. It was the custom for the formation leader to bring his pilots to the briefing tent in order to study the bomb line, dispositions of friendly and enemy troops, enemy flak batteries, enemy vehicle recognition, weather forecast etc. It was the duty of the Wing Commander Flying to be present at all these small briefings and also at the interrogation of the pilots concerned after the operation was completed. The ALOs were found to be extremely valuable and they stimulated the pilot's interest in the land battle a great deal.

Conclusion

It must be appreciated that Battle Tactics are entirely dependent upon the existing circumstances and it is impossible to lay down any hard and fast rules. A close study of tactics which have been used successfully, along with the conditions existing at the time of their use can, however, be invaluable as very often it is possible to adapt well tried ideas to a new set of circumstances. The chief requirement for successful tactics is, however, for the Wing Leaders to 'keep abreast of the times' and constantly review their tactics in the face of new developments.

'Parky' – comparing the Spitfire to the Typhoon

Flight Lieutenant Antony Parkinson – better known to most as 'Parky' – has flown a wide variety of types during his RAF career, including the McDonnell Douglas Phantom, Panavia Tornado F.3 and the General Dynamics F-16 Fighting Falcon on exchange with the Royal Netherlands Air Force. 'Parky' was the Tornado F.3 display pilot for the 1999 and 2000 seasons, before four years of flying with the Red Arrows.

On leaving the 'Reds' he became an instructor on 29(R) Squadron, the Typhoon Operational Conversion Unit, at RAF Coningsby. He became the first pilot to amass 1,000 hours on the Typhoon. 'Parky' joined the RAF Battle of Britain Memorial Flight (BBMF) for its 50th anniversary season in 2007 and is now its operations officer.

Here he compares the different generations of RAF fighters, and describes his first flight in the recently rebuilt Spitfire XVI TE311:

Left: Spitfire XVI TE311 transits away from RAF Coningsby while being flown by Officer Commanding BBMF Squadron Leader Andy Millican. Jarrod Cotter

The Typhoon is agile, powerful and a delight to fly, but we can build the vices out of a modern aircraft. We have over 70 computers on the Typhoon – the aircraft is relatively easy to fly and can go to 55,000ft and Mach 1.8 in a heartbeat.

The Spitfire is a beautiful aircraft to fly, but difficult to land. It was designed to land into wind on a grass strip, but landing on tarmac in a crosswind is a different situation. I had never been taught on taildragger aircraft and didn't realise how difficult it is – it's real flying! The Spitfire is such an evocative aircraft, it gets your heart racing just carrying out the walk-round.

The Hurricane is a beautiful aircraft to fly too. It's 'heavier' but it's the aircraft we fly first. It is the first time you fly an aircraft that you have never flown without an instructor before. The Hurricane has a special place in our hearts as it was the first aircraft we flew after that 'tap on the shoulder'.

It's an emotional overload. Everything you have ever been taught through flying training holds true, but it's magnified in a warbird. You are totally aware they are priceless pieces of the nation's heritage. It has been fabulous meeting the veteran RAF pilots. Their landing was one of the benign aspects of the sortie after heavy fighting with maybe 100 enemy aircraft. You feel privileged. Talking to them is like talking to a mate in the crewroom. Nothing has changed in over 60 years.

First flight in Spitfire Mk XVI TE311
Flight Lieutenant Antony Parkinson
On a typically blustery Sunday in late September 2013, I pulled the fuel cut-off lever rearwards for the last time in Mk XIX PM631, signalling for me the end of another busy BBMF summer season. As the mighty five bladed propeller ground to a halt, I was filled with the usual tinge of sadness that I would not have the privilege of flying one of these wonderfully iconic aircraft for another six months. Even the faded gold autumnal leaves drifting down nearby seemed to reflect my mood. Or maybe not. …

The Boss, Squadron Leader Dunc Mason, had mentioned that a few shake down sorties would be required over the winter on our latest addition to the hangar – Spitfire Mk XVI TE311 – which I'd slowly seen take shape over the last decade. Quite surprisingly (and without any coercion required) he had agreed that it would be beneficial for another pilot – me – to fly her. Genius, I was in!

So with pride and a whiff of envy, I watched as 'Smithy' [Squadron Leader Ian Smith MBE] and then Dunc flew the new Spit. I observed them both linger a little longer than usual post shut-down, not wanting to leave the cockpit; flying any new Spitfire for the first time is incredibly special, but they both seemed more moved by the event than I had expected. I listened intently as they answered the obvious question, 'What's she like to fly?', and I remember phrases like 'utterly beautiful' and 'brilliant' being flashed around. It was my turn next.

As 6 December 2012 dawned it proved to be a beautiful clear winter's day. TE311 glinted resplendently in the low sun and waited patiently for me to strap in and perform my various checks. I imagined she was as keen as I was to be off, to get back to where she belonged after her 58-year lay-off. I had already ground run her and given her a taxi check, but yet again I was amazed how smooth her Merlin 266 engine ran. The view out front was much the same as other Spits – that long nose pointing up at the sky and impairing forward vision – but it was so different when looking sideways and rearwards. The clipped wings seemed ridiculously short from the cockpit and even with the bubble canopy closed the view from the low back cockpit was spectacular for 'checking six'. The ratchet handle on the right-hand side was instinctive to operate to close the canopy and here I was cocooned in the beautifully detailed cockpit, waiting for her to slowly warm up.

As the oil temperature crept up to 40°C, I completed my power checks and lined up on the runway. I often find myself subconsciously talking to these beautiful pieces of machinery; it was no different now. It was time for us to get airborne together. Concentrate now. Power coming up smoothly, blending in right rudder, checking 3,000rpm, +4 on the boost and easing the stick forward. Tail's up nice and quick and she's as straight as a die; 80kts and pull her off the ground. Squeeze the brakes on and off and gear up. Nice and slow with the cadence. UP/UP red lights lit. Happy days. Throttle back to 2,400rpm and up into the blue we go.

Dunc had briefed me to take her up to around 5,000ft, produce a couple of stalls in the clean and dirty (gear and flaps down) configuration to get the feel of her, before some aerobatics in the overhead for 10 minutes, then pop her back down. As she'd had a complete rebuild and such a long stint on the ground, manoeuvring her up to +3G would perhaps reveal any 'gremlins' she may have. Best place to be was in the overhead of the airfield; if anything untoward happened with the engine I would have the height and energy to glide her back to the main runway at Coningsby.

Prior to stalling I couldn't resist seeing how she rolled. I'd flown our Mk IX Spit, MK356, when she had clipped wings, but I couldn't really notice the intended improved roll rate (to counter the Fw 190) that clipping the wings was intended to generate (at the penalty of slightly reduced lift from the shorter wings and poorer high altitude performance). But this was different. Stick fully left with a blend of left rudder and, wow, spectacular! Now to the right (against the torque from the powerful four blade propeller) and again noticeably quicker. What a beauty!

Time for the stalling and she exhibited the usual benign Spitfire stall characteristics, a reluctance to stop flying even when the airspeed is deliberately bled to below 50kts. Heavy buffet but no wing drop and instant recovery when the control column is moved forwards to unstall the wings and power is applied. Testament to how the wartime fighter pilots must have loved these forgiving qualities when taking their Spitfires to the edge, and often beyond, the flying envelope in combat.

Now for some aeros. Lined up with the runway, power on and nose down. Speed rapidly building to 250kts and gently ease straight back on the stick. Squint at the G meter, a little over +3G, easing in right rudder initially during the pull, then blending in left rudder as

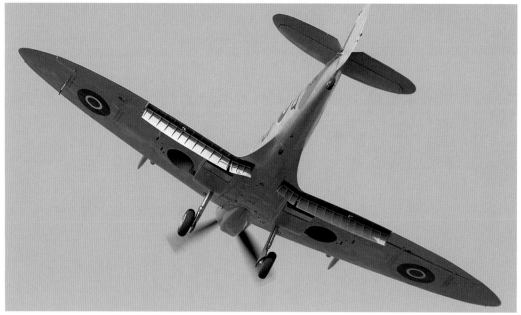

she slows inverted at the top of the loop. Gyroscopic effect then torque from the mighty Merlin engine doing their bit on the Spitfire airframe. Head back (no mirror on this Spit) to keep her straight and picking up the line of the runway below. No buffet and just light inputs on the stick to pull her out of the ensuing dive. Fantastic. Might as well go straight into another one. … The next ten minutes passed by in a blur with 'TE' and myself enjoying seeing the world revolve around us.

Time to land. Engine 'T&Ps' (Temps and Pressures) all normal so position for a 'hangar break'. Throttle back to cruise power and let the speed build for a low pass over the BBMF hangar at 240kts – that's nice and fast for the power setting – and a climbing turn to downwind. Throttle back and pop the radiator flaps open. Speed bleeding back to 150kts, wind the canopy handle backwards to get the bubble canopy open. Much easier than on the other Spits and no need to swap hands to lock the canopy with the door. Smoothly select fine pitch, 100kts and now swap hands to select the gear down. Nice slow cadence and the reassuring 'clunk, clunk' as the gear locks thump into place. Green lights (gear locked down indicators) lit so select the flap lever down. Feel the drag as the flaps bite and a quick glance left and right to see both flap down indicators have popped up on the wings. Turn finals and trim her out. Squeeze the brakes on and off and check the brake pressures. All good. She's ready to land.

Speed trickling back to just under 90kts with a trickle of power, that's OK. Concentration now between airspeed and runway picture. Roll out on finals and that long nose now obscuring the view out front. Speed just above 80kts.

No real crosswind to contend with today and I'm now aware of the ground getting closer as the sides of the runway come into my peripheral vision. Gently arrest the rate of descent, but keep her coming down. Going to touch soon so gently throttle back to idle. The rotation of the propeller seems so slow. Stick still further back and we gently touch down. She's lovely and straight. Phew! Let the tailwheel drop the last few inches. The nose rising still further and then smoothly fully back on the stick to hold the tail down.

Concentrate now. This is where a Spit often darts off line – maybe to the right but could be left – as the various tail-dragger landing nuances are magnified by the Spit's narrow track undercarriage. But nothing. Only tiny rudder inputs required to keep her straight. Time to breathe again.

Taxi in and shut down. Helmet off. No rush. Think I'll linger here just a little bit longer than usual.

After I signed her in, I had one last job to do. Chief Technician Paul Blackah, who led the rebuild of this magnificent Spitfire, was away that day so a quick text message to him. 'I reckon you've built the best handling Spitfire in the world.' Enough said!

Left: A wide angle view of the cockpit of Spitfire XVI TE311. Crown Copyright

Below left: MK356 curves around on finals ready to land at RAF Coningsby. Jarrod Cotter

PILOT'S NOTES
FOR
SPITFIRE
XIV & XIX
GRIFFON 65 or 66 ENGINE

'The main development effort went into achieving continuous improvement in the basic characteristics required for better fighting in the air – more speed, higher rate of climb, better manoeuvrability, more fire-power, more range and endurance. These central objectives determined the main march of events and the other role variants benefitted from them. The Photographic Reconnaissance Mk XIX, for example, an aircraft of spectacular performance, derived directly from the Mk XIV fighter.' Jeffrey Quill

**Pilot's Notes for
Spitfire XIX and
April 1946
Griffon 65 or 66 Engine**

Part I Descriptive

Introduction
The Spitfire PR.XIX is basically an F Mk XIV, powered by a Griffon 65 or 66 engine, and differs from it only in the fuel system, canopy and armament/camera fit. Later aircraft are fitted with a pressure cabin.

Fuel, Oil and Coolant Systems

Fuel tanks The two wing tanks, the capacities of which are increased to 66 gallons each, feed direct to the engine through separate on/off cocks and non-return valves. The total tank capacity is 217 gallons.

Pressure cabin aircraft have an additional tank of 20 gallons capacity in each wing from which fuel is fed automatically into the top main tank by means of air pressure and a float operated cut-off valve.

Fuel cocks The cocks of the two 66-gallon wing tanks are operated by two levers, one for each tank, mounted together on a bracket below the left-hand side of the instrument panel.

Fuel booster pump There are three electric fuel booster pumps, one in each 66-gallon wing tank and one in the bottom main tank. The three pumps are controlled by a master switch and a three-way selector switch, mounted together on the right-hand side of the cockpit. A test push-button for each pump is fitted below the two switches.

NOTE: The fuel cut-off lever must be kept in the fully aft position when a booster pump is on and the engine is not running, otherwise fuel will be injected into the supercharger at high pressure and there will, in consequence, be a serious risk of fire.

Fuel contents gauges and warning light There is a contents gauge for each 66-gallon wing tank on the corresponding side of the cockpit.

Oil system Oil is supplied from a tank of 9 gallons oil capacity and 3 gallons air space, mounted between the top main fuel tank and the fireproof bulkhead. The oil passes through a filter before entering the engine. A cooler is fitted inside the fairing of the port wing radiator and oil pressure and temperature gauges are mounted on the right-hand side of the instrument panel. An oil dilution system is fitted. It is controlled by a shielded push-button on the electrical panel.

Coolant system The header tank is mounted above the reduction gear casing and is fitted with a relief valve. The radiator flaps are fully automatic and are designed to open at a coolant temperature of 115°C. A push-button on the electrical panel is fitted for ground testing, and there is a coolant temperature gauge on the right-hand side of the instrument panel.

Main Services

Hydraulic system Oil is contained in a reservoir on the fireproof bulkhead and passes through a filter to an engine-driven pump for operation of the undercarriage and tailwheel.

Electrical system A 12-volt generator charges an accumulator which supplies the whole of the electrical system. A red light on the electrical panel, marked **GEN FAILURE**, is illuminated when the generator is not charging the accumulator.
NOTE: If the electrical system fails, or is damaged, the supercharger will remain in (or return to) low gear and the radiator flaps will remain closed.

Pneumatic system An engine-driven air compressor feeds two storage cylinders for the operation of the brakes, flaps, radiator flaps and supercharger gear change ram. The cylinders each hold air at a pressure of 300lb/in².
NOTE: If the pneumatic system fails, the supercharger will remain in (or return to) low gear, but the position of the radiator flaps will depend on the nature of the failure. The brakes and flaps will also be inoperative.

Flying controls (i) The control column is of the spade-grip pattern and incorporates the brakes lever.
(ii) The rudder pedals have two positions for the feet and are adjustable for reach by rotating the star wheels on the sliding tubes.

Flying controls locking gear Two struts are stowed on the right-hand cockpit wall. The longer strut and the arm attached to it lock the control column to the seat and to the starboard datum longeron, and the shorter strut, attached to the other strut by a cable, locks the rudder pedals. The controls should be locked with the seat in its highest position.

Trimming tabs controls i) The elevator trimming tabs are controlled by a handwheel on the left-hand side of the cockpit and their setting is shown on an indicator on the bottom left-hand side of the instrument panel.
ii) A smaller handwheel aft of the elevator trimming tab control operates the rudder trimming tab. No indicator is provided.
NOTE: When this handwheel is wound clockwise it tends to turn the aircraft to the right.

Undercarriage selector lever The undercarriage selector lever moves in a gated quadrant on the right-hand side of the cockpit. To raise the undercarriage, the lever must be moved downwards and inwards to disengage it from the gate, and then moved forward smartly in one movement to the full extent of the quadrant. When the undercarriage is locked up the lever will automatically spring into the forward gate. To lower the undercarriage, the lever must be held forward for about two seconds, then pulled back in one movement to the full extent of the quadrant. When the undercarriage is locked down the lever will spring into the rear gate. Warning: The lever must never be moved into either gate by hand as this will cut off the hydraulic pressure.

An indicator in the quadrant shows DOWN, IDLE or UP, depending on the position of the hydraulic valve. UP or DOWN should show only during the corresponding operation of the undercarriage, and IDLE when the lever is in either gate. If, when the engine is not running, the indicator shows DOWN, it should return to IDLE when the engine is started; if it does not, probable failure of the hydraulic pump is indicated.

Undercarriage indicator The electrically operated visual indicator has two semi-transparent windows on which the words UP (on a red background) and DOWN (on a green background) are lettered; the words are illuminated according to the position of the under-carriage. The indicator switch incorporates a sliding bar which prevents the ignition switches from being switched on until the indicator is also switched on. The indicator switch also operates the tailwheel indicator light and the fuel pressure warning light.

Flaps control The split flaps have two positions only, up and fully down. They are controlled by a finger lever fitted on the top left-hand side of the instrument panel.

Wheel brakes The brakes lever is fitted on the control column spade grip and a catch for retaining it in the on position for parking

is fitted below the lever pivot. A triple pressure gauge, showing the air pressures in the pneumatic system and at each brake, is mounted on the left-hand side of the instrument panel.

Main Services

Throttle control The throttle lever moves in a quadrant gated at the take-off position. Mixture control is fully automatic and there is no pilot's control lever. The short lever on the inboard side of the quadrant is a friction adjuster for the throttle and propeller speed control levers; forward movement increases the friction damping or locking.

Propeller control On early aircraft the propeller speed control on the throttle quadrant varies the governed rpm from 2,750 down to below 1,800. Speeds below this figure should, however, not be used except in the event of a forced landing when it is necessary to lengthen the glide. On later aircraft the propeller speed control is interconnected with the throttle control. The interconnection is effected by a lever similar to the normal speed control lever and known as the override lever. When this is pulled back to the stop in the quadrant (the AUTOMATIC position) the rpm are controlled by the positioning of the throttle lever. When pushed fully forward to the MAX REVS position it overrides the interconnection device and rpm are then governed at approximately 2,750. The override lever can be used in the same way as the conventional propeller speed control lever to enable the pilot to select higher rpm than those given by the interconnection. It must be remembered that the interconnection is effected only when the override lever is pulled back to the stop in the quadrant; indiscriminate use of the lever in any position forward of this stop will increase fuel consumption considerably.
At low altitudes the corresponding rpm for a given boost with the override lever set at AUTOMATIC are as follows:

Boost (lb/in^2)	rpm
+ 3 and below	1,800 to 1,850
+ 7 (cruising)	2,250 to 2,400
+ 12 (at the gate)	2,725 to 2,775
+ 18 (fully open)	2,725 to 2,775

Supercharger controls The two-speed two-stage supercharger is controlled by a switch marked MS and AUTO, NORMAL POSITION, mounted on the right-hand side of the instrument panel. When this switch is set to MS the supercharger remains in low gear at all altitudes; when it is set to the AUTO, NORMAL POSITION an electro-pneumatic ram, which is controlled by an aneroid, automatically engages high gear at about 13,000ft when the aircraft is climbing and re-engages low gear at about 12,000ft when the aircraft is descending. There is a push-button on the electrical panel for ground testing the gear change and a red light on the instrument panel, next to the supercharger switch, comes on whenever high gear is engaged, either on the ground or in flight.

Radiator flaps control The radiator flaps are fully automatic and there is no manual control. A push-button for ground testing the operation of the flaps is fitted on the electrical panel.

Fuel cut-off control The fuel cut-off control, which is used when starting and stopping the engine, is mounted outboard of the throttle lever. It is spring-loaded and is set forward to allow the carburettor to deliver fuel to the engine. The fuel supply is cut off when the lever is pulled back and engaged in the gate.

Cylinder priming pump and cock A Ki-gass type K.40 pump for priming the engine is mounted immediately forward of the undercarriage selector lever. The priming selector cock just forward of the Ki-gass pump is marked MAIN, GROUND and ALL OFF. The first position is used for priming with normal fuel from the main fuel tanks, and the GROUND position for priming with high volatility fuel from an outside source in cold weather. In flight the cock must be in the ALL OFF position.

Ignition switches The ignition switches on the left-hand side of the instrument panel cannot be moved to the ON position until the undercarriage indicator is switched ON.

Cartridge starter re-indexing control The Coffman starter breech re-indexing control is a pull-grip toggle below the right-hand side of the instrument panel. The magazine for the starter holds five cartridges which are fired by the engine starter push-button. This also operates the booster coil.

Hand starting No provision is made for starting the engine by hand.

Carburettor air-intake filter control – The filter control lever on the left-hand side of the cockpit, forward of the elevator trimming tab control, has two positions, NORMAL INTAKE and FILTER IN OPERATION. The latter position must be used for all ground running, for take-off and landing and when flying in sandy or dust laden conditions.
NOTE: The lever must always be moved slowly.

Camera Equipment and Controls

Alternative groups of cameras may be installed in the rear fuselage.

Right: In this modern day view as PM631 banks away from the camera aircraft its camera ports are shown to good effect. Jarrod Cotter

Below: Because of the high altitudes at which photographic reconnaissance aircraft mostly flew, apart from early examples the cockpit of the Spitfire PR.XIX was pressurised and hence the pilot's access door on the left side of the cockpit was removed. Here Squadron Leader Ian Smith is seen having returned to RAF Coningsby after a local sortie. Jarrod Cotter

Opposite page: PM631 is seen flying straight and level just as it would have needed to do in order to get the photographs needed by the photographic interpreters – a situation which was far from ideal for the photo recce pilots who flew in the skies of hostile enemy territory. Jarrod Cotter

The cameras are controlled by four switches on the electrical panel and a type 35 control mounted at the top of the instrument panel. A green light at the side of each of the three switches comes on when the corresponding camera is switched ON. The fourth switch is a master switch. The oblique camera can also be operated separately by the push-button in the throttle lever.

Pressure Cabin

Automatic valve The differential pressure in the cabin is automatically controlled by a valve to a maximum of +$2\frac{1}{2}$lb/in^2 and commences to build up at about 11,000ft, the maximum being reached and maintained at heights of 28,000ft and above. The reverse holds on the descent.

Air supply Air is drawn through an intake just below the port exhaust manifolds, passes through a filter to an engine-driven blower and then enters the cabin by an inlet at the rear of the pilot's seat. A spill valve in the supply line, operated by a control on the right-hand side of the cockpit, diverts the air supply to atmosphere when pressurising of the cabin is not required.

Cabin hood The hood is fitted with a rubber seal in the gap between the hood and the fuselage, pressure for which is taken from the air supply line inside the cockpit and controlled by a lever on the left-hand side of the cockpit.

Cabin ventilation Two hand-operated ventilators are provided in the cockpit, an intake incorporated in the rear view mirror and an extractor in the right-hand cockpit wall.
NOTE: If, at low altitudes, the cockpit is uncomfortably warm, the direct vision panel should be opened.

Cabin instruments The cabin instruments on the right-hand side of the instrument panel comprise an altimeter to which the pilot refers when adjusting the oxygen supply, and a red warning light which comes on when the differential pressure in the cabin has fallen by 1lb/in^2.

Operation of cabin controls

i) To pressurise the cabin:
a) Close the intake and extractor ventilators.
b) Close the spill valve by moving the lever to PRESSURISE.
c) Turn ON the HOOD SEAL PRESSURE cock.
NOTE: It is recommended that the cabin be pressurised before or immediately after take-off. If the cabin is pressurised or exhausted at altitude the hood sealing control should be moved slowly to avoid the risk of damage to the ears by a sudden change of pressure.

ii) To exhaust cabin pressure:
a) Turn OFF the HOOD SEAL PRESSURE cock.
b) Open the spill valve and ventilators to cool the cabin.

Part II Handling

Management of the fuel system

a) Start the engine, warm up, taxi and take off on the main tanks; then change over to one of the wing tanks at 2,000ft. (If a drop tank is carried, fuel should be used from that first). Fly on each wing tank alternately for 20 minutes until the fuel in both has been used up; this will be indicated by the fuel pressure warning light. Then change back to the main tanks.
NOTE: By operating the wing tank cocks every 20 minutes the possibility of them freezing up at altitude is lessened.
b) For each change of tanks, first turn ON the cock of the next tank in sequence, select the appropriate booster pump and then turn OFF the cock of the tank just used.

Use of the booster pumps

a) The main tanks booster pump should be switched on for starting the engine, take-off and landing and at all times when these tanks are in use in flight.
b) The booster pumps master switch must be switched OFF when the pumps are not in use.

Preliminaries

i. Switch on the undercarriage indicator and check the contents of the fuel tanks. See that both wing tank cocks are off. If a drop tank is fitted, check that the cock is OFF.
ii. Check that the undercarriage selector lever is down and that the indicator light shows DOWN and the tailwheel light is on.
iii. Test the operation of the flying controls and trimming tab controls and adjust the rudder pedals for equal length.
iv. Ensure that the fuel cut-off lever is in the fully aft position, then check the operation of the booster pumps by sound.

i) Set the main fuel cock ON.
ii) Set the controls as follows:

Ignition switches	OFF
Throttle	1½ inches open
Propeller control	Fully forward
or override lever	MAX REVS
Fuel cut-off control	Fully aft
Supercharger switch	AUTO, NORMAL POSITION
Carburettor air-intake filter switch	FILTER IN OPERATION
Priming selector cock	MAIN (GROUND for HV fuel)

NOTE: High volatility fuel should be used for priming at air temperatures below freezing.

iii) Operate the Ki-gass priming pump until the fuel reaches the priming nozzles; this can be judged by a sudden increase in resistance.
iv) Switch on the main tanks booster pump.
NOTE: When the engine is not running the booster pump must not be switched on unless the fuel cut-off control is in the fully aft position.
v) Index the cartridge starter. The following types of cartridge should be used:

| At air temperatures above +10°: | No. 4 Mk I |
| At air temperatures below +10°: | No. 5 Mk I |

vi) Immediately before attempting to start switch ON the ignition and prime with the following number of strokes if the engine is cold:

Air temperature °C:	+30	+20	+10	0	-10	-20
Normal fuel:	1	1	2	5	–	–
High volatility fuel:	–	–	–	1	2	3

Leave the priming pump plunger out and press the cartridge starter push-button. As soon as the engine fires release the fuel cut-off control. (Keep the button pressed until the engine is running steadily as it also controls the booster coil.)
NOTE: (a) It may be necessary to continue priming until the engine picks up on the carburettor. (b) A visual all-clear signal must be obtained from the ground crew before each cartridge is fired.
vii) Screw down the priming pump and turn OFF the priming selector cock.
viii) Open up slowly to 1,200rpm then warm up at this speed.
ix) Switch off the booster pump and check that the fuel pressure warning light does not come on. Then switch the pump on again.
x) If the engine fails to start on the first cartridge the fuel cut-off control must be returned immediately to the fully aft position and the booster pump must be switched off. No further priming should be given except for half a stroke as each subsequent cartridge is fired.
NOTE: If a cartridge fails to fire, a wait of at least one minute must be allowed before the next cartridge is inserted in the Coffman breech.

Testing the engine and services
While warming up:
NOTE: If a drop tank is carried it should be selected and the flow of fuel from it checked by running on it for at least one minute.
i) Check temperatures and pressures.
ii) Check the operation of the flaps.
iii) Press the radiator test push-button and have the ground crew check that the flaps open.
iv) Test each magneto in turn as a precautionary check before increasing power further.

After warming up to at least 15°C oil temperature and 60°C coolant temperature:
v) Open up 0lb/in^2 boost and exercise and check the operation of the supercharger by pressing and holding in the test push-button. Boost should rise slightly and the red warning light should come on when high gear is engaged. Release the push-button after 30 seconds.
vi) At the same boost exercise at least twice and check the operation of the constant speed propeller. Check that the generator is charging.
NOTE: The following comprehensive checks should be carried out after repair, inspection other than daily, or at any time at the discretion of the pilot. When these checks are performed the tail of the aircraft must be securely lashed down. Normally they may be reduced in accordance with local instructions and the tail need not then be lashed down:
vii) With the propeller speed control or override lever fully forward, open the throttle to the gate and check take-off boost and static rpm.
viii) Throttle back to +9lb/in^2 boost or further if necessary to ensure that rpm fall below the take-off figure, then test each magneto in turn. The single ignition drop should not exceed 100rpm.
ix) If an interconnection is fitted, throttle back to +3lb/in^2 boost and set the override lever to AUTOMATIC; rpm should fall to 1,800–1,850. Return the lever to MAX REVS.
x) Before taxying check brake pressure (80lb/in^2) and the pneumatic supply pressure (220lb/in^2).

Check list before take-off

T – Trimming tabs –	Rudder: Fully left (hand-wheel fully back) Elevator: a) At typical service load (but no rear fuselage tank fuel) 8,375lb: Neutral b) At typical service load plus rear fuselage tank fuel, but no external stores, 9,000lb: NOSE DOWN c) At typical service load plus rear fuselage tank fuel and full 90-gallon drop tank, 9,772lb: Neutral-½-1 division NOSE UP
P – Propeller control	Fully forward
Control or Override lever	MAX REVS
F – Fuel Main tanks cock	Main tanks cock ON Main tanks booster pump on Transfer valve selector cock NORMAL Drop tank cock OFF
F – Flaps	UP
Supercharge Switchr	AUTO, NORMAL POSITION, red light out
Carburettor air intake filter control	FILTER IN OPERATION

NOTE: It is particularly important on these aircraft to clear the engine before take-off.

Take-off

i) Whenever possible open the throttle slowly up to +7lb/in^2 boost only. This is important as there is a strong tendency to swing to the right and to crab in the initial stages of the take-off run. If too much power is used tyre wear is severe. +12lb/in^2 boost may be used at heavy load, and should in any case be used on becoming airborne to minimise the possibility of lead fouling of the sparking plugs, but +7lb/in^2 boost is sufficient for a normal take-off.

ii) After raising the undercarriage, see that the red indicator light – UP – comes on and that the tailwheel light goes out. It may be necessary to hold the selector lever hard forward against the quadrant until the light does come on. Failure of the main wheels to lock up will spoil the airflow through the radiators and will result in excessive temperatures.

iii) If fitted, move the override lever smoothly back to AUTOMATIC when comfortably airborne.

iv) Unless operating in sandy or dust-laden conditions, set the carburettor air intake filter control to NORMAL INTAKE at 1,000ft.

Climbing

The recommended climbing speed from sea level to 22,000ft, is 180mph (155kts) IAS.

NOTE: i) With the supercharger switch at AUTO high gear is engaged automatically when the aircraft reaches a height of about 13,000ft. This is the optimum height for the gear change if full combat power is being used, but if normal climbing power (2,600rpm +9lb/in^2 boost) is being used, the maximum rate of climb is obtained by delaying the gear change until the boost in low gear has fallen to +5lb/in^2. This is achieved by leaving the supercharger switch at MS until the boost has fallen to this figure.

ii) Use of the air intake filter reduces the full throttle height considerably.

General flying

Controls: The elevator, and the rudder and elevator trimming tabs, are powerful and sensitive and must be used with care.

Changes of trim:

Undercarriage down	Nose down
Undercarriage up	Nose up
Flaps down	Initially nose up, finally little change
Flaps up	Nose down.

Changes of power and speed induce marked changes in directional trim. These should be countered by careful and accurate use of the rudder trimming tab.

Flying at low altitude in conditions of bad visibility:
Reduce speed to 160mph (140kts) IAS and lower the flaps. Set the propeller speed control or override lever to give 2,400rpm and open the cockpit hood. Fly at about 160mph (140kts) IAS, keeping a close watch on oil and coolant temperatures.

Spinning

i) Spinning is not permitted when external stores are carried.

ii) Recovery from a spin by the standard method is normal, but the loss of height involved may be very great and the following limits are to be observed.

a) Spins are not to be started below 10,000ft.

b) Recovery is to be initiated before two turns are completed.

iii) The spin itself is erratic, the nose rising and falling and the rate of rotation varying, increasing as the nose falls and decreasing almost to a stop as it rises. Considerable tail buffeting persists throughout the spin.

iv) A speed of 180mph (155 kts) IAS should be attained before starting to ease out of the resultant dive.

Diving

i) As speed is gained, the aircraft becomes increasingly tail heavy and should, therefore, be trimmed into the dive. The tendency to yaw to starboard should be corrected by accurate use of the rudder trimming tab.

ii) No attempt should be made to reach the maximum diving speed (470mph, 410kts IAS) at heights above 20,000ft, otherwise compressibility effects may be encountered. These effects produce a nose-down change of trim. If such a change of trim is observed, it must be held on the control column alone and no attempt must be made to correct it with the elevator trimming tab, for while this action will not immediately prove effective, it is likely to render the recovery violent when the Mach number falls at a lower altitude. It is equally important to avoid yawing the aircraft in an attempt to reduce speed.

iii) The speeds in excess of which compressibility effects become apparent are as follows:

Up to 20,000ft	470 mph IAS
20,000–25,000ft	430
25,000–30,000ft	390
30,000–35,000ft	340

Aerobatics

i) The following speeds in mph (kts) IAS are recommended:

Roll	220–250 (190–220)
Loop	320–350 (230–300)
Half roll off the top of the loop	350–400 (300–350)
Climbing roll	350–450 (300–400)

ii) Aerobatics are not permitted when carrying any external stores (except the 30-gallon 'blister' type drop tank) or when there is any fuel in the rear fuselage tank.

iii) Flick manoeuvres are prohibited.

Check list before landing

(i) Reduce speed to 160mph (140kts) IAS, open the sliding hood and check:

U – Undercarriage	DOWN (check indicator)
Tailwheel	Light on
P – Propeller control or override lever	Set to give 2,400rpm (fully forward on final approach)
Supercharger	Red light out
Carburettor air intake filter control	FILTER IN OPERATION
F – Fuel Main tanks booster pump	Main tanks cock ON ON
F – Flaps	DOWN

(ii) Check brake pressure (80lb/in²) and pneumatic supply pressure (220lb/in²).
NOTE: The undercarriage operation takes considerably longer with the engine 'off' than with it 'on'.

Approach and landing

The recommended final approach speeds in mph (kts) IAS are as follows:

At typical service load (8,375lb)

	Flaps down	Flaps up
Engine assisted	100 (87)	110 (96)
Glide	110 (96)	112 (100)

NOTE: The initial straight approach should be made at a speed some 20–25mph (17–22kts) IAS above these figures.

Mislanding

i) The aircraft will climb away easily with the undercarriage and flaps down and the use of full take-off power is unnecessary.
ii) Open the throttle steadily to give the desired boost.
NOTE: The torque effect of the Griffon engine is opposite to and more powerful than that of the Merlin engine, and is of opposite sign.
iii) Raise the undercarriage immediately.
iv) With the flaps down climb at about 160mph (140kts) IAS.
v) Raise the flaps at 300ft and retrim.

After Landing

i) Before taxying:
a) Raise the flaps.
b) Switch off the booster pump.

ii) On reaching dispersal:
Open up to 0lb/in² boost and exercise the supercharger once.
Throttle back to 800–900rpm and idle at this speed for a few seconds, then stop the engine by moving the fuel cut-off control fully aft.

When the propeller has stopped rotating switch off the ignition and all other electrical services.
Turn off the fuel.

iii) Oil dilution
The correct dilution period for these aircraft is:
1 minute at atmospheric temperatures above 10°C
2 minutes at atmospheric temperatures below 10°C

Part III Operating Data

Engine data – Griffon 65 and 66

i) Fuel – 100 octane only.
ii) The principal engine limitations are as follows:

	Supercharger Gear	Rpm	Boost Lb/In²	Temp. °C Coolant	Oil
Max Take-Off to 1,000ft	Low	2,750*	+12	–	–
Max Climbing 1 Hour Limit	Low High }	2,600	+12	125	90
Max Continuous	Low High }	2,400	+7	105 (115)	90
Combat 5 Mins Limit	Low High }	2,750*	+18	135	105

* With interconnected controls there is a tolerance on 'maximum' rpm. The figure in brackets is permitted for short periods.

Minimum Temperature for Take-Off

Oil	15°C
Coolant	60°C

Flying limitations

i) Maximum speeds in mph (kts) IAS.

Diving (without external stores)*	470 (410)
Undercarriage down	160 (140)
Flaps down	160 (140)

ii) Maximum weights
Overload:

Take-off and gentle manoeuvres only	9,400lb

Normal:

Take-off and all forms of flying	8,600lb
Landing (except in emergency)	8,600lb

Above right: PM631's photographic reconnaissance blue paintwork takes on a perfect look when flying at higher altitudes. Jarrod Cotter

Right: Spitfire XIX PS853 was one of the early aircraft to equip the Historic Aircraft Flight which later became the BBMF, and in those early days with fewer airworthy aircraft on its books the Flight's personnel painted the PR.XIXs in camouflage to better represent a fighter variant which it lacked for quite some years. Crown Copyright

iii) Flying restrictions

a) Spinning is not permitted when carrying any external stores.

b) Aerobatics and combat manoeuvres are not permitted when carrying any external stores (except the 30-gallon 'blister' type drop tank).

c) When a 90-gallon drop tank is carried, the aircraft is restricted to straight flying and only gentle manoeuvres.

d) When jettisoning a drop tank, the aircraft should be flown straight and level at a speed not greater than 300mph (260kts) IAS.

Maximum performance

i) Climbing:

a) The speed for maximum rate of climb is 180mph (155kts) IAS from sea level to 22,000ft, thereafter reducing speed by 3mph (2kts) per 1,000ft.

b) With the supercharger switch at AUTO high gear is engaged automatically when the aircraft reaches a height of about 13,000ft. This is the optimum height for the gear change if full combat power is being used but if normal climbing power (2,600rpm +9lb/in^2 boost) is being used, the maximum rate of climb is obtained by delaying the gear change until the boost in low gear has fallen to +5lb/in^2. This is achieved by leaving the supercharger switch at MS until the boost has fallen to this figure.

c) Combat evasion:

Set the supercharger switch to AUTO and open the throttle fully.

Economical flying

i) Climbing:

On aircraft not fitted with interconnected throttle and propeller controls:

a) Set the supercharger override switch to MS, the propeller speed control lever to give 2,400rpm and climb at the speeds given above, opening the throttle progressively to maintain a boost pressure of +7lb/in^2.

b) Set the supercharger override switch to AUTO when the maximum obtainable boost is +3lb/in^2, throttling back to prevent overboosting as the change to high gear is made.

On aircraft fitted with interconnected throttle and propeller controls:

a) Set the supercharger override switch to MS, set the throttle to give +7lb/in^2 boost and climb at the speeds given above.

b) As height is gained the boost will fall, but the throttle should not be advanced to restore it, since rpm will then be increased beyond the maximum permitted for continuous operation.

c) When the boost has fallen to +3lb/in^2 set the supercharger override switch to AUTO.

Cruising

The recommended speed for maximum range is 200–210mph (175–185kts) IAS.

On aircraft not fitted with interconnected throttle and propeller controls:

With the supercharger override switch at MS fly at the maximum obtainable boost (not exceeding +7lb/in²) and obtain the recommended speed by reducing rpm as required.
NOTE: i) Rpm should not be reduced below a minimum of 1,800. At low altitudes therefore it may be necessary to reduce boost or the recommended speed will be exceeded.
ii) As the boost falls at high altitudes it will not be possible to maintain the recommended speed in low gear, even at maximum cruising rpm and full throttle. It will then be necessary to set the supercharger override switch to AUTO. Boost will thus be restored and it will be possible to reduce rpm again (as outlined in (a) above).
iii) In both low and high gears rpm which promote rough running should be avoided.

On aircraft fitted with interconnected throttle and propeller controls:
Set the supercharger override switch to MS and adjust the throttle to obtain the recommended speed. Avoid a throttle setting which promotes rough running.
NOTE: At moderate and high altitudes it will be necessary to advance the throttle progressively to restore the falling boost and thus maintain the recommended speed. Now as the throttle is opened rpm will increase and at a certain height the recommended speed will be unobtainable at a throttle setting which gives 2,400rpm. At this height the supercharger override switch should be set to AUTO and the throttle then adjusted as before to maintain the recommended speed.

Fuel capacities and consumption
i. Fuel capacities:
a) Normal fuel capacities

Top main tank	36 gallons
Bottom main tank	49 gallons
2 wing tanks (each 66 gallons)	132 gallons
2 wing tanks (each 20 gallons)*	40 gallons
Total all tanks	257 gallons

*Pressure cabin aircraft only.
b) Long-range fuel capacities (gallons):

With 1 x 30 gal drop tank	287
With 1 x 45 gal drop tank	302
With 1 x 50 gal drop tank	307
With 1 x 90 gal drop tank	347

(ii) Fuel consumption (approximate gals/hour)
a) Weak mixture and low gear at 5,000ft

Boost lb/in² rpm	2,400	2,200	2,000	1,800
+7	88	85	80	–
+4	74	71	67	60
+2	65	63	59	52
0	57	55	51	46
-2	50	47	43	41

NOTE: For every 5,000ft increase in height add 4 gallons per hour.

b) Weak mixture and high gear at 20,000ft

Boost lb/in² rpm	2,400	2,200	2,000	1,800
+7	95	92	87	–
+4	82	78	74	70
+2	73	70	66	63
0	66	63	59	56
-2	59	56	52	49

c) Rich mixture and low gear at 5,000ft

Boost lb/in² rpm	2,750	2,600
+18	180	–
+12	130	–
+9	–	103

Spitfire PR.XIX Air Test

Squadron Leader Dunc Mason, OC BBMF

As we reach the end of each and every display season, the BBMF tucks its precious aircraft safely into 'the shed' and peels off the panels to start the winter servicing programme. The air and ground crews look forward to having the weekends at home again with their families, but such is the nature of flying these aircraft that we are soon itching to get them back in the air!

Normally, the first of these flights is an air test after one of the fighters emerges from the rigours of its annual service. In 2014 the first aircraft to become ready, in later February, was PM631, one of our two PR Mk XIX Spitfires. The air test requires good weather to climb the aircraft to 7,000ft, clear of cloud, before conducting stalling and tests of the undercarriage, flaps and engine. On 27 February the wind was down the strip but, with a 1,500ft cloud base, things were not looking terribly promising. However, being the eternal optimist, I started the preliminary processes that I go through before launching off into the wild blue yonder in a newly readied aircraft.

Preliminaries

Firstly, a chat with the engineers about what faults have been found and rectified so that I know if there is anything out of the ordinary that I should be looking for.

Then to the F700, the aircraft's 'military logbook', where I check the maintenance carried out, how much fuel the aircraft has (normally full) and if there are any accepted 'Deferred Defects', such as the tail wheel being locked down or the compass not having been 'swung'.

All appears good on 'PM' so I poke my head out of the door for a check of the weather. As I look skyward, a big blue gap appears in the cloud to the south, so I grab my helmet, gloves and the Flight Test Schedule, and head out to the aircraft. (The Flight Test Schedule is a sort of 'crib sheet' and questionnaire for the air test sortie, laying down the elements to be covered, with spaces for the pilot to write in the figures obtained.)

Walk round

A small crowd of the BBMF ground crew has gathered to witness

the first flight of the year as I wander out. The two ground crew 'seeing me off' have got the cockpit open with the harness straps ready. A hard look as I walk toward the aircraft to make sure that nothing is leaking out of it and, after a check inside the cockpit, the 'walk round'. This is normally a quick but thorough inspection of both the cockpit and the exterior of the aircraft to look for leaks, loose fastenings and to ensure all the bits that should 'wobble', wobble correctly and that there are no bits that shouldn't wobble that do! On an initial, post-winter servicing air test, this is a much slower and more in-depth affair, paying close scrutiny to all parts of the aircraft.

Start-up

After strapping in I complete the pre-start checks and then prime the engine with fuel; ignition on; stick fully back and hit the start button. The tips of the prop swing past a couple of times on the starter motor and then a mighty roar, and a kick on the control column as the 37-litre Rolls-Royce Griffon bursts into life. As all this occurs I have to note that the fuel pressure is good and the generator comes on line before settling her at 1,200rpm and completing the after start checks.

Take-off

Having taxied out to the runway and completed the engine run-up and pre-take-off checks, I note a few more figures down and brief myself carefully what I'll do if the engine quits during, or worse, just after take-off. With take-off clearance given, I line up the aggressively long nose of the Mk XIX down the runway and push the throttle forward gently to +6 inches of manifold pressure, known as 'boost'. I feel the torque from the mighty V12 Griffon engine push the right wheel hard onto the runway and progressively more left rudder is required to hold her straight as I gently raise the tail as she charges down the strip. A look in at temperatures and pressures (known as 'Ts and Ps') to see that all is well and then she is airborne! Noting the 'unstick' (rotate) speed, I quickly raise the undercarriage to avoid it being in transit above the limiting speed. Aside from engine considerations this is the first real test of the aircraft since the previous year; if the landing gear doesn't move at all, things are not too bad as you can just turn downwind and land. However, in the unlikely event

that it only moves halfway this would present you with a much more worrying and troublesome prospect!

Climb

No problem this time, though, the undercarriage gives a satisfying 'thump, thump' and the red UP light illuminates on the front panel. I close the radiator flaps and bring the revs back to 2,400, leaving the boost at +6 inches; a quick check of Ts & Ps and then start the stopwatch to time the climb to 7,000ft. Up into the blue gap, keeping the speed pegged at 160kts and squeezing the throttle lever to maintain the boost as I climb. No time to relax, I scribble down the unstick speed on the take-off on my schedule and tick off the checks as I climb, ensuring the radio, instruments and avionics work as expected, and within three minutes I'm up at 7,000ft, having noted the height every 30 seconds. This check confirms that the engine is producing the power expected of it and 'PM' doesn't disappoint; she's a power house!

Stalling

Levelling off, I note the Ts & Ps once more and bring the throttle back to slow down and check the stalling characteristics. I put the radiator flaps down and the rpm to max (2,750) and trim the aeroplane for level flight. Deliberately stalling the aircraft feels utterly wrong, the huge nose of the aircraft pointing skyward and little noise from either engine or airflow. As the speed approaches 65kts there is a small shudder and the left wing drops slightly. A check of the vertical speed indicator and we are descending like a stone, but it really is a benign stall. A squeeze of power as I ease the control column forward and she's flying again. I furiously scribble the numbers down and drop the landing gear and flaps, noting the time it takes for the gear to lower and any asymmetry with the flaps, and repeat the stalling exercise, the only difference being that the speed is roughly 8kts slower and there is a bit more of a wing drop. No problems, I get her flying again and then time how long it takes for the gear to retract and note down that the flaps raise symmetrically too.

Flight regimes

Clean again, I reduce the rpm, ease the boost up a little so she is at cruise power and give her a couple of minutes to settle the engine after a relatively long period at max rpm. I dive down 1,000ft, level off again and let the speed settle before noting it down. This test shows that the relationship between the power setting and propeller pitch produces the requisite amount of thrust and that in the cruise the Ts & Ps are as expected.

You've probably noticed that 'Ts & Ps' feature a lot in the test. It is vitally important that the engine is rock solid throughout, and other than smell, sound and vibration, the three engine gauges and the pressure lights are the main indication of how it is performing, hence the constant noting of Ts & Ps!

Enough of cruising! Time to check full power. Max rpm and +6 inches boost. After a few moments, I note the engine parameters are in limits and dive, level off, let the speed settle and check it, then push the boost up to maximum permissible, +12 inches at maximum rpm for 20 seconds, a cacophony of noise as the aircraft accelerates, the engine instruments as solid as a rock!

Aerobatics

Now the fun part. The next part of the schedule calls for a check that the aircraft performs satisfactorily under display conditions. Setting display power of 2,650rpm and +6 inches boost, I pull the aircraft into a series of loops, rolls, and half horizontal eights. Wonderful! After a few moments of this it is time to perform the last airborne check. This is a dive from 7,000ft at 100kts with the boost set at zero and 2,400rpm, increasing speed to 270kts (the BBMF's normal operating speed limit) to level at 1,000ft, noting what happens to the boost and rpm. This test is to ensure that the automatic engine controls function correctly. On all the BBMF fighters the constant speed unit should maintain 2,400rpm during this high speed dive, and the boost will either remain static or increase slightly as altitude is lost, depending on the type and mark of engine. The Griffon in 'PM' lets the boost increase as expected.

Successful air test

After completing the obligatory and traditional flypast over the BBMF hangar to let the expectant ground crew waiting below know that all is well and that their hard work has produced a successful air test, I turn the Spitfire downwind to land. Final

checks of pneumatics and magnetos, after taxying back in and it's done! 'PM' has performed very nicely and so I write up the figures and chat it through with the engineers.

Test flying

If only they all performed as well as 'PM'! As an air test pilot I really earn my money when things don't go as planned. Sometimes, something doesn't perform quite as it should but the rest of the test flight can be completed. Sometimes, such as when the engine cut during the climb in one of the Hurricanes (thankfully it started again), it can't. Whatever the severity of the fault it must be analysed by the engineers and myself, the necessary rectification then has to be carried out and the air test must be re-flown. Hurricane PZ865 took 12 test flights this year before being declared serviceable.

Test flying occurs throughout the year on the Flight, all of it geared to ensuring that our wonderful aircraft are completely safe to display to the public. It is an interesting and rewarding part of my job and I hope that the article has provided an insight into a little known part of these responsibilities of the Flight and of the Officer Commanding – the BBMF Fighter Air Test Pilot – in particular.

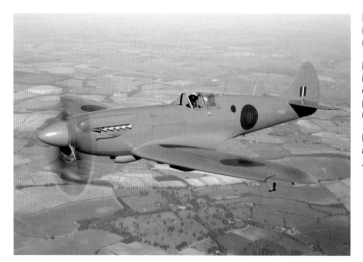

Left: With a Griffon engine for its power unit, a PR.XIX has a noticeably longer nose than a Spitfire powered by the more iconic Rolls-Royce Merlin. Note also in this view of PM631 the position of the port facing oblique camera port just in front of the fuselage roundel. Jarrod Cotter

Right: PR.XIX PM631 caught in a steep bank to starboard. Jarrod Cotter

'Personally I, and most others at Supermarine felt extremely proud of the Spitfires 22 and 24. ... I remember setting the trimmers carefully, with a small amount of power on, for a gently curving and steady landing approach, and as I chopped the throttle at the threshold of the runway the aircraft virtually landed itself. I had the same thought that I had had so many years before after my first flight in the prototype – that this aeroplane was a real lady; albeit by then a much more powerful, noisy, tough and aggressive lady, but a lady all the same. Jeffrey Quill

Pilot's Notes for Spitfire 22 & 24 Griffon 61 Engine
AP2816B & C
Air Ministry September 1947

Part I Descriptive

Introduction
The Spitfire Mk 22 and Mk 24 are fitted with a Griffon 61 engine having two-speed two-stage supercharging and a Bendix Stromberg carburettor, and a Rotol 35° five-bladed propeller. The aircraft have rear-view fuselages, are fully tropicalised and have an armament of four 20mm cannon. Bombs may be carried beneath the fuselage.

Fuel, Oil and Coolant Systems

Fuel tanks Fuel is carried in six tanks, two main tanks mounted one above the other in the fuselage and two interconnected tanks in the leading edge of each wing.

The lower main tank and wing tanks are self-sealing. The top main tank feeds into the lower tank and fuel in the wing tanks is transferred to the top main tank by air pressure. An engine-driven pump supplies fuel to the carburettor through a filter. The vapour return line from the Stromberg carburettor is connected to the top main tank. A drop tank of 30, 45, 50, or 90 gallons capacity can be fitted under the fuselage. The drop tanks cannot be pressurised.

The main and rear fuselage tanks are vented to atmosphere with the pressurising cock set to OFF. With this cock ON the tanks are automatically pressurised above 15,000ft provided that the fuel transfer selector cock is in the NORMAL VENTING or PRESSURISING position. With the transfer selector cock set to PORT (or STARBOARD) WING TANKS, fuel is transferred by air pressure from the corresponding pair of wing tanks to the main tanks. Pressurising of the main and rear fuselage tanks is then inoperative even with the pressurising cock ON.

Pressurising impairs the self-sealing qualities of the tanks and the pressurising cock should be turned OFF in the event of a tank being holed.

Permanent tanks capacities are:

Top tank	36 gallons
Bottom tank	48 gallons
Two wing tanks (12½ gallons each)	25 gallons
Two wing tanks (5½ gallons each)	11 gallons
Total	120 gallons

Mk 24 aircraft have rear fuselage tanks. They are in two sections, upper and lower, the capacity of each being 33 gallons. The upper tank drains into the lower and thence to the engine. The lower tank is fitted with a booster pump and the tanks are pressurised in the same way as the main tank.

Fuel cock The cock control for the main tanks is a lever mounted below the engine-starting push-button: the pressurising cock is on the right-hand side of the cockpit, to the right of the seat. It should be left ON for automatic pressurising above 15,000ft. The transfer valve selector cock, for admitting air pressure to either pair of wing tanks, is below and slightly forward of the throttle quadrant. It is important that this cock be returned to the NORMAL position after use, or pressurising of the main tanks will not be effective. The cock control and jettison lever for the auxiliary drop tank are mounted together on the right-hand side of the cockpit below the undercarriage control. The jettison lever is pulled up to jettison the drop tank, but cannot be operated until the cock control is moved forward to the OFF position. The cock control for the rear fuselage tanks is to the left and forward of the seat.

Booster pump Two electric fuel booster pumps are fitted, one in the bottom of the lower main tank and one in the lower rear fuselage tank. They are controlled by a three-position switch on the electrical panel. A test push-button for each pump is also fitted. NOTE: The cut-off lever must be in the fully aft position when either booster pump is on and the engine is not running.

Fuel contents gauges and warning lights The contents gauge on the right-hand side of the instrument panel has two dials, which give readings for the combined capacity of the top and bottom main fuel tanks. A red mark on the left-hand dial indicates the level of fuel at which fuel should be transferred from the wing tanks. A contents gauge for the rear tank is situated to the left of the main tanks gauges. It indicates the quantity of fuel in the lower rear tank only. The fuel pressure warning light is to the left of the super-charger change switch on the instrument panel, and it comes on when the fuel pressure drops to 10lb/in². The contents gauges and warning light are switched on and off by the GROUND/FLIGHT switch.

Previous page: Spitfire F.24 PK713. Note the doors on the outer edges of the wheel bays, which unlike most Spitfire variants covered the wheels to give a smoother surface. British Official

Left: The Spitfire F.22 and F.24 represented the far end of the Spitfire's evolution, and had a performance that matched the early jets of the era. This is a very clear view of Spitfire F.22 PK312. British Official

Below left: This photo, taken from the rear turret of a Lancaster, shows a late Spitfire F.22 on an air test out of Castle Bromwich. British Official

A low fuel level warning light is fitted to the right of the main contents gauge. It comes on when sufficient fuel for only 30 minutes' flying at max economical cruising conditions remain in the main tanks.

Oil system Oil is supplied by a tank of 9 gallons oil capacity and 3 gallons air space, mounted between the top main fuel tank and the fireproof bulkhead. The oil passes through a filter before entering the engine. A cooler is fitted inside the fairing of the starboard wing radiator and oil pressure and temperature gauges are fitted on the right-hand side of the instrument panel.

Coolant system The header tank is mounted above the reduction gear casing and is fitted with a relief valve. The radiator flaps are fully automatic and are designed to open at a coolant temperature of 115°C. A push-button on the electrical panel is fitted for ground testing and there is a coolant temperature gauge on the instrument panel.

Main Services

Hydraulic system Oil is contained in a reservoir on the fireproof bulkhead and passes through a filter to an engine-driven pump for operation of the undercarriage and tailwheel.

Electrical system A generator supplies a 24-volt battery which in turn supplies the whole of the electrical installation. A red light on the electrical panel, marked GEN FAILURE, is illuminated when the generator is not charging the battery. NOTE: If the electrical system fails or is damaged, the supercharger will remain in (or return to) low gear and the radiator flaps will remain closed.

A GROUND/FLIGHT switch is on the electrical panel. With this switch set to GROUND, all electrical services can be tested by means of a ground battery plugged into the external ELECTRICAL & RADIO socket; the switch should be set to FLIGHT before starting the engine.

Pneumatic system An engine-driven air compressor feeds two storage cylinders for the operation of the flaps, radiator flaps, supercharger gear change ram, and brakes. The cylinders each hold air at 300lb/in^2 pressure. The flap system differs from that on earlier marks in that the flaps are returned to the UP position by air pressure instead of a spring.
NOTE: If the pneumatic system fails, the supercharger will remain in (or return to) low gear, but the position of the radiator flaps will depend on the nature of the failure. The flaps and brakes may also be inoperative.

Aircraft Controls

Flying controls The control column is of the spade-grip pattern and incorporates the brake lever and gun firing control. The rudder pedals have two positions for the feet and are adjustable for reach by rotating the star wheels on the sliding tubes. Mk 24 aircraft have a spring tab elevator fitted and an extra inertia weight in the elevator circuit.

Trimming tabs The elevator trimming tabs are controlled by a handwheel on the left-hand side of the cockpit, the indicator being on the instrument panel. The rudder trimming tab is controlled by a small handwheel and is not provided with an indicator. The servo tabs on the ailerons may be adjusted on the ground to alter the ratio of aileron to tab movement.

Undercarriage control The undercarriage selector moves in a gated quadrant on the starboard side of the cockpit. To raise the undercarriage, the lever must be moved downwards to disengage if from the slot, inwards through the gate, and then forward to the full extent of the quadrant. The lever should spring outwards through the upper gate and when the undercarriage is locked up it will automatically spring back into the upper slot.

To lower the undercarriage, the lever must be held forward for about two seconds, pulled through the upper gate and then back in one movement to the full extent of the quadrant. The lever should spring outwards through the lower gate and when the undercarriage is locked down it will automatically spring into the lower slot.

When operated in either direction the lever must be permitted to spring outboard when it reaches the end of its travel; this ensures that it can spring into the appropriate slot when the undercarriage is locked up or down. The lever must not be forced into either slot by hand. An indicator in the quadrant shows DOWN, IDLE or UP, depending on the position of the hydraulic valve. UP or DOWN should show only during the corresponding operation of the undercarriage, and IDLE when the lever is in either slot. If mishandled or out of adjustment it is nevertheless possible for the lever to be on the wrong side of the gate, and yet for the indicator to show IDLE. It is important to check, therefore, that the lever is correctly positioned in the slot. If, when the engine is not running, the indicator shows DOWN, it should return to IDLE when the engine is started; if it does not, probable failure of the hydraulic pump is indicated.

Undercarriage indicator The electrically operated visual indicator has two semi-transparent windows on which the words UP on a red background and DOWN on a green background are lettered; the words are illuminated according to the position of the undercarriage. The tailwheel light is illuminated green when the tailwheel is down. All three lights are switched on and off by the GROUND/FLIGHT switch.

Flaps control The split flaps have two positions only, up and fully down. They are controlled by a three-position lever on the top left-hand side of the instrument panel marked UP, AIR OFF, and DOWN. The lever should be set DOWN to lower the flaps and left in that position. To raise the flaps the lever is set to UP and when they have been raised should be set and left at AIR OFF.

Wheel brakes The brake lever is fitted on the control column spade grip and a catch for retaining it in the on position for parking is fitted below the lever pivot. A triple pressure gauge, showing the air pressures in the pneumatic system and at each brake, is mounted on the instrument panel.

Flying controls locking gear Two struts are stowed on the right-hand side of the cockpit, aft of the seat. The longer strut and the arm attached to it lock the control column to the seat and to the starboard datum longeron, and the shorter strut, attached to the other strut by a cable, locks the rudder pedals. The controls should be locked with the seat in its highest position.

Engine Controls

Throttle The throttle quadrant is gated at the take-off position. Mixture control is fully automatic and there is no pilot's control lever. The short lever on the inboard side of the quadrant is a friction adjuster for the throttle and propeller control levers; forward movement increases the friction damping or locking.

Propeller control The aircraft have interconnected throttle and propeller controls. The interconnection is controlled by a lever similar to the normal propeller control lever, known as the override lever. When this lever is set fully back to the AUTOMATIC position the rpm are controlled by the positioning of the throttle lever. When pushed fully forward to the MAX RPM position it overrides the interconnection device and rpm are then governed at 2,750.

The override lever can also be used in the same way as the conventional propeller control lever to enable the pilot to select higher rpm than those given by the interconnection. The automatic controlling of rpm is effected only when the override lever is set fully back and indiscriminate use of the lever in any position will increase fuel consumption considerably.

At low altitudes the corresponding rpm for a given boost with the override lever set at AUTOMATIC are as follows:

Boost (lb/in^2)	rpm
+ 3 and below	1,800 to 1,850
+ 7 (cruising)	2,250 to 2,400
+ 12 (at the gate)	2,725 to 2,775
+ 18 (fully open)	2,725 to 2,775

Supercharger controls The two-speed two-stage supercharger is controlled by a switch marked MS and AUTO, NORMAL POSITION, mounted on the right-hand side of the instrument panel. When this switch is set to MS the supercharger remains in low gear at all altitudes; when it is set to the AUTO, NORMAL POSITION an electro-pneumatic ram, which is controlled by an aneroid, automatically engages high gear at about 11,000ft when the aircraft is climbing and re-engages low gear at about 10,000ft when the aircraft is descending.

There is a push-button on the electrical panel for ground testing the gear change and a red light beside the supercharger switch comes on whenever high gear is engaged, either on the ground or in flight.

Radiator flap control The push-button for testing the radiator flaps is on the electrical panel.

Fuel cut-off control The fuel cut-off control, which is used for starting and stopping the engine, is mounted outboard of the throttle lever. It is spring-loaded and is set forward to allow the carburettor to deliver fuel to the engine. Fuel is cut off when the lever is pulled back and engaged in the gate.

Cylinder priming pump and cock A Ki-gass type K.40 pump for priming the engine is fitted immediately forward of the under-carriage control. The priming selector cock on the right-hand side of the cockpit, is marked MAIN, GROUND and ALL OFF. The first position is used for priming with normal fuel from the main fuel tanks, and the GROUND position for priming with high volatility fuel from an outside source in cold weather. In flight the cock must be in the ALL OFF position.

Ignition switches These are on the left-hand side of the instrument panel.

Cartridge starter The Coffman starter breech control is a pull-grip toggle below the right-hand side of the instrument panel. The

magazine for the starter holds five cartridges which are fired by the engine starter push-button. This also operates the booster coil.

Hand starting No provision is made for hand-starting the engine.

Carburettor air-intake control On Mk 22 aircraft the filter control lever on the left-hand side of the cockpit has two positions. NORMAL INTAKE and FILTER IN OPERATION. The latter position must be used for all ground running, take-offs and landings, and when flying in sandy or dust-laden conditions.
NOTE: In the air it may be necessary to reduce speed to 180mph IAS before the control lever can be operated. It must always be moved slowly.

On the Mk 24, the filter is controlled from an electrical switch on the undercarriage selector quadrant marked NORMAL & CLEAN (filter in operation). On both marks the filter is always in circuit with the undercarriage down independent of the setting of the control.

Oil dilution The push-button for operating the solenoid valve is on the electrical panel.

Operational Equipment

Guns The guns are fired pneumatically (electrically on later Mk 24s) by means of a selective push-button on the control column spade grip. Pressing the top of the button fires the outboard guns, pressing the bottom of the button fires the inboard guns, and all four guns are fired simultaneously if the centre of the button is pressed. It is locked in the SAFE position by a catch at the bottom of the button casing. When the catch is pushed up to FIRE, a stud projects from the top of the casing.

Gyro gunsight The sight is mounted above the instrument panel. The selector is on the right-hand side of the cockpit. The caging button is on the control column to the right of the firing button.

Cine cameras A G.45 cine camera is mounted in the starboard wing root and is pneumatically operated by the gun firing button, or on some aircraft by separate push-button on the spade grip. There is a master switch on the electrical panel which must be ON before the camera will operate.

Bomb and R/P [Rocket Projectile] controls The bomb master switch and fusing switches, the PAIRS/SALVO and R/P-bomb selector switches are on the left-hand side of the cockpit. The bomb release-R/P firing button is fitted in the throttle lever grip.

Previous page: Spitfire F.24 VN485 was the 11th from last Spitfire to be delivered to the RAF. In September 1950 it was shipped to Hong Kong and served with No. 80 Squadron based at Kai Tak. In April 1955 it flew its last official sortie as part of a four-ship Spitfire formation for the Queen's Birthday Flypast. It was then placed in storage at Kai Tak having accrued just 242 hours of flying time. In 1989 it was gifted to the Imperial War Museum and is now on display inside 'AirSpace' at Duxford. VN465 is seen here on 10 August 1980 having been taken outside at Kai Tak. Via Doug Fisher

Left: The cockpit of a Spitfire F.22

Other Controls and Equipment

Cockpit door The cockpit door is fitted with a two-position catch which allows it to be partly open to ensure that the hood cannot slide shut when taking off and landing, and in the event of a forced landing. The catch operates more easily when the aircraft is airborne than when it is on the ground. Any attempt to wind the hood forward when the door is partly open may strain the hood or mechanism.

Windscreen de-icing A tank containing de-icing fluid is mounted on the lower right-hand side of the cockpit. There is a cock on the starboard side of the cockpit and a pump and needle valve further aft to control the flow of the fluid which is pumped to a spray at the base of the windscreen, over which it is blown by the slipstream. When no longer required the plunger should be locked down by the catch and the cock returned to the OFF position.

Navigation and identification lights The switch controlling the navigation lights is on the top of the electrical panel. The downward recognition lights are controlled by a signalling box on the right-hand side of the cockpit. Amber, red or green lights may be selected by a three-way switch on the right-hand side of the cockpit below the coaming.

Cockpit lighting This is provided by two lights mounted one on each side of the cockpit. The right-hand light may be moved vertically and the left-hand light may be moved in all directions. Both lights are shielded to prevent glare, and are operated by dimmer switches on the centre of the instrument panel.

Sliding hood
i. The 'teardrop' hood is opened and closed by a crank handle mounted on the right-hand cockpit wall, above the undercarriage selector lever. The handle must be pulled inwards before it can be operated. To lock the hood in any desired position it is only necessary to release the crank handle which then engages with the locking ratchet.
ii. From outside the cockpit the hood may be opened and closed by hand provided the push-button below the starboard hood rail is held depressed.
iii. The hood may be jettisoned in emergency.

Part II Handling

Final Checks for Take-Off

Trim	Rudder: Fully left (hand-wheel fully back)
Prop	Override lever fully forward
Fuel	Contents
	Main cock On
	Booster pump On
	Transfer cock Normal
Flaps	Up

Final Checks for Landing

Fuel	Contents
	Main cock On
	Booster Pump On
	Transfer cock Normal
Brakes	Off
	Check pressures
Wheels	Down and locked
Prop	2,600 RPM
Flaps	Down

Management of the fuel system
i) Order of use of the tanks
Main fuel system only
a) Start and warm up on the main tanks.
b) Take off on the main tanks and when the contents of the tank drops to the red mark on the gauge, transfer the fuel from one pair of wing tanks. Return the transfer valve selector cock to NORMAL after 5 minutes, then transfer the fuel from the other pair of wing tanks and return the selector to NORMAL after a further 5 minutes.
c) When all the fuel has been transferred, the selector cock must be left in the NORMAL position, otherwise pressurising of the main and rear tanks will not be effective.

When rear fuselage tanks are used
d) Start, warm up and take off on the main tanks.
e) At 2,000ft select the rear tanks by switching main booster pump OFF, rear tank cock ON, main tank cock OFF, and use rear booster pump as required.
f) When two to three gallons remain in the rear tank, turn ON the main tank cock and turn OFF the rear cock. For extreme range, turn ON the main cock leaving the rear cock and booster pump on until the rear tank empties. This happens quickly and to prevent damage to the pump by running dry it must be switched off not more than 5 minutes after turning ON the main tank. Proceed as in b) and c) above.

When fitted with a drop tank

g) Start, warm up and take off on the main tanks and change over to the drop tank at a safe height (2,000ft). Turn OFF the main tanks.

h) Owing to a possible delay in picking up after the engine-driven pump has run dry, it is recommended that the main tanks are turned ON and the drop tank is turned OFF before the drop tank is completely empty, working on a time basis. If it is essential to use all fuel from the drop tank proceed as follows:

(i) It must be run dry only at a safe height.

(ii) The drop tank cock should be turned OFF immediately and the main tank cock then turned ON.

(iii) The main booster pump should be turned on. Windmilling at high rpm will assist the engine to pick up.

i) If a tank has to be jettisoned before it is empty, first turn ON the main tanks then turn OFF the drop tank.

NOTE: It is necessary to ensure that the drop tank cock is in the fully OFF position when the tank is empty or has been jettisoned; otherwise, air may be sucked into the main fuel system.

When flying with full rear tanks and full drop tank

j) Use the rear tanks first as described in d), e) and f) above. Then use the drop tank as in g) and h) above, and finally the main and wing tanks as in b) and c).

Use of the booster pumps

The main tank booster pump should be switched on for take-off and landing. This, or the rear tank booster pump if that tank is in use, should be switched on at any time should the fuel pressure warning light come on. When climbing to high altitude the appropriate booster pump should be on for the tank in use.

Starting the engine and warming up

After carrying out the external, internal and cockpit checks, confirm:

Main fuel cock	ON
Wing transfer selector cock	NORMAL
Rear fuselage tank cock	OFF
Drop tank cock	OFF
Fuel cut-off control	Fully aft
Throttle	1½ inches open
Rpm override lever	Max rpm position
Priming selector cock	MAIN (GROUND for HV fuel)
Carburettor air-intake filter control	FILTER IN OPERATION (Mk 24: CLEAN)

With the fuel cut-off control fully aft, switch on the main tank booster pump for 30 seconds to prime the system. Switch off the booster pump

and after a few seconds, set the cut-off control fully forward.

Index the cartridge starter breech.

Operate the priming pump until the fuel reaches the priming nozzles; this may be judged by a sudden increase in resistance. High volatility fuel should be used for priming at air temperatures below freezing. Switch on the ignition. Prime with the following number of strokes if the engine is cold:

Air temperature °C:	+30	+20	+10	0	-10	-20
Normal fuel:	½	1	2	3	–	–
HV fuel:	–	–	–	1	2	3

If engine is warm after recent running it will not require priming.

Leave the priming pump plunger out and press the engine starter push-button: keep the button pressed until the engine is running steadily as it also operates the booster coil. It may be necessary to continue priming gently until the engine picks up on the carburettor.

Screw down the priming pump and turn off the priming selector cock.

Open up slowly to 1,200rpm and warm up at this speed.

If the engine fails to start on the first cartridge, subsequent priming action will depend on whether the engine was initially over or under primed. Normally no further priming should be given except for half a stroke as each subsequent cartridge is fired, or less if the air temperature is high.

Testing the engine and installations

After warming up until the oil temperature is 15°C, and the coolant temperature is 40°C:

i) Test each magneto for a dead cut as a precautionary check before increasing power further.

ii) Open up to the static boost reading (zero under standard atmosphere conditions) and check the operation of the supercharger by pressing and holding in the test push-button. Boost should rise slightly and the red light comes on when high gear is engaged. Release the test push-button, boost should then fall slightly and the red light goes out on return to low gear.

iii) At the same boost, exercise and check the operation of the constant speed unit by moving the rpm override lever through its full governing range, at least twice and then return it fully forward. Check that the rpm are within 50 of those normally obtained, and check that the generator warning light is out.

iv) Test each magneto in turn. The single ignition drop should not exceed 100rpm. If it exceeds 100rpm but there is no undue vibration, a full power check should be carried out. If there is marked vibration, the engine should be shut down and the cause investigated.

v) The following full power checks (for which the tail must be securely tied down) may also be carried out after repair, inspection other than

Right: Four Spitfires lined up in Hong Kong on 21 April 1955 ready for the Queen's Birthday Flypast. From nearest the camera they are VN318, VN485, PS854 and PS852. Courtesy Adrian Rowe-Evans

Far right: Flight Lieutenant Adrian Rowe-Evans taxies VN485 in after flying in the Queen's Birthday Flypast in Hong Kong on 21 April 1955. Courtesy Adrian Rowe-Evans

Below right: Spitfire F.24 VN485 on a sortie out of Kai Tak during the early 1950s. Courtesy Adrian Rowe-Evans

daily, when the single ignition drop at the static boost reading exceeds 100rpm or at the discretion of the pilot. Except in these circumstances no useful purpose will be served by a full power check.

The full power checks should be carried out as follows:

a) Open the throttle fully and check take-off boost and rpm.

b) Throttle back until the rpm fall, thus ensuring that the propeller is not constant speeding and test each magneto. If the single ignition drop exceeds 100rpm the aircraft should not be flown.

c) Throttle back to +4lb/in^2 boost and set the rpm override to AUTOMATIC when rpm should fall to 1,800. Return the override lever to the maximum rpm position.

vi) After completing the checks either at static boost or full power, steadily move the throttle lever to the fully closed position and check the minimum idling rpm, then open up to 1,200rpm.

Take-off

i) For normal take-off, open the throttle slowly up to about +7lb/in^2 only. There is a strong tendency to swing to the right and to crab in the initial stages, and if too much power is used, tyre wear is severe. Power should be increased, consistent with rudder control, to +12lb/in^2 boost on becoming airborne, to ensure adequate clearing of the engine. The aircraft should be flown off at a speed of approximately 90kts. At the maximum load with the rear fuselage tanks full, the aircraft may tend to pitch slightly immediately after leaving the ground.

ii) After raising the undercarriage, see that the red indicator light – UP – comes on and the tailwheel light goes out. It may be necessary to hold the lever hard forward against the quadrant until the red indicator light does come on. Failure of the wheels to lock up will spoil the airflow through the radiators and oil cooler and result in excessive temperatures.

NOTE: The undercarriage should always be raised before a speed of 140kts (160mph) IAS has been attained; otherwise the fairing doors may be damaged.

iii) Move the override lever smoothly to AUTOMATIC when comfortably airborne.

iv) Unless operating in sandy or dust-laden conditions, set the air-intake filter control to NORMAL INTAKE at 1,000ft.

Climbing

i) The recommended speed for a normal climb is 150kts (175mph) IAS from sea level up to 25,000ft, reduced speed thereafter by 2kts per 1,000ft.

ii) On a combat climb the supercharger will automatically change to high gear at 11,000ft, but under normal conditions (2,600rpm and +9lb/in^2 boost) the maximum rate of climb is obtained by delaying the gear change until the boost has dropped to +6¼lb/in^2. To do this, fly with the override switch in the MS position until the boost has fallen to this figure.

iii) Use of the air-intake filter considerably reduces the full throttle height.

General flying

i) Stability

At all altitudes with the rear fuselage tanks empty and at low altitudes with those tanks full, the aircraft is easy to trim and there is no tendency to tighten in turns. At high altitudes, with the rear fuselage tanks full, the aircraft will not maintain trimmed flight with hands off the controls and there is a tendency to tighten in turns. In this condition the aircraft should be restricted to gentle manoeuvres only. Excessive supplication of yaw induces a marked change in longitudinal trim. This characteristic becomes very noticeable at high altitudes.

ii) Controls

The ailerons remain very light and effective throughout the speed range. Both the rudder, elevator and their trimming tabs are powerful and sensitive but the rudder becomes heavier as speed increases.

iii) Changes of trim

Flaps down – Nose up

Flaps up – Nose down

Movement of the undercarriage in either direction or operation of the hood promotes little change of trim. Changes of power and speed induce marked changes in directional trim. These should be countered by careful and accurate use of the rudder trimming tab.

iv) Flying at reduced airspeed

Reduce speed to 140kts and lower the flaps. Set the rpm override lever to AUTOMATIC and open the hood. Fly at about 140kts keeping a close watch on oil and coolant temperatures. The stalling speed under these conditions is about 60kts.

v) Cruising at lower powers

To avoid the possibility of lead fouling of the plugs when operating at reduced rpm and low inlet temperatures, it is recommended that the engine be cleared at climbing power for at least one minute each hour in cruising flight and before landing.

Stalling

i) The stalling speeds (engine off) in knots (mph) IAS are:

	Typical service load	Typical service load plus 90-gal tank
Undercarriage and flaps up	75 (85)	80 (92)
Undercarriage and flaps down	65 (75)	70 (80)

ii) On Mk 24 aircraft with full rear fuselage tanks the above stalling speeds are increased by approximately 4kts (or mph)

Left: Spitfire F.22 PK312 flying in formation with two Spitfire Mk.XVIIIs. British Official

iii) When carrying RP, bombs or other external stores, the above speeds are increased by approx 5kts (or mph).

iv) There is little warning of the approach of the stall. At the stall either wing or the nose may drop, accompanied by snatching of the ailerons, which is more marked with the undercarriage and flaps down. Recovery is straight-forward and easy.

v) High-speed stall. If the aircraft is stalled in a turn or in the recovery from a dive, some warning is given by juddering. The aircraft will flick to the right with strong aileron snatching. Recovery is immediate if the pressure on the control column is relaxed.

Spinning

i) Practice spinning is permitted and recovery by the standard method is normal.

ii) The spin itself is erratic, the nose rising and falling and the rate of rotation varying, increasing as the nose falls and decreasing as it rises. This characteristic is more marked at high altitude.

NOTE: (a) Practice spinning should not be commenced below 10,000ft.
(b) Recovery action should be initiated after not more than two turns of the spin have been completed.

iii) Spinning is not permitted when carrying a drop tank or external stores.

Diving

i) As speed is gained the aircraft becomes increasingly tail heavy and should, therefore, be trimmed into the dive. The tendency to yaw to port should be corrected by accurate use of the rudder trimming tab.

ii) No attempt should be made to reach the maximum diving speed at heights above 10,000ft; otherwise, compressibility effects may be encountered. These effects produce a nose down change of trim. If such a change of trim is observed it must be held on the control column alone and no attempt must be made to correct it with the elevator trimming tab, for while this action will not immediately prove effective, it is likely to render the recovery violent when the Mach number falls at a lower altitude. It is equally important to avoid yawing the aircraft in an attempt to reduce speed.

Aerobatics

The following speeds in knots (mph) IAS are recommended:

Loop	280–300 (320–350)
Roll	190–220 (220–250)
Half roll off loop	300–340 (350–400)
Upward roll	300–390 (350–450)

Flick manoeuvres are not permitted.

Approach and landing

The recommended final approach speeds in knots (mph) IAS are

	At normal landing weight
	9,300lb (Mk 22)
	9,650lb (Mk 24)

	Flaps down	Flaps Up
Engine assisted	90 (100)	95 (110)
Glide	95 (110)	100 (115)

NOTE: i) The initial straight approach should be made some 20kts or mph IAS above these figures.

ii) When landing with a drop tank, RP, bombs or full rear fuselage tanks, the above speeds should be increased by about 5 to 8kts or mph.

iii) Pilots should be prepared for a tendency to swing after landing.

Mislanding

i) The aircraft will climb away easily with the undercarriage and flaps lowered, and the use of full take-off power is unnecessary. The throttle should be opened slowly, and care taken to ensure that adequate control is maintained. The torque effect of the Griffon engine is opposite to that of all Merlin engines and is considerably greater.

ii) Raise the undercarriage.

iii) Climb at 130–140kts (150–160mph) IAS with the flaps lowered.

iv) Raise the flaps at a safe height (300–400ft) and retrim.

After Landing

i) After reaching dispersal, if the serviceability of the engine is in doubt, such items of the run up given earlier as may be necessary should be carried out. In all cases, however, the engine should be idled at 800–900rpm for half a minute and then stopped by moving the fuel cut-off control to the fully aft position.

ii) Oil dilution

a) The oil level should be adjusted to the normal full level.

b) To ensure a satisfactory start without pre-heating at the following outside air temperatures, dilution for the periods quoted is required:

| 10°C to 15°C | 1 min |
| 15°C to 26°C | 2 mins |

c) No special partial boiling off precautions are necessary.

Part III

Engine data – Griffon 61

i) Fuel – 100 octane.
ii) Engine limitations:

		Rpm	Boost Lb/In^2	Temp. °C Coolant	Oil
Max Take-Off to 1,000ft	M	2,750	+12	–	–
Max Climbing 1 Hour Limit	M } S }	2,600	+9	125	90
Max Continuous	M } S }	2,400	+7	105 (115)	90
Combat	M }	2,750*	+18	135	105
5 Mins Limit	S }				

NOTE: The figure in brackets is permitted for short periods.
IMPORTANT: (a) Rpm must not exceed 2,600 when changing gear.
(b) Combat boost must not be used at less than 2,600rpm.

Oil Pressure

Normal	60–80lb/in^2
Minimum	45lb/in^2

Minimum Temp for Take-Off

Oil	15°C
Coolant	60°C

Flying limitations
i) (a) The following diving speed limitations apply to both marks:

Between	knots	mph
SL and 10,000ft	450	520
10,000–15,000ft	410	475
15,000–20,000ft	375	435
20,000–25,000ft	340	390
25,000–30,000ft	300	345
30,000–35,000ft	270	310
Above 35,000ft	240	275
Undercarriage down	170	200
Flaps down	140	160

(b) With Triplex RP a speed of 408kts (470mph) IAS must not be exceeded below 15,000ft. Above this height as in (a).
(c) When carrying 500lb or 200lb No. 2 Mark 2, smoke floats, a speed of 390kts (450mph) IAS must not be exceeded below 15,000ft. Above this height as in (a).

(d) With a 90-gallon drop tank, the following speeds must not be exceeded:

	knots	mph
SL and 10,000ft	380	440
10,000–15,000ft	350	405
15,000–20,000ft	315	365
20,000–25,000ft	280	325
25,000–30,000ft	250	290

NOTE: With 30-, 45- or 50-gallon drop tanks the above restrictions do not apply.

ii) Maximum weights

	Mk 22	Mk 24
For take-off and gentle manoeuvres only	11,350lb	12,150lb
For all forms of flying	9,300lb	10,150lb
For landing except in emergency	9,300lb	9,650lb

ii) Restrictions
Practice spinning is prohibited and violent manoeuvres should be avoided when a drop tank or other external stores are carried.
At high altitudes with the rear fuselage tank more than half full the aircraft should be restricted to gentle manoeuvres only.
Drop tanks should be jettisoned in straight flight at a speed of not more than 260kts (300mph) IAS.

Maximum Performance
i. Climbing:
a) The recommended speed for a normal climb is 150kts (170mph) IAS from sea level up to 25,000ft, reducing speed thereafter by 2kts or 3mph per 1,000ft.
b) On a combat climb the supercharger will automatically change to high gear at 11,000ft, but under normal climbing conditions (2,600rpm and +9lb/in^2 boost) the maximum rate of climb is obtained by delaying the gear change until the boost has dropped to +6½lb/in^2. To do this, fly with the override switch in the MS position until the boost has fallen to this figure.
c) Use of the air-intake filter considerably reduces the full-throttle height.
Combat:
ii. Set the supercharger override switch to AUTO and open the throttle fully.

Economical flying

i. Climbing:

a) With the propeller override lever at AUTO set the supercharger switch to MS, set the throttle to give +7lb/in^2 boost and climb at the speeds given above.

b) As height is gained the boost will fall, but the throttle should not be advanced to restore it, since rpm will then be increased beyond the maximum permitted for continuous operation.

When the boost has fallen to +3lb/in^2 set the supercharger switch to AUTO.

ii. Cruising:

a) The recommended speed for maximum range is 170–180kts (200–210mph) IAS.

b) With the propeller override lever at AUTO set the supercharger switch to MS and adjust the throttle to obtain the recommended speed. Avoid a throttle setting which promotes rough running.

NOTE: At moderate and high altitudes, it will be necessary to advance the throttle progressively to restore the falling boost and thus maintain the recommended speed. Now, as the throttle is opened, rpm will increase and at a certain height, the recommended speed will be unobtainable even at a throttle setting which gives 2,400rpm. At this height, the supercharger switch should be set to AUTO, and the throttle then adjusted as before to maintain the recommended speed.

Fuel capacities and consumptions

i. Normal fuel capacity

Top tank	36 gallons
Bottom tank	48 gallons
Two wing tanks (12½ gallons each)	25 gallons
Two wing tanks (5½ gallons each)	11 gallons
Mk 22 Total	**120 gallons**

Two rear fuselage tanks (33 gallons each)
66 gallons

Mk 24 Total	186 gallons

ii. Long-range fuel capacities

	Mk 22	Mk 24 with rear fuel
(a) With 30-gallon drop tank	150 gals	216 gals
(b) With 45-gallon drop tank	165 gals	231 gals
(c) With 50-gallon drop tank	170 gals	236 gals
(d) With 90-gallon drop tank	210 gals	276 gals

Below left: A profile study of F.24 VN315. Air Ministry

Below VN485 seen at Sek Kong in 1954 during an armament practice camp while serving with the Hong Kong Auxilliary Air Force.

Below: Alex Henshaw seen on an air test in F.22 PK312 during April 1945. Via François Prins

Below right: A nice topside view of F.22 PK312 showing this variant's four cannon arrangement nicely. British Official

Following page: While there are no airworthy Spitfire F.22s or F.24s in the world today, the closely related Mk.XVIII can be seen at UK air shows in the form of SM845 seen here being flown by Squadron Leader Ian Smith MBE at Duxford. Jarrod Cotter

iii. Fuel consumptions (approx. gals/hr)
a) Weak mixture (as obtained at +7lb/in² boost and below) in low gear at 5,000ft:

Boost lb/in² rpm	2,400	2,200	2,000	1,800
+7	88	85	80	–
+4	74	71	67	60
+2	65	63	59	52
0	57	55	51	46
-2	50	47	43	41

NOTE: For every 5,000ft increase in height add 4gals/hr.

b) Weak mixture (as obtained at +7lb/in² boost and below) in high gear at 20,000ft:

Boost lb/in² rpm	2,400	2,200	2,000	1,800
+7	95	92	87	–
+4	82	78	74	70
+2	73	70	66	63
0	66	63	59	56
-2	59	56	52	49

NOTE: For every 5,000ft increase in height add 4gals/hr.

c) Rich mixture (as obtained above +7lb/in² boost) in low gear at 5,000ft.

Boost lb/in² rpm	rpm	Gals/hr
+18	2,750	180
+12	2,750	130
+9	2,600	103

Flying the Mk 24

Flying Officer Gordon H.G. Bowtle flew Spitfire F.24s with 80 Squadron at Kai Tak, Hong Kong, from 1949 to 1951. In 1967 he wrote about his experiences of this, and edited extracts follow here:

The Spitfire 24 was not an easy aircraft to fly, totally lacking the docility displayed by earlier marks. With its increased weight, high speed wing, far more power, and lengthened undercarriage legs, take-offs and landings were invariably interesting; the aircraft had a marked inclination to swing with little reason when groundborne, and the results were amusing to watch – from a safe distance. Flying high performance fighters from Kai Tak was an engrossing occupation, most of the interest and hazard arising from the geographical features.

It was soon found that the dangers of flying near to and in the lee of mountains had to be ignored. Each pilot averaged at least 10 hours each month flying at very low altitude in close or battle formation up and down the twisting valleys, and learned how to judge the effects of turbulence. Constant practice taught them how to operate and attack targets at the base of cliffs, on hill flanks, and in the steep-sided valleys. With its great manoeuvrability and power, the Mk 24 was an ideal aircraft for these conditions.

The Griffon-engined Mk 24 was an improved Mk 22, with a new fin and rudder, longer and stronger undercarriage and other minor changes. Compared with earlier Marks, the brakes were powerful and free from fading. The highly efficient flying controls gave outstanding and initially disturbing response over the whole speed range. Once a pilot had grown accustomed to the increased engine noise and relative roughness, and mastered the sensitive feel, the Spitfire 24 became an exhilarating aircraft and a challenge to the pilot's skill. With the combination of small airframe, high power, it could be put through a full aerobatic schedule in a limited airspace; and with the big, tabbed ailerons, rolling was a delight, very slow rolls and hesitation being performed with precision. Loops were possible from level flight at 200kts, but needed constant change of rudder trim to counteract torque effects with the varying speed.

The aircraft was basically stable, and one pilot (Sgt Bennett) flew one back with inoperative elevator controls, completing an overshoot and landing with throttle and trim tabs. The Mk 24 was

easy to fly in the circuit, but had to be handled with care on landing, and required a threshold speed of 90kts. The landing roll in zero wind and high ambient temperature was 500–600 yards. Weapons training included the novel experience of rocket firing at a moving target – a splash target towed by HMS Charity. The Spitfire 24 was equipped with four pairs of zero length RP launchers and bomb carriers on each wing. A typical load would be four 60lb rockets, two 250lb bombs and 175 rounds per cannon. Thirty degree dives from 3,000ft were standard for air-to-ground strafing and RP firing, sixty degree dives from 8,000ft with release at 3,000ft for dive-bombing. The Mk 24 was a good gunnery platform, and its fine control response permitted a good steady run even in turbulent conditions. During pull-out from a dive, the pilot could easily become completely blacked out, recovering in the climb back up. Low level bombing was complicated by the target disappearing under the nose before the release point was reached, and similarly, large angle deflection shooting became a question of guesswork. If one cannon stopped, the asymmetric recoil yawed the aircraft and the shoot had to stop. Napalm was not used.

The aircraft were dispersed in the open, exposed to extremes of heat, humidity, and rain, yet serviceability was good; the little hangar accommodation available was reserved for major repairs and inspections. The Spitfires proved to be prone to radiator damage from flying debris during ground attacks, and several aircraft were damaged in take-off and landing incidents.

Early in 1950 the Royal Engineers bulldozed a landing strip amongst the paddy fields in a valley at Sek Kong, covering the rolled earth with long strips of tarred felt. The pounding of the Spitfires and the fierce biting slipstream broke the welded seams of the felt strips, and very soon each Spitfire taking off was chased by a billowing wave of felt as high as the top of the rudder. The squadron returned to Kai Tak.

The Sek Kong strip was in due course resurfaced with PSP, and No. 80 Squadron returned to life in the paddy fields. Unfortunately, this coincided with monsoon rains and the camp was flooded over-night. With the outbreak of the Korean War the Wing was alerted, invasion stripes were painted on the aircraft, the aircrew were armed with revolvers and dusk-to-dawn patrols were reinstated.

The dawn patrol produced new problems, for take-off was at dawn minus 30 minutes. In the absence of runway lighting, two hurricane lamps were hung from poles on either side of the end of the runway. With the engine running and producing long orange flames from the exhaust stubs, the aircraft lined up. Take-off was started on instruments, and sometimes completed without catching sight of the lamps through the exhaust glare. When the aircraft were pointing toward the tents, only the braver remained in situ, the rest taking cover in the ditches. Landing in the early morning on the narrow strip, into a low sun, was handicapped by the blinding flashing of the prop blades, only the clanking of the PSP proving that the landing was on target.

In direct comparison with contemporary jet fighters, the Spitfire 24 came out well ahead in all respects except level flight at medium altitudes. With a limiting speed Mach 0.15 higher than the Meteor or Vampire, a service ceiling and speed at height better than the Meteor, Vampire, Phantom 1 or F-80, ability to out-turn all-comers and the ability to operate from 1,200-yard strips with a full service load, it was hard to believe that no further use could be found for this superb fighting machine. How long can the too few survivors be kept flying, to wring our hearts with nostalgia?

It is no longer just a dream!

Until recently the opportunity for an enthusiast to fly in a Spitfire in the UK was extremely rare, as for a long time the Civil Aviation Authority (CAA) had not allowed paid-for flights to be made in warbirds that were given a 'Permit to Fly' only. Therefore, for an author who was privileged and lucky enough to go on such a flight it was mostly considered 'taboo' to write about it, as it could make them unpopular with their readership!

However, in these modern times, with such an increase in the demand for adventure sports that involve far greater risks than flying in an immaculately maintained aircraft, attitudes have changed and the CAA has now issued guidelines allowing passenger flights in aircraft such as the Spitfire Tr.IX. The guide-lines predominantly state that the passenger must have the slightly enhanced risks involved in flying in a Spitfire, as opposed to an airliner, clearly explained to them and they must be fully understood.

Among the pioneers who offered this experience was Aero Legends, with flights available from Headcorn in Kent or Sywell in Northamptonshire. Would-be 'Spitfire pilots' have the option to participate in a multiple package, which takes them through three stages of a pilot's training – the de Havilland Tiger Moth, then the more powerful North American Harvard and culminates with a 30-minute flight in the Aircraft Restoration Company's (ARC's) Spitfire Tr.IX PV202. Alternatively, a Spitfire passenger flight is available on its own and, as already mentioned, at one time this was not possible so it really is a chance for enthusiasts now to be able to take that once in a lifetime experience.

The thrill begins long before you walk out to the iconic fighter you are about to fly in – in fact the night before if not even earlier! But after your briefing as you approach the open side hatch you really get the sense of reality that this is going to happen. Once you climb aboard and settle into the seat, your immediate action is to look around at your surroundings, something you've done many times before but perhaps only in books and on the screen, before you take an impulsive look out over the Spitfire's trademark elliptical wings from the position of being inside the cockpit – instead of viewing them from on the ground. You are then strapped into your parachute, before

'The thrill begins long before you walk out to the iconic fighter you are about to fly in – in fact the night before if not even earlier!'

Right: The view ahead from Spitfire Tr.IX PV202 on a sortie out of Headcorn in Kent. Jarrod Cotter

the harness straps are fastened secure. It's then time for a final safety briefing of the emergency handles and on goes your flying helmet, which is plugged in, to the immediate accompaniment of radio crackle. Then the groundcrew will close and secure your access door, and the pilot takes over your care via the intercom. He will firstly check that you feel comfortable, something that will be a frequent question throughout the flight as your comfort in the air will be vital to your enjoyment and appreciation of the flight. The pilot will then go through the pre-start checks, and as the engine bursts into life a mist of exhaust smoke will drift past you on both sides before it quickly disappears, and the characteristic sound of a Rolls-Royce Merlin fills the air around you. Now you have entered the world of the Spitfire pilot!

The next job is to carry out the after-starting checks, which include seeing that the oil pressure is rising and making sure that the magnetos are functioning correctly. This procedure is followed by the taxying checks, and as soon as the radiator temperature and brake pressures are within limits the pilot will ask that you are still ok and then taxi out towards the in-use runway, weaving from side to side to ensure he has a clear view ahead as crackles and pops erupt from the exhaust stubs as small amounts of power are applied and reduced as necessary.

When the Spitfire is out at the holding point the pilot will turn it into wind, ask you to make certain that your canopy is closed, then go through the power checks. Once he has established that the engine is in good order to make the flight, it's time for the pre-take-off tests, which after the technical checks conclude with asking you again to confirm that your canopy is closed and that your harness is tight and locked, then once more that you are still comfortable. You're now ready to get airborne!

With clearance granted from Air Traffic Control, out you go and line up in the direction of take-off. With one final check from the pilot that you're good to go, he will increase the throttle slowly up through the gate to take-off boost and as the Merlin in front of you roars loudly your speed increases rapidly and in a short space of time the elliptical wings distance themselves from the ground below you. That's it, no one can take it away from you – you have become airborne in an iconic piece of Britain's aviation heritage.

But the best is yet to come. On a beautiful sunny day you will climb into the wild blue yonder, soon skimming around the edges of puffy white cumulus clouds, looking out over the Spitfire's wings in amazement and thinking that this moment will remain dominant in your memory for the rest of your life, a moment you have probably dreamt of on so many occasions while watching Spitfires flying at air shows.

'I have control'

My chance to fly a Spitfire came at Headcorn on 22 June 2014, when an informal launch of Aero Legends was arranged on a summer Sunday at this charming facility, which is the last grass aerodrome left in Kent. The airfield's location in the heart of Kent allows passengers to fly through the same airspace in which the Battle of Britain was fought in 1940, plus its close proximity to the coast allows for flying over the White Cliffs of Dover and the emotive clifftop Battle of Britain Memorial at Capel-le-Ferne.

I had flown solo while in the Air Cadets and have since been very fortunate to take the controls of numerous Second World War and historic aircraft and modern jets. These include the Tiger Moth, Chipmunk, Harvard, Mustang and Harrier, so I had experienced a reasonable range of handling characteristics and was consequently afforded the opportunity to take the controls of the Spitfire. I had often heard it called a 'pilot's aeroplane' and witnessed even modern RAF fighter pilots who have flown hundreds and even thousands of hours in state-of-the-art fast jets be very emotional after their first flight in a Spitfire, so there I was about to try it for myself and see why all that had been said and done.

My pilot was a good friend, Dave 'Rats' Ratcliffe of ARC, and once I had announced to him that 'I have control' in a calm and reassured voice (but with a massive grin hidden away in the rear cockpit behind him as I grasped the famous spade grip), I was immediately impressed by the lightness of the inputs required to manoeuvre those broad, elliptical wings of the Spitfire due to the superbly harmonised controls of this masterpiece of design. On commenting on this to Rats he replied, 'Yeah, it almost flies itself!'

Then it was time for the moment I think would be pinnacle of almost any pilot's flying career – to perform a victory roll in a Spitfire! Dave had taken control back from me and gone through the manoeuvre with me himself, all the time describing what control inputs he was putting in while I followed him through with my right hand lightly placed on the spade grip, before handing control over, and then beginning a talk through of the control inputs I was to do. As the victory roll is a climbing manoeuvre and we had gained several hundred feet during Dave's perfectly flown example, I firstly needed to put the Spit into a shallow dive to reach at least 180kts. Dave then told me to begin to pull back on the control column to climb at 20° of pitch, which effected a force of about +3G on to us. I then began a gentle roll to the left and as the wings tilted over looked out of the top of the canopy until I saw the ground directly 'above' me, which gave me the situational awareness that I had reached the inverted position as I continued the roll, all the time still climbing. As I regained a normal attitude I had climbed about 600–700ft, and had now flown the famous Spitfire victory roll myself!

Flying in a Spitfire used to be 'every schoolboy's dream' as people have said for several generations, and for many years I believed it would remain just a dream for me. But thanks to the hard work of those who run Aero Legends it had become a reality. I now had a far greater appreciation of all that I had read about for so many years from the likes of Jeffrey Quill, Alex Henshaw, 'Johnnie' Johnson and their peers.

Even if I was never to fly again, the disappointment could soon be overcome by thinking back to that day I looked out over those beautiful elliptical wings skirting around perfectly puffy white clouds in the skies over Kent.

Previous page 160, clockwise from top left: The author in the rear cockpit of PV202 just before fulfilling all those boyhood dreams of flying a Spitfire. Andrea Featherby

Having been put into a shallow dive to build up speed, PV202 is pulled skywards into a loop. Jarrod Cotter

Dave Ratcliffe retracts the undercarriage of PV202 just after take-off with the author in the rear cockpit. Andrea Featherby

Previous page 161, top PV202 being flown by Dave Ratcliffe on a local sortie out of Headcorn. Andrea Featherby

Previous page 161, below Over goes the Spitfire at the top of a loop. Jarrod Cotter

Below: Looking out over the iconic elliptical wing of PV202 as the Spitfire pulls up in a steep climb during an aerobatic manoeuvre.
Jarrod Cotter

Right: The view from the rear cockpit of PV202 turning in the summer skies over Kent.
Jarrod Cotter

Appendix 1
Spitfire Mk IX Pilot's Check Lists

Ensure that the Spitfire is in a suitable position for starting and taxying, and that its wings are level, there are no fuel, oil or coolant leaks, a ground fire extinguisher is available and that the chocks are in position.

Cockpit

Hood	Operation And Cleanliness
Hood Jettison Knob	Not Pulled
Mirror	Secure And Clean
Ignition Switches	Off
Ground/Flight Switch	Ground
Landing Gear Selector	Down, In The Gate. Idle Indicated
Cockpit Access Door	Condition Of Hinges And Bolts
Crowbar	Secure
Dinghy (If Fitted)	In Position
Pneumatic Pressure	120psi Minimum
Control Locks	Removed
Radiator Flaps	Auto

External Checks

Carry out a systematic check of the aircraft for obvious signs of damage, leaks, loose panels or fairings. At the same time make the following specific checks:

Port mainplane

Flap	Up, mechanical indicator flush
Aileron	Full/free movement. Leave neutral
Nav light	Secure. Condition
Pitot mast	Secure. Condition
Pressure head	Cover removed. Condition
Oil cooler	Intake and matrix unobstructed
Radiator	Matrix unobstructed

Landing gear:

Wheel well	General condition
D door	Secure. Undamaged
Oleo	Condition. Extension

Brake pipe	Secure. Check for leaks and chafing. Ensure clear of wheel and ground
Tyre	Cuts, creep and wear. Correct inflation and valve free
Engine air intake	Unobstructed. No excess fuel
Engine cowling fasteners	Secure
Port exhaust stubs	Secure. No undrilled cracks
Propeller blades	Undamaged
Starboard exhaust stubs	Secure. No undrilled cracks
Engine cowling fasteners	Secure

Starboard mainplane

Starboard landing gear	As for port landing gear
Cooling radiator	Intake and matrix unobstructed. Fuel vent pipe undamaged
Nav light	Secure. Condition
Aileron	Neutral. Full/free movement
Flap	Up. Mechanical indicator flush

Tail unit

Elevators	Full and free movement. Condition of tabs
Rudder	Full and free movement. Condition of tab
Tail wheel tyre	Cuts, creep and wear. Correct inflation and valve free

Port fuselage

Baggage pannier panel	Secure
Radio mast	Secure. Condition

Internal Checks

Strap in and adjust seat and rudder pedals

Ground/flight switch	Flight
Landing gear lights	DOWN (green)
Flying controls	Full, free and correct movement

Wheelbrakes lever	On, parked
	(minimum 120psi per wheel)
Radio	On and checked
Cockpit access door	Closed or half cock.
	Check front and rear bolts properly
	engaged
Fuse box	Cover secure
Pressure head heater	OFF
Rudder trim	Fuel and free movement. Set fully right
	(white lines aligned)
Elevator trim	Full and free movement checked
	against indicator. Set ½ division up
	from 3 o'clock
Supercharger selector	Wire-locked MS.
	Warning light out
Radiator flaps	AUTO (Mk IX)

Throttle quadrant:

Mixture control	Fully back
Friction wheel	Adjusted
Propeller pitch control	Fully forward
Throttle	Set ¼ inch open
Ignition switches	OFF
Pneumatic pressure	Min. 120psi
Nav lights	Off
Flap selector	UP
Generator warning light	On
Accelerometer	Reset
Fuel press warning light	On
Voltmeter	24 volts
Flight instruments	Condition
Compass and DI	Serviceable. Synchronise DI, leave caged
Engine instruments	Condition
Fuel gauge	Contents
Fuel cock	ON, gated
Priming pump	Unscrewed and loaded
Start isolate switch	ON
Harness release	As required

Landing gear emergency	
Air bottle	Lever vertical and wire-locked

Starting

Prime the engine normally	
5–7 strokes, then:	
Groundcrew	Pilot to call 'prop clear' and hear
	response
Ignition switches	ON
Control column	Fully back
Start and Boost Coil buttons	Press BOOST then both together
When the engine fires:	Release the START button keeping the
	BOOST COIL button pressed until the
	engine runs smoothly.
	WARNING: Do not pump the throttle
	during engine start.

Failure to start

1. Engine turns freely but does not fire. Check:

Ignition switches	ON
Air intake for excessive fuel	
Throttle ¼ inch open	

If there is no obvious reason for failure to start, use one more stroke of the priming pump and try a further start.

2. Engine turns, flames appear from the exhaust banks but the engine does not run. Continue to turn the engine on the starter until the flames are extinguished. Then, if the engine does not start:

Ignition switches	OFF
Throttle	Fully open
START button	Press for 9 propeller tips
Throttle	Set ¼ inch open

Ignition switches	ON
START and BOOST COIL buttons	Press BOOST then both together

3. Engine does not turn: Check:

Start isolate switch	ON

Note: The engine starter motor operating limits are:

a. Maximum 20 seconds continuous.
b. 30 seconds cooling time between each operation.
c. After 3 operations, each of 20 seconds, wait 3 minutes before a further operation.

After-starting checks

Oil pressure	Rising
RPM	Set 1,000rpm
Fuel pressure warning light	Out
Generator warning light	Out
Starter isolate switch	OFF
Priming pump	Screwed fully down
Ignition switches	Check magnetos (maximum drop 1,000rpm)
Radiator flaps (Mk IX)	Manual OPEN
Radio	Taxi clearance
Altimeter	Set
DI	Synchronised, uncaged

Taxying Checks

Flight instruments	Checked
Radiator temperature and brake pressures	Make frequent checks

Testing the Engine

Face the aircraft into the wind, set the brakes on and parked and

hold the control column fully back. Ensure:

Oil temperature	15°C minimum
Radiator temperature	40°C minimum
RPM	Set 1,500rpm
Ignition switches	Switch OFF each in turn (maximum drop 100rpm)
Throttle	Closed, idle 550 to 650rpm
RPM	Reset 1,000rpm

Take-Off Checks

Checks before take-off

Trim	Elevator set ½ division up from 3 o'clock Rudder fully right
Throttle friction	Tight
Mixture control	Fully back
Propeller pitch control	Fully forward
Pressure head heater	As required

Fuel:

Fuel cock	ON
Low pressure warning light	Out
Priming pump	Screwed fully down
Contents	Sufficient
Flaps	UP, mechanical indicators flush
Radiator flaps	Open
Gyros	DI synchronised, uncaged.
Artificial horizon erect	
Hood	As required
Harness	Tight and locked

Runway checks

DI	Check against runway heading
Temperatures and pressures	Within limits

After-take-off checks

Brakes	On, then off
Landing gear	UP, red lights on
Boost	+4psi
RPM	2,400rpm
Hood	As required
Engine instruments	Temperatures and pressures
Radiator flaps	As required

Landing Checks

Field approach checks

Fuel	Check contents
QFE	Set
DI	Synchronised with compass
Radiator flap(s)	Open
Harness	Tight and locked
RPM	2,650rpm

Pre-landing checks

Pneumatic pressure	Sufficient
Landing gear	Down (below 120kts (VNO)/140kts (VNE)) Indicates DOWN (green). Hydraulic indicator IDLE. Lever in gate
Propeller pitch control	Fully forward
Flaps	Down (below 120kts), mechanical indicators up
Hood	As required

Checks on final approach

Landing gear	DOWN (green). IDLE
Pneumatic pressure	Checked

Overshoot or mislanding

Throttle	Set +4psi boost

Landing gear	UP
Climb initially at 75–80kts	
At a minimum height of 200ft:	
Flaps	UP
Increase IAS to 90kts	

After-landing checks

Pressure head heater	OFF
Flaps	UP, indicators flush
Radiator flaps	Check open
Pneumatic and brake pressures	120psi minimum
Throttle friction	Adjusted

Shutdown Checks

Carry out a magneto check at 1,500rpm. Run the engine at 800 to 900rpm for 30 seconds then:

Radiator flaps	AUTO
Throttle	Closed
Slow running cut-out	Operate
Ignition switches	OFF when propeller stops
Fuel cock	OFF
Radio	OFF
Nav and cockpit lights	OFF if used
DI	Caged
Ground/flight switch	Ground
Braked	Off when chocks in place

Appendix 2
Wartime Emergency Procedures

Undercarriage emergency operation
(i) If the selector lever jams and cannot be moved to the fully down position after moving it out of the gate, return it to the fully forward position for a few seconds to take the weight of the wheels off the locking pins and allow them to turn freely, then move it to the DOWN position.
(ii) If, however, the lever is jammed so that it cannot be moved either forward or downward, it can be released by taking the weight of the wheels off the locking pins either by pushing the control column forward sharply or inverting the aircraft. The lever can then be moved to the DOWN position.
(iii) If the lever springs into the gate and the indicator shows that the undercarriage is not locked down, hold it fully down for a few seconds. If this is not successful, raise and then lower the undercarriage again.
(iv) If the undercarriage still does not lock down, ensure that the lever is in the DOWN position (this is essential) and push the emergency lever forward and downward through 180°.
NOTE: (a) The emergency lever must not be returned to its original position and no attempt must be made to raise the undercarriage until the CO_2 cylinder has been replaced.
(b) If the CO_2 cylinder has been accidentally discharged with the selector lever in the up position, the undercarriage will not lower unless the pipeline from the cylinder is broken, either by hand or by means of the crowbar.

Failure of the pneumatic system
(i) If the flaps fail to lower when the control is moved to the DOWN position, it is probably due to a leak in the pipeline, resulting in complete loss of air pressure and consequent brake failure.
(ii) Alternatively, if a leak develops in the flaps control system the flaps will lower, but complete loss of air pressure will follow and the brakes will become inoperative. (In this case a hissing sound may be heard in the cockpit after selecting flaps DOWN.)

(iii) In either case the flaps control should immediately be returned to the UP position in order to allow sufficient pressure to build up, so that a landing can be made with the brakes operative but without flaps.
NOTE: As a safeguard pilots should always check the pneumatic pressure supply after selecting flaps DOWN.

Hood jettisoning
The hood may be jettisoned in an emergency by pulling the knob inside the top of the hood forward and downward and then pushing the lower edge of the hood outwards with the elbows.
WARNING: Before jettisoning the hood the seat should be lowered and the head then kept well down.

Forced landing
In the event of engine failure necessitating a forced landing:
(i) If a drop tank or bomb load is carried it should be jettisoned.
(ii) The fuel cut-off control (if fitted) should be pulled fully back.
(iii) The booster pump (if fitted) should be switched OFF.
(iv) The sliding hood should be opened and the cockpit door set on the catch.
(v) A speed of at least 150mph (130kts) IAS should be maintained while manoeuvring with the undercarriage and flaps retracted.
(vi) The flaps must not be lowered until it is certain that the selected landing area is within easy gliding reach.
(vii) If oil pressure is still available the glide can be lengthened considerably by pulling the propeller speed control (or override) lever fully back past the stop in the quadrant.

Ditching
(i) Whenever possible the aircraft should be abandoned by parachute rather than ditched, since the ditching qualities are known to be very poor.

(ii) When ditching is inevitable any external stores should be jettisoned (release will be more certain if the aircraft is gliding straight) and the following procedure observed:
(a) The cockpit hood should be jettisoned.
(b) The flaps should be lowered in order to reduce the touchdown speed as much as possible.
(c) The undercarriage should be kept retracted.
(d) The safety harness should be kept tightly adjusted and the R/T plug should be disconnected.
(e) The engine, if available, should be used to help make the touchdown in a taildown attitude at as low a forward speed as possible.
(f) Ditching should be along the swell, or into wind if the swell is not steep, but the pilot should be prepared for a tendency for the aircraft to dive when contact with the water is made.

Crowbar
A crowbar for use in emergency is stowed in spring clips on the cockpit door.

Appendix 3
Spitfire Sortie

We follow a hypothetical Spitfire sortie to fly over the clifftop national Battle of Britain Memorial at Capel-le-Ferne in Kent from pre-flight briefing to post-flight. All photographs are by the author.

1 A scene from a pre-flight briefing by the Battle of Britain Memorial Flight at RAF Coningsby in Lincolnshire. Note that on the whiteboard is a drawing of the formation to be flown, in this case comprising the BBMF's Avro Lancaster accompanied by two fighters to form the Flight's famous three-ship configuration of Lancaster, Spitfire and Hurricane. As this formation will fly over London, needing to be over its 'target' precisely on time, it will be led by the Lancaster, because there is a navigator on board who will take on the responsibility of ensuring this occurs to the very second of its flight plan using maps with timing annotations marked on them, a stop-watch and a GPS. This too means that the briefing is led by the Lancaster's captain, in this case Flight Lieutenant Ernie Taylor. Here fighter pilot Flight Lieutenant Antony 'Parky' Parkinson, MBE, asks a question. When the fighters fly alone the pilots have to navigate as well as fly their aircraft, which is a high workload as they often also need to fly to a very precise timing.

2 Having discussed the question raised in the pre-flight briefing, Parky makes notes on his map for the sortie.

3 Briefing over, it's time to walk out to the awaiting Spitfire, which will have been prepared for flight by the groundcrew. This is HF.IX TD314 owned by Keith Perkins, and seen out on the grass at Headcorn on a beautiful summer's day.

4 After checking the cockpit and having stowed his flying helmet and paperwork close to or in it, the pilot's next job is to begin his exterior walk-round check of the Spitfire, which begins at the port wing's inner trailing edge and goes all around the aircraft in a clockwise direction. Here Parky has gone around most of the port wing of Spitfire IIa P7350 and is seen checking the leading edge.

5 Continuing in a clockwise direction Parky is now seen checking the exhaust stubs.

6 All the control surfaces must be inspected to ensure they are securely attached and move freely. Here Parky has reached the rudder on the walk-round.

7 Having completed his pre-flight walk-round, here Flight Lieutenant Charlie Brown has donned his life-jacket and flying helmet and is seen about to climb aboard the Historic Aircraft Collection's Spitfire Vb BM597.

8 The pilot's parachute will be placed in position before he climbs into the seat, as getting in with the parachute already on would be quite difficult. Seen here placed in Spitfire I P9374 is one of the Aircraft Restoration Company's Air Ministry 1940 parachutes. These are modern parachutes with very quick-deploying canopies that give a high margin of safety in case of a low-level exit; however, they were specially commissioned to be more historically authentic by ARC managing director John Romain. After going to such great lengths to ensure the superbly restored early Mk I Spitfires were refurbished in every authentic way, John felt disappointed to be only able to place modern black or blue parachutes into the aircraft so

came up with this new innovation. As well as being khaki in colour, with white webbing straps, visible on the ripcord cover is a crown and 'A.M. 1940' stamping in black.

9 Seen here entering BM597, Charlie Brown has stepped on to the parachute seat pan, is holding on to the windscreen framework and lowering himself down.

10 With his parachute secured, Charlie's next job is to secure his

harness, which comprises lap and shoulder straps that snap into place into a quick-release box. He is seen here fitting the lap straps first, as the quick-release box is attached to one of those.

11 The pilot then goes through the pre-start checks, which Charlie Brown is seen doing here in BM597.

12 On start-up, as the Merlin engine starts to turn, the propeller flames will often exit the exhaust stubs, burning off any extra primed fuel.

13 The flames will quickly give way to smoke as the engine gathers momentum, then as the Merlin kicks into life a cloud of smoke will

pour down the fuselage sides to the rear of the Spitfire, being blown away by the wash of the propeller.

14 Time to taxi out to the runway. Here John Romain is at the controls of Bremont-sponsored Tr.IX PV202.

15 In order to keep a good view

ahead with the engine pointing sky-wards directly in front of them, the pilot will weave from side to side and occasionally even put their head outside the cockpit.

16 One of the final procedures that needs to be carried out before take-off are the power checks,

which ensure that the engine is functioning correctly. For these the Spitfire will be turned into wind.

17 Seen here during a power check on PV202, the rpm gauge is seen reading 1,800rpm.

18 If all is ok with the power checks, take-off time nears as the Spitfire taxies out to the active runway, where its pilot may have to hold to await any incoming arrivals before being given clearance to move out on to the runway for take-off.

19 Power is applied here as BM597 begins its take-off run at Duxford.

20 It doesn't take long on the take-off run before the tailwheel is

brought clear of the ground as the Spitfire's speed rapidly increases. This is The Fighter Collection's Mk V EP120 at Duxford.

21 Once clear of the ground the undercarriage is retracted, as seen in the early stages here on Mk IX TD314, gaining height at Headcorn.

22 Now TD314 is in 'clean' configuration and can gain speed and height easily.

23 BM597 cruises towards its venue on the outward leg of the sortie.

24 Flight Lieutenant Charlie Brown has reached the south coast of England close to Folkestone and is about to make a turn to position himself for a west to east course over the national Battle of Britain Memorial at Capel-le-Ferne.

25 With a crowd of spectators in place at the emotive clifftop memorial, which comprises three giant propeller blades with a lone

pilot statue gazing out to sea at its centre, BM597 flies over to commemorate a Battle of Britain anniversary on 15 September.

26 Having carried out his flypast, Charlie Brown turns inland to head for home as he skirts BM597 around the edge of the village of Capel-le-Ferne.

27 Charlie Brown levels BM597 out after the turn has been completed, with the memorial visible below the Spitfire's tail and Folkestone seen ahead and above the aircraft's nose.

28 BM597 then sets course for its home airfield as the Spitfire begins its return leg.

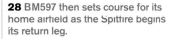

29 On reaching home and having flown into circuit and getting clearance to land, BM597 has its undercarriage and flaps down on finals.

30 A view on finals to RAF Coningsby's runway 07, with four Typhoons on hold waiting for this arrival.

31 The Spitfire V is now close to touching down on short finals.

32 Charlie Brown points the Spitfire's nose slightly up as he rounds out for landing.

33 Having safely landed, the Spitfire will exit the runway and taxi

back to its slot. In this case Mk XVI TD248 is seen at Duxford.

34 Another wonderful Spitfire sortie has been flown for the enjoyment of many people, and here Spitfire I P7308 sits at rest at Duxford either awaiting another flight later in the day or to be put back inside its hangar until another occasion.

Appendix 4
Spitfire Ladies

It was not just men who flew Spitfires during the Second World War; there were also some very gifted and determined ladies who had the same desire to fly this icon of aviation, with the Air Transport Auxiliary (ATA) delivering Spitfires to RAF stations. The first woman to fly a Spitfire was Margaret Fairweather, daughter of Lord Runciman, who prior to the war already had 1,000 hours of civilian flying and was an instructor with the Civil Air Guard. This ground-breaking flight opened the doors for women of the ATA to progress to powerful single-seat fighters. To highlight the important work they did just a handful are featured here.

Among the best known female ATA pilots was **Diana Barnato Walker**, the daughter of a motor-racing champion. She flew 260 Spitfires between 1942 and 1945 and became the first woman to fly a Spitfire across the Channel. In 1944 she married decorated pilot Derek Walker, and the newly married couple took a honeymoon trip to Brussels, each piloting their own Spitfire! Diana said of the Spitfire: 'It was, beyond doubt, a wonderful aircraft.'

Joy Lofthouse, pictured right in 1945, remarked of the Spitfire: 'I would never pass up the opportunity to fly one. It was such a small cockpit but it handled very well and was very responsive.' Talking about joining the ATA with her sister Yvonne, Joy continued: 'When the war broke out all our boyfriends would talk about was flying, so when we saw the advert we both decided to apply. Once we were there, there was no sex discrimination. In fact, I don't think those words had been invented back then. It really was the best job to have during the war because it was exciting, and we could help the war effort. In many ways we were trailblazers for female pilots in the RAF.'

South African **Jackie Sorour**'s description of her first flight in a Spitfire is a literary delight: 'It seemed the most natural thing in the world to be sitting in the cockpit, as though my entire life had led to this moment. I started up inexpertly and felt the power coursing through the Spitfire's frame. A little awed but stimulated by the urgent throb of the Merlin engine that seemed to tremble with eagerness to be free in its own element, I taxied cautiously to the downwind end of the field. A few seconds later I found myself soaring through the air in a machine that made poetry of flight. Carefully I familiarised myself with the controls as the ground fell away at fantastic speed and felt exhilarated by the eager, sensitive response. Singing with joy and relief I dived and climbed and spiralled round the broken clouds. …'

'I always wanted to fly. I nearly broke my neck a couple of times jumping off a ledge at the top of the hill behind our house, until I was absolutely forbidden to do it when I was eight or nine years old.' **Maureen Dunlop**, who was born in Argentina and gained the requisite number of hours flying solo to join the ATA, sailed to England in 1940/41. After initial postings, Maureen moved to the all-female Ferry Pool at Hamble, Southampton, which only flew Spitfires from the Supermarine factory. She gained fame overnight after being caught by a photographer following a delivery flight on a hot summer's day, when wearing a blue shirt with sleeves rolled up she removed her flying helmet and ran her hand through her long dark hair to unfurl it, looking away from the camera as her bracelet contrasted with the functional metal ring on one of the parachute straps hanging over her shoulder. The photograph was used on the cover of the 16 September 1944 edition of the Picture Post, and Maureen became the cover-girl of the ATA. Maureen Dunlop wished that women could have flown in combat, and is well known for having remarked: 'I thought it was the only fair thing, why should only men be killed?'

While it is well known that numerous male Polish pilots escaped their country after the German invasion to fly with the RAF, it is not common knowledge that four female pilots did the same and flew with the ATA. This is **Barbara Wojtulanis**, who is seen studying her maps before a Spitfire delivery flight. She had been a popular pre-war air racer and was initially turned down by the Polish Air Force but, on escaping to Paris before the fall of France, that was to change and all four were commissioned as pilot officers, and so became the only women from the Western Allies to wear full air force pilots' uniforms during the entire war.

Lettice Curtis, seen climbing into a Spitfire, wrote: 'In the air the Spitfire was without vice, and I never heard of anyone who did not enjoy flying it. It has a personality uniquely of its own. The Hurricane was dogged, masculine and its undercarriage folded inwards in a tidy, businesslike manner. The Spit, calling for more sensitive handling, was altogether more feminine, had more glamour and threw its wheels outward in an abandoned, extrovert way. The cockpit of any single-seater aircraft is a very snug, private world, but to sit in the cockpit of a Spitfire, barely wider than one's shoulders, with the power of a Merlin at one's fingertips, was a poetry of its own. The long, flat-topped cowling and pop-popping exhaust stubs gave an almost breathtaking feeling of power, and the exhilaration of throwing it around, chasing clouds or low flying – strictly unauthorised in our case – was something never to be forgotten by those who experienced it.'

Glossary and Abbreviations

A&AEE	Aircraft & Armament Experimental Establishment
AFDU	Air Fighting Development Unit
AP	Air Publication (an official manual containing the information required on how to fly or maintain a military aircraft)
ASI	Air speed indicator
Bf	An abbreviation for Baycriooho Flugzougworlo AG, the company that designed the Bf 109 but later changed its name to Messerschmitt (hence Bf 109, not Me 109)
Boost	The amount of additional pressure created by a supercharger. (In operation the piston aero-engine is subject to two separate stresses. Inertia stresses are caused by the speed at which it rotates (rpm). Gas pressure stresses are caused by the manifold air pressure, or boost as it is more commonly known. Consequently, the two main power ratings of the piston aero-engine involve changes in both rpm and boost. For this purpose there are two controls fitted in the cockpit – the rpm lever and the boost lever, or throttle. The rpm lever is connected via the constant-speed unit to control the pitch of the propeller, while the throttle is connected to the engine to control fuel flow and consequently the power delivered by the engine.)
CofG	Centre of gravity
FOD	Foreign object damage
hp	Horsepower – the measurement used to denote the power of an engine
IAS	Indicated air speed
IFF	Identification friend or foe
IFR	Instrument flight rules
MU	Maintenance Unit (RAF)
NDT	Non-destructive testing
NOTAM	Notice to airmen. Advisory notice giving information on the establishment, condition or change in any aeronautical facility, service, procedure or hazard
OC	Officer commanding
OTU	Operational Training Unit
psi	Pounds per square inch (lb/in^2) – a measurement of pressure
RAAF	Royal Australian Air Force
RAE	Royal Aircraft Establishment
RAF	Royal Air Force
RCAF	Royal Canadian Air Force
RNZAF	Royal New Zealand Air Force
rpg	Rounds per gun
rpm	Revolutions per minute
R/T	Radio telegraphy – sending voice messages over a radio
SAAF	South African Air Force
Supercharger	A device to increase the inlet pressure of a piston engine to boost its power
TAF	Tactical Air Force
Trim Tab	A small additional control surface on the trailing edge of an aileron, rudder or elevator that can be adjusted to aid the stability of an aircraft at different weights of intended flight regimes
UHF	Ultra-high frequency (radio), in the wavelengths 225–400MHz (mainly used for military aircraft communications)
UK	United Kingdom
US	United States
VFR	Visual Flight Rules
VHF	Very high frequency (radio), in the wavelengths 118–136MHz
VNE	Velocity to Never Exceed
VNO	Velocity of Normal Operations
W/T	Wireless telegraphy – sending Morse code messages by radio

Bibliography

A&AEE Ref: 4493/44 – AS.56/8, AM Ref: B.8242/39/AD/RDL, Spitfire Mark I Performance Trials, Aeroplane & Armament Experimental Establishment, Boscombe Down, 19 March 1940

Air Publication 1565B, Pilot's Notes, Spitfire IIa and IIb Aeroplanes, Merlin XII Engine, Air Ministry, July 1940

Air Publication 1565E, Pilot's Notes, Spitfire Va, Vb and Vc Aircraft, Merlin 45, 45M, 46, 50, 50A, 50M, 55 or 55M Engine, Air Ministry, May 1941

Air Publication 1565G & H, Pilot's Notes, Spitfire Mark F.VII Merlin 64 or 71 Engine, Mark F.VIII 63, 66 or 70 Engine and Mark PR.X Merlin 64, 71 or 77 Engine, Air Ministry, December 1943

Air Publication 1565T & W, Pilot's Notes XIV & XIX, Griffon 65 or 66 Engine, Air Ministry, April 1946

Air Publication 1565J, P & L, Pilot's Notes 3rd Edition, Spitfire IX, XI & XVI, Merlin 61, 63, 66, 70 or 266 Engine, Air Ministry, September 1946

Air Publication 2816B & C, Pilot's Notes, Spitfire 22 & 24, Griffon 61 Engine, Air Ministry, September 1947

Report No. M/692/Int. 2, Aeroplane & Armament Experimental Establishment, Handling trials of the Spitfire K5054, September 1936

R.J. Mitchell – Schooldays to Spitfire, Mitchell, Gordon, Tempus Publishing, 2002

Spitfire: A Test Pilot's Story, Quill, Jeffrey, John Murray (Publishers) Ltd, 1983

Tactical Paper No. 1, Air Ministry, Air Fighting Tactics used by Spitfire Fighter Squadrons of 2 TAF during the campaign in Western Europe

The Aeroplane, 1 July 1936, Temple Press, Grey, C.G.

The Aeroplane, 1 July 1936, Temple Press, James, Thurstan

Index